KU-271-906

Interpreting the French Revolution

This book is published as part of the joint publishing agreement established in 1977 between the Fondation de la Maison des Sciences de l'Homme and the Press Syndicate of the University of Cambridge. Titles published under this arrangement may appear in any European language or, in the case of volumes of collected essays, in several languages.

New books will appear either as individual titles or in one of the series which the Maison des Sciences de l'Homme and the Cambridge University Press have jointly agreed to publish. All books published jointly by the Maison des Sciences de l'Homme and the Cambridge University Press will be distributed by the Press throughout the world.

Cet ouvrage est publié dans le cadre de l'accord de co-édition passé en 1977 entre la Fondation de la Maison des Sciences de l'Homme et le Press Syndicate of the University of Cambridge. Toutes les langues européennes sont admises pour les titres couverts par cet accord, et les ouvrages collectifs peuvent paraître en plusieurs langues.

Les ouvrages paraissent soit isolément, soit dans l'une des séries que la Maison des Sciences de l'Homme et Cambridge University Press ont convenu de publier ensemble. La distribution dans le monde entier des titres ainsi publiés conjointement par les deux établissements est assurée par Cambridge University Press.

LIVERPOOL JOHN MOORES UNIVERSITY
Aldham Roberts L.R.C.
TEL. 051 231 3701/3634

**Books are to be returned on or before
the last date below.**

2 1 MAR 1995 A

-8 FEB 1996 A

12 MAR 1996

2 1 MAR 1997

1 1 NOV 1997

2 5 MAR 1998 A

2 5 JAN 1999 A

1 3 MAY 2003

LIBREX —

LIVERPOOL JMU LIBRARY

3 1111 00605 4942

Interpreting the French Revolution

FRANÇOIS FURET

TRANSLATED BY ELBORG FORSTER

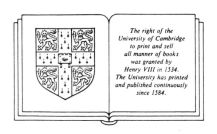

CAMBRIDGE UNIVERSITY PRESS

Cambridge

New York   Port Chester   Melbourne   Sydney

EDITIONS DE
LA MAISON DES SCIENCES DE L'HOMME

Paris

Published by the Press Syndicate of the University of Cambridge
The Pitt Building, Trumpington Street, Cambridge CB2 1RP
40 West 20th Street, New York, NY 10011, USA
10 Stamford Road, Oakleigh, Melbourne 3166, Australia
and
Editions de la Maison des Sciences de l'Homme
54 Boulevard Raspail, 75270 Paris Cedex 06

Originally published in French as *Penser la Révolution Française* by
Editions Gallimard Paris, 1978, and © Editions Gallimard 1978.

First published in English by the Maison des Sciences de l'Homme and
the Cambridge University Press, 1981 as *Interpreting the French Revolution*
Reprinted 1985, 1986, 1988, 1989, 1990

English translation © Maison des Sciences de
l'Homme and Cambridge University Press 1981

Printed in Malta by Interprint Limited

British Library Cataloguing in Publication Data

Furet, François
Interpreting the French Revolution.
1. France – History – Revolution, 1789–1799
– Historiography
I. Title II. Penser la Révolution française,
English
944.04   DC155   80-42290

ISBN 0 521 23574 X hard covers
ISBN 0 521 28049 4 paperback

Let us set our souls free to revolutionise the Revolution and, above all, let us resolve never to accuse an impartial mind of insulting the Revolution. For the term 'insult to Religion' has been so abused that we shall strike it from our language, since nothing is to be more avoided than the style and cast of mind of a public prosecutor when they are brought into historical and philosophical criticism.

Edgar Quinet,
Critique de la Révolution (Paris, 1867)

Contents

Preface

The two parts of this book were written at two distinct moments, and the order in which they appear reverses the order of their composition.

The first part aims at providing a synthetic solution to a problem that has been a constant concern of mine ever since I started studying the French Revolution: how does one interpret such an event? The second part presents the successive stages of my attempt to answer that question and the sequence of my intellectual encounters so as to chart the itinerary I have followed.

It begins with a brief against the communist historians of the French Revolution, focusing on the inconsistencies of what is today the dominant interpretation of that event. That essay originated in the give-and-take of intellectual life and debate at a particular time; but I did not feel that I should rewrite it, seven years later, in an artificially neutral tone. As it stands, it testifies in its own way to the special importance of the French Revolution as an issue in the French academic community. I can only hope that what it owes to circumstance will not detract from its explanatory character, which is all that matters to me.

That somewhat massive clearing operation is followed by two studies, devoted to the two authors who have been instrumental to the development of my intellectual position: Alexis de Tocqueville and Augustin Cochin. The reader will understand why as these pages unfold: Tocqueville and Cochin were the only historians to propose a rigorous conceptualisation of the French Revolution and to have dealt with the question raised in this book. Their analyses, which seem to me not so much contradictory as complementary, are the basis of my proposed system of interpretation, which will be found in the first part of the book. It is their path that I have taken, and it gives me pleasure to inscribe their names in this preface.

Note to the English edition

I should like to express here all my appreciation to Mrs Elborg Forster for having translated a text that involved not a few difficulties. I am also deeply grateful to Mr Jonathan Mandelbaum, with whom I was able, in Paris, to review the English typescript and update a number of bibliographical references. Thanks to him, the present translation is in many respects fuller than the French original, published in 1978.

Part I

The French Revolution is over

I

Historians engaged in the study of the Merovingian Kings or the Hundred Years War are not asked at every turn to present their research permits. So long as they can give proof of having learned the techniques of the trade, society and the profession assume that they possess the virtues of patience and objectivity. The discussion of their findings is a matter for scholars and scholarship only.

The historian of the French Revolution, on the other hand, must produce more than proof of competence. He must show his colours. He must state from the outset where he comes from, what he thinks and what he is looking for; what he writes about the French Revolution is assigned a meaning and label even before he starts working: the writing is taken as his *opinion*, a form of judgment that is not required when dealing with the Merovingians but indispensable when it comes to treating 1789 or 1793. As soon as the historian states that opinion, the matter is settled; he is labelled a royalist, a liberal or a Jacobin. Once he has given the password his history has a specific meaning, a determined place and a claim to legitimacy.

What is surprising here is not that the history of the Revolution, like all histories, involves intellectual presuppositions. There is no such thing as 'innocent' historical interpretation, and written history is itself located in history, indeed *is* history, the product of an inherently unstable relationship between the present and the past, a merging of the particular mind with the vast field of its potential topics of study in the past. But if all history implies a choice, a preference within the range of what might be studied, it does not follow that such a choice always involves a preconceived opinion about the subject chosen. For that to happen, or to be assumed, the subject must arouse in the historian and his public a capacity for identifying with political or religious passions that have survived the passing of time.

1

The passing of time may weaken that sense of identification, or on the contrary preserve and even strengthen it, depending on whether the subject treated by the historian does or does not continue to express the issues of his own times, his values and his choices. The theme of Clovis and the Frankish invasions was of burning interest in the eighteenth century because the historians of that era saw it as the key to the social structure of their own time. They thought that the Frankish invasions were the origin of the division between nobility and commoners, the conquerors being the progenitors of the nobility and the conquered those of the commoners. Today the Frankish invasions have lost all relevance, since we live in a society where nobility has ceased to act as a social principle. No longer serving as the mirror of an existing world, the Frankish invasions have lost the eminent place in historiography that that world once assigned to them, and have moved from the realm of social polemic to that of learned debate.

The fact is that beginning in 1789 the obsession with origins, the underlying thread of all national history, came to be centred precisely on the Revolutionary break. Just as the great invasions were the myth of a society dominated by the nobility, the saga of its origins, so 1789 became the birth date, the year zero of a new world founded on equality. The substitution of one birth date for another, in other words, the definition in time of a new national identity, is perhaps one of the *abbé* Sieyès's greatest strokes of genius, especially if one remembers that he anticipated the founding event by several months[1] and yet gave it its full meaning in advance:

The Third Estate has nothing to fear from going back into the past. It will refer back to the year preceding the conquest; and since it is today strong enough not to be conquered, its resistance will no doubt be more effective. Why should it not send back to the forests of Franconia all those families who cling to the mad claim that they are descended from the race of conquerors and have inherited their rights? Thus purified, the nation will easily console itself, I believe, for no longer imagining itself composed only of the descendants of Gauls and Romans.[2]

These few lines tell us not only that the nobles' proprietary claims over the nation are fictitious, but also that, even if those claims were well founded, the Third Estate would have only to restore the social contract in force before the conquest or, rather, to found it by obliterating centuries of violent usurpation. In either instance it is a matter of

---

1. *Qu'est-ce que le Tiers Etat?* was written at the end of 1788 and published in January 1789.
2. *Qu'est-ce que le Tiers Etat?*, ed. Edme Champion (Paris: Société d'histoire de la Révolution française, 1888), ch. II, p. 32.

constituting a 'true' origin for the nation by giving a legitimate date of birth to equality: that is what 1789 is all about.

But Revolutionary historiography has had the function of keeping alive that account of society's origins. Consider, for example, the manner in which studies are divided for the teaching of history in France. 'Modern' history ends in 1789 with what the Revolution christened the 'Ancien Régime', a period which, if it lacks a clearly marked birth-certificate, is thus given a duly signed death-certificate. Thereafter, the Revolution and the Empire form separate and autonomous fields of study, each with its own professorships, students, learned societies and journals, and the quarter-century separating the storming of the Bastille from the Battle of Waterloo is assigned a special place: it is both the end of the 'modern' era and the indispensable introduction to the 'contemporary' period, which begins in 1815; it is the period of transition that gives meaning to both, the watershed from which the history of France either flows back to its past or rushes toward its future. By remaining faithful to the conscious experience of the actors of the Revolution, despite all the intellectual absurdities implicit in such a chronological framework, our academic institutions have invested the French Revolution and the historian of that period with the mysteries of our national history. The year 1789 is the key to what lies both upstream and downstream. It separates those periods, and thereby defines and 'explains' them.

But it is not enough to say that the Revolution explains what lies downstream – the period beginning in 1815 that the Revolution is supposed to have created, made possible, inaugurated. The Revolution does not simply 'explain' our contemporary history; it *is* our contemporary history. And that is worth pondering over.

For the same reasons that the Ancien Régime is thought to have an end but no beginning, the Revolution has a birth but no end. For the one, seen negatively and lacking chronological definition, only its death is a certainty; the other contains a promise of such magnitude that it becomes boundlessly elastic. Even in the short term, it is not easy to 'date': depending on the significance the historian attributes to the main events, he may encapsulate the Revolution within the year 1789, seeing in it the year in which the essential features of the Revolution's final outcome were fixed, when the final page of the Ancien Régime was turned – or he may go up to 1794 and the execution of Robespierre, stressing the dictatorship of the Revolutionary committees and of the *sections*, the Jacobin saga and the egalitarian crusade of the Year II. Or he may use 18 Brumaire 1799 as the terminus, if he wants to acknowledge the extent to which Thermidorians had remained Jacobins, and include the government of the regicides and the war against the European monarchies. He may even integrate the Napoleonic adventure into the Revolution, perhaps to the end of the Consular period, or to Napoleon's Habsburg marriage, or even to the Hundred Days: a case can be made for any of these time frames.

One could also envisage a much longer history of the French Revolution, extending even farther downstream, and ending not before the late nineteenth or early twentieth century. For the entire history of nineteenth-century France can be seen as a struggle between Revolution and Restoration, passing through various episodes in 1815, 1830, 1848, 1851, 1870, the Commune and 16 May 1877. Only the victory of the republicans over the monarchists at the beginning of the Third Republic marked the definitive victory of the Revolution in the French countryside. The lay schoolteacher of Jules Ferry was a missionary for the values of 1789, and was more than an instrument; he was the embodiment of victory in that long battle. Integration of France's villages and peasant culture into the republican nation on the basis of the principles of 1789 was to take at least a century, and no doubt considerably longer in such regions as Brittany or the Southwest, which lagged in more than one respect.[3] That recent history of the French countryside is still, for the most part, unwritten; yet it too constitutes a history of the Revolution. Republican Jacobinism, dictated for so long from Paris, won its victory only after it could count on the majority vote of rural France at the end of the nineteenth century.

But its electoral 'victory' did not mean that it was honoured or assimilated as a value, something so unanimously accepted as to be no longer debated. The celebration of the principles of 1789, the object of so much pedagogical solicitude, or the condemnation of the crimes of 1793, which usually serves as a screen for the rejection of those principles, has remained at the core of the set of notions that shaped French political life until the middle of the twentieth century. Fascism, by its explicit rejection of the values of the French Revolution, gave an international dimension to that conflict of ideas. But, interestingly enough, the Vichy régime, set up after the German victory, was less specifically fascist than traditionalist, and was obsessed with 1789. France in the 1940s was still a country

---

3. The expression 'lagging' has only a descriptive value. The analysis of this 'lag' and of integration into the Republic through the school system and politics is the central topic of Maurice Agulhon's work (especially in *La République au village* [Paris: Plon, 1970]). That process is also analysed in Eugen Weber's recent book *Peasants into Frenchmen: the modernization of rural France* (Stanford: Stanford Univ. Press, 1976).

whose citizens had to *sort out* their history, date the birth of their nation, choose between the Ancien Régime and the Revolution.

In that form, the reference to 1789 disappeared from French politics with the defeat of fascism. Today the discourse of both Right and Left celebrates liberty and equality, and the debate about the values of 1789 no longer involves any real political stakes or even strong psychological commitment. But if such unanimity exists, it is because the political debate has simply been transferred from one Revolution to the other, from the Revolution of the past to the one that is to come. By shifting the conflict to the future, it is possible to create an apparent consensus about the legacy of the past. But in fact that legacy, which is one of conflict, lives on by dominating the representations of the future, just as an old geological substratum, covered with later sedimentation, still moulds the features of the earth and the landscape. For the French Revolution is not only the Republic. It is also an unlimited promise of equality and a special form of change. One only has to see in it not a national institution but a matrix of universal history, in order to recapture its dynamic force and its fascinating appeal. The nineteenth century believed in the Republic. The twentieth century believes in *the* Revolution. The same founding event is present in both images.

And indeed, the socialists of the late nineteenth century conceived of their action as both coordinated with and distinct from that of the republicans. Coordinated, because they felt that the Republic was the prerequisite of socialism. Distinct, because they saw political democracy as a historical stage of social organisation that was destined to be superseded, and because they perceived 1789 not as the foundation of a stable State but as a movement whose logic required it to go beyond that first stage. The struggle for democracy and the struggle for socialism were the two successive forms assumed by a dynamic of equality originating in the French Revolution. Thus was formed a vision, a linear history of human emancipation whose first stage had been the maturing and the dissemination of the values of 1789, while the second stage was to fulfil the promise of 1789 by a new, and this time socialist, revolution. This two-pronged mechanism is implicit in Jaurès's socialist history of the Revolution, for example, but the great socialist authors were at first unable to give an account of the second stage; understandably so, since it was still in the future.

All that changed in 1917. Now that the socialist revolution had a face, the French Revolution ceased to be the model for a future that was possible, desirable, hoped for, but as yet devoid of content. Instead, it became the mother of a real, dated, and duly registered event: October 1917. As I suggest in one of the essays below, the Russian Bolsheviks never – before, during or after the Russian Revolution – lost sight of that filiation. But by the same token the historians of the French Revolution projected into the past their feelings or their judgments about 1917, and tended to highlight those features of the first revolution that seemed to presage or indeed anticipate those of the second. At the very moment when Russia – for better or worse – took the place of France as the nation in the vanguard of history, because it had inherited from France and from nineteenth-century thought the idea that a nation is *chosen* for revolution, the historiographical discourses about the two revolutions became fused and infected each other. The Bolsheviks were given Jacobin ancestors, and the Jacobins were made to anticipate the communists.

Thus, for almost two hundred years now, the history of the French Revolution has been a story of beginnings and so a discourse about identity. In the nineteenth century that history was virtually indistinguishable from the event it purported to retrace, for the drama begun in 1789 was played over and over, generation after generation, for the same stakes and around the same symbols, an unbroken memory that became an object of worship or of horror. Not only did the Revolution found the political culture that makes 'contemporary' France intelligible, but it also bequeathed to France conflicts between legitimacies and a virtually inexhaustible stock of political debates: 1830 was 1789 all over; 1848 re-enacted the First Republic; and the Commune echoed the Jacobin dream. It was not until the end of the century, with the spread of a republican consensus, first in the Parliament, then in the nation at large, and with the founding of the Third Republic, that the Revolution – at last, after a century – began to acquire academic respectability. Under pressure from the *Société d'histoire de la Révolution française*, founded in 1881 by a group of republican intellectuals, the Sorbonne offered in 1886 a 'course' in the history of the Revolution, taught by Alphonse Aulard. In 1891, that course became a 'chair'.

Did the Revolution, once it was officially taught, become national property, like the Republic? As in the case of the Republic, the answer is: yes and no. Yes, because in a sense, with the founding of the Republic on the vote of the people, and no longer on the Parisian insurrection, the French Revolution was finally 'over'; it had become a national institution, sanctioned by the legal and democratic consent of citizens. Yet, on the other hand, the republican consensus built on the political culture born in

1789 was conservative and obtained by default from the ruling classes, who could not agree on a king, and from the peasants and minor notables, who wanted a guarantee of security: indeed, it was the repression of the Commune that made the Republic acceptable in the provinces. However, a victorious French Revolution, finally accepted as a closed chapter of history, as a patrimony and a national institution, contradicted the image of change it implied, for that image involved a far more radical promise than lay schools and the separation of Church and State. Once the Revolution had succeeded in imposing the Republic, it became clear that it was much more than the Republic. It was a pledge that no event could fully redeem.

That is why, in the very last years of the nineteenth century, when the historiographical debate between royalists and republicans was still over what had been the political stakes of 1789, socialist thinking seized upon the notion of the Revolution as prefiguration. Aulard had criticised Taine for reconstructing the 'Origins of Contemporary France'. Jaurès saw the French Revolution as the beginning of a beginning, as a world that would give birth again: 'The least of its greatness is the present ... Its pro-longations are unlimited.'[4] The Russian Revolution of October 1917 seemed made to order to fulfil that expectation of a renewed beginning. Henceforth – as Mathiez made quite explicit[5] – the inventory of the Jacobin legacy was overlaid with an implicit discourse for or against Bolshevism, a development that hardly made for intellectual flexibility. In fact, the overlap of those two political debates extended the nineteenth into the twentieth century, and transferred onto communism and anti-communism the passions previously aroused by the king of France and by the Republic, *displacing* but not weakening them. Quite the contrary, for those passions were re-implanted in the present and given new political stakes to be culled, like so many still indistinct promises, from the events of 1789 or rather 1793. But in becoming the positive or negative pre-figuration of an authentically communist revolution, in which the famous 'bourgeoisie' would not come to confiscate the victory of the people, the French Revolution did not gain in meaning or in conceptual clarity. It simply renewed its myth, which became the poorer for it.

I should like to avoid a misunderstanding here: that contamination of the past by the present, that endless capacity for assimilation, which by definition characterises a Revolution conceived as a starting point, does

---

4. Jean Jaurès, *Histoire socialiste de la Révolution française* (Paris: Éditions Sociales, 1968); preface by Ernest Labrousse, p. 14.
5. Cf. below, p. 85.

not preclude partial progress in certain areas of scholarship. After all, the
Revolution has been an academic 'field' since the end of the nineteenth
century, and since then each generation of historians has had to do its
share of archival work. In that respect, the emphasis on the popular
classes and their action in the French Revolution has brought advances in
our knowledge of the rôle played by the peasants and the urban masses
that it would be absurd to ignore or underestimate. But those advances
have not appreciably modified the analysis of what we usually refer to as
the 'French Revolution' taken as a whole.

Take the problem of the peasantry, which has been studied and re-
evaluated in many works since the beginning of the century, from
Loutchiski to Paul Bois, an area in which, it seems to me, Georges Lefebvre
made his main contribution to the historiography of the French
Revolution. From his analysis of the question and of peasant behaviour,
Georges Lefebvre came to two ideas: first, that, from the social point of
view, there were several revolutions within what is called *the* French
Revolution; second, that the peasant revolution was not only largely
autonomous and distinct from the other revolutions (those of the aristoc-
rats, the bourgeois, and the *sans-culottes*, for example), but also anti-
capitalist, that is, in his opinion, traditionalist and backward-looking.[6]
Right off, those two ideas are difficult to reconcile with a vision of the
French Revolution as a homogeneous social and political phenomenon
opening the way to a capitalist or bourgeois future that the 'Ancien
Régime' had blocked.

But there is more. Georges Lefebvre also noted that, in the rural history
of the Ancien Régime, capitalism was increasingly present, and that its
'spirit' had deeply penetrated the landed aristocracy. Consequently, as
Paul Bois showed later,[7] the same peasantry could successively come into
conflict with the seigneurs in 1789 and with the Republic in 1793 without
the 'Revolution' having changed anything in the nature of the social
pressures exerted by the peasantry or the struggle in which it was
engaged. As early as 1932, Georges Lefebvre could write: 'The Ancien
Régime started the agrarian history of France on the road to capitalism;
the Revolution abruptly completed the task that the Ancien Régime had
begun.'[8] But this conclusion, which sounds almost like Tocqueville, does not
lead the historian of Jacobin tradition, like his legitimist ancestor, to a critique of the very concept of revolution. He does not try to understand how

6. Georges Lefebvre, 'La Révolution française et les paysans' (1932), in *Études sur la
   Révolution française* (Paris: P.U.F., 1954; 2nd edn, introduction by Albert Soboul, 1963).
7. Paul Bois, *Les Paysans de l'Ouest* (Paris and The Hague: Mouton, 1960).
8. Lefebvre, 'La Révolution française et les paysans', p. 263.

one might reconcile the idea of radical change with that of an actual continuity. He simply juxtaposes, without attempting to make them compatible, an *analysis* of the peasant problem at the end of the eighteenth century and a contradictory *tradition* that consists in seeing the Revolution, through the eyes of its participants, as a break, an advent, a time both qualitatively new and different, as homogeneous as a brand-new fabric. It would not be difficult to show that the twentieth century's greatest university scholar of the French Revolution, the man who had a richer knowledge and a surer grasp of the period than anyone, based his synthetic vision of the immense event to which he devoted his life on nothing more than the convictions of a militant adherent of the *Cartel des Gauches* and the Popular Front.[9]

The fact is that scholarship, although it may be stimulated by pre-occupations stemming from the present, is never sufficient in itself to modify the conceptualisation of a problem or an event. In the case of the French Revolution, scholarship could, under the influence of Jaurès, 1917 and Marxism, take a turn toward social history and conquer new territories in the twentieth century. Yet it remains attached – indeed more closely than ever – to the old recital of origins, which was both renewed and made more rigid by deposits of socialist thinking. For the takeover of the history of the Revolution by social history, if it has opened new fields of research in specific areas, has only shifted elsewhere the question of origins: the advent of the bourgeoisie has been substituted for the advent of liberty, but it remains no less an advent. The durability of that notion is the more extraordinary since the idea of a radical rending of the social fabric of a nation is even more difficult to conceive of than the political break; in that sense, the historiographical shift from a political to a social emphasis shows the lasting power of the notion that the Revolution was an advent, precisely because such a shift is even more incompatible with 'revolution'. That intellectual contradiction is masked by the celebration of the beginnings. For in the twentieth century, more than ever before, the historian of the French Revolution commemorates the event he narrates or studies. The new materials he brings to bear are no more than supplementary ornaments offered up to his tradition. Lineages are per-petuated along with the debates: just as Aulard and Taine debated the Republic when writing about the French Revolution, so Mathiez and Gaxotte discussed the origins of communism.

This infinite capacity for commemoration, always an expression of

9. See the intellectual portrait of Lefebvre by Richard Cobb in *A second identity: essays on France and French history* (London, New York and Toronto: Oxford University Press, 1969).

national pride, explains why in France the Revolution has become a special field in historical studies. It was dignified as an academic specialty not because it contains demonstrably special problems, but because it allows the historian to identify with his heroes and 'his' event. The French Revolution therefore has its royalist, liberal, Jacobin, anarchist, or libertarian histories, and this list is neither exclusive – for those tendencies do not necessarily always contradict each other – nor above all restrictive. Mother of the political culture into which all of us are born, the Revolution allows everyone to look for filiations. But all those histories, which have bitterly fought each other for the last two hundred years in the name of the origins of their opposition, in fact share a common ground: they are all histories in quest of identity. No Frenchman living in the second half of the twentieth century can perceive the French Revolution *from the outside*. One cannot practise ethnology in so familiar a landscape. The event is so fundamentally, so tyrannically rooted in contemporary French political consciousness that any attempt to consider it from an intellectual 'distance' is immediately seen as hostility – as if identification, be it a claim to descent or rejection, were inevitable.

Yet we must try to break the vicious circle of that commemorative historiography. It has long been fashionable among people of my generation, who were brought up under the double influence of existentialism and Marxism, to stress that the historian is rooted in his own times, his own choices and his own constraints. By now the continued harping on those truisms – however useful they may have been for combating the positivist illusion that 'objectivity' is possible – is liable to perpetuate professions of faith and polemics that have had their day. Today the historiography of the Revolution is hampered, even more than by political ideology, by mental laziness and pious rehashing. Surely, it is time to strip it of the elementary significations it has bequeathed to its heirs, and to restore to it another *primum movens* of the historian, namely, intellectual curiosity and the free search for knowledge about the past. Moreover, a time will come when the political beliefs that have sustained the disputes within our societies over the last two centuries will seem as surprising to men as the inexhaustible variety and violence of the religious conflicts in Europe between the fifteenth and the seventeenth century seem to us. The very fact that the study of the French Revolution could become a political arena will probably be seen as an explanatory factor and as a psychological commitment of a bygone age.

But that 'cooling off' of the object 'French Revolution', to speak in Levi-Straussian terms, is not to be expected from the mere passing of time.

One can define the conditions needed to bring it about, and even spot the first signs of it, in our own time. I do not claim that those conditions will at last provide us with historical *objectivity*; but they are already deeply modifying the relation between the historian of the French Revolution and his subject, making less spontaneous and therefore less compelling the historian's identification with the actors, his commemoration of the founders, or his execration of the deviants.

I can see two routes to that divestment, which I consider beneficial for the renewal of the history of the Revolution. The first is emerging gradually, belatedly, but ineluctably, from the contradictions between the myth of Revolution and the societies that have experienced it. The second is inherent in the mutations of historical knowledge.

The impact of the first, the contrast between myth and reality, is becoming increasingly clear. I am writing these lines in the spring of 1977, at a time when the criticism of Soviet totalitarianism, and more generally of all power claiming its source in Marxism, is no longer the monopoly, or near monopoly, of right-wing thought and has become a central theme in the reflections of the Left. What is important here, in referring to the historically related entities of Right and Left, is not that criticism from the Left, which has occupied a culturally dominant position in France since the end of the Second World War, carries more weight than criticism from the Right. Much more important is that in indicting the U.S.S.R. or China the Right has no need to adjust any part of its heritage and can simply stay within the bounds of counter-revolutionary thought. The Left, on the other hand, must face up to facts that compromise its beliefs, which are as old as those of the Right. That is why, for so long, the Left was loath to face up to such facts, and why, even today, it would often rather patch up the edifice of its convictions than look into the history of its tragedies. That will not matter in the long run. What does matter is that a left-wing culture, once it has made up its mind to think about the facts – namely, the disastrous experience of twentieth-century communism – in terms of its own values, has come to take a critical view of its own ideology, interpretations, hopes and rationalisations. It is in left-wing culture that the sense of distance between history and the Revolution is taking root, precisely because it was the Left that believed that all of history was contained in the promises of the Revolution.

The history of the French Left in relation to the Soviet Revolution remains to be written. It would show that Stalinism took root in a modified Jacobin tradition that consisted in grafting onto the Soviet phenomenon the ideas of a new beginning and of a nation in the vanguard of history. Moreover, it would show that during a long period, by no means over, the notion of *deviation* from an unsullied beginning made it possible to salvage the pre-eminent value of revolution as an idea. But these two notions – of a new beginning and of a vanguard nation – are now giving way. Solzhenitsyn's work has become the basic historical reference for the Soviet experience, ineluctably locating the issue of the Gulag at the very core of the revolutionary endeavour. Once that happened, the Russian example was bound to turn around, like a boomerang, to strike its French 'origin'. In 1920, Mathiez justified Bolshevik violence by the French precedent, in the name of comparable circumstances. Today the Gulag is leading to a rethinking of the Terror precisely because the two undertakings are seen as identical. The two revolutions remain connected; but while fifty years ago they were systematically absolved on the basis of excuses related to 'circumstances', that is, external phenomena that had nothing to do with the nature of the two revolutions, they are today, by contrast, accused of being, consubstantially, systems of meticulous constraint over men's bodies and minds.

Thus the exorbitant privilege assigned to the idea of revolution, a privilege that placed it beyond the reach of internal criticism, is beginning to lose its standing as a self-evident fact. Academic historiography – in which the communists, almost as a matter of course, have taken over from the socialists and the radicals as the keepers of republican commemoration – still clings to that privilege and does not make light of its traditions. Holding on ever more closely to their short period of 'ancestral' history as if it were their social patrimony, those historians are not simply faced with the conceptual devaluation of their patrimony among intellectuals; they have trouble embracing, or even imagining, the intellectual changes that are indispensable to progress in the historiography of the Revolution.

In fact, this historiography should be made to show, not its colours, but its concepts. History in general has ceased to be a body of knowledge where the 'facts' are supposed to speak for themselves, once they have been established according to the rules. It must state the problem it seeks to analyse, the data it uses, its working hypotheses and the conclusions at which it arrives. If the history of the Revolution is the last one to adopt that method of *explicitness*, it is partly because all its traditions have drawn it, generation after generation, toward the myth of the beginnings; but, in addition, that myth has been taken over and canonised by a 'Marxist' rationalisation that does not change its character in any fundamental way but, on the contrary, consolidates the myth by making it appear a conceptual elaboration having the elemental power derived from its function as a new beginning.

I have explained my position in one of the essays below:[10] that rationalisation does not exist in Marx's writings, which do not include any systematic interpretation of the French Revolution; it is instead the product of a confused encounter between Bolshevism and Jacobinism, predicated upon a linear notion of human progress and punctuated by the two successive 'liberations', nested like a set of Russian dolls. The most hopelessly confused aspect of the 'Marxist' vulgate of the French Revolution is the juxtaposition of the old idea of the advent of a new age – the seminal idea of the French Revolution itself – with an enlargement of the field of history that is part of the very substance of Marxism. In fact Marxism – or perhaps one should say the kind of Marxism that penetrated the history of the French Revolution with Jaurès – has shifted the centre of gravity of the *problem* of the Revolution toward economic and social matters. It seeks to root in the progress of capitalism both the slow rise of the Third Estate (a theme dear to the historiography of the Restoration) and the apotheosis of 1789. In so doing, Marxism includes economic life and the fabric of society as a whole in the myth of a revolutionary break: before the Revolution, feudalism; after, capitalism; before, the nobility; after, the bourgeoisie. But since those propositions are neither demonstrable, nor in fact even likely, and since, in any case, they shatter the accepted chronological framework, the Marxist approach amounts to no more than joining an analysis of causes carried out in the economic and social mode to a narrative of events written in the political and ideological mode.

At least that incoherence has the advantage of underscoring one of the essential problems of the historiography of the Revolution, which is how to fit the various levels of interpretation into the chronology of the event. If one is determined to preserve at any cost the idea of an objective break in the continuity of history, and to consider that break the alpha and omega of the history of the Revolution, one is indeed bound to end up with a number of absurdities, whatever the interpretation advanced. And those absurdities become the more inevitable as the interpretation becomes more ambitious and encompasses more and more levels. One could say, for example, that between 1789 and 1794 the entire political system of France was radically transformed because the old monarchy then came to an end. But the idea that between those same dates the social or

10. Cf. below, p. 81ff.

economic fabric of the nation was renewed from top to bottom is obviously much less plausible. The 'Revolution', then, is not a useful concept for making such assertions even if it is true that some of the causes of the Revolution were not exclusively political or intellectual.

In other words, any conceptualisation of the history of the Revolution must begin with a critique of the idea of revolution as experienced and perceived by its actors, and transmitted by their heirs, namely, the idea that it was a radical change and the origin of a new era. So long as that critique is absent from a history of the Revolution, superimposing a more social or more economic interpretation upon a purely political inter- pretation will not change what all those histories share, a fidelity to the revolutionary consciousness and experience of the nineteenth and twen- tieth centuries. Nonetheless, the social and economic deposits added by Marxism may have one advantage, for the absurdities to which they lead bring into sharp focus the dilemmas of any history of the Revolution that remains founded on the personal consciousness of those who made that history.

It is here that I encounter Tocqueville, and that I take the measure of his genius. At the very time when Michelet was working out the most penetrating of the histories of the Revolution written in the mode of personal identification – a history without concepts, made up of disco- veries of the heart and marked by an intuitive grasp of men's souls and actors' motives – Tocqueville, and Tocqueville alone, envisaged the same history in the inverse mode of a sociological interpretation. It does not matter, therefore, that the Norman aristocrat did not hold the same *opinions* as the son of the Jacobin printer. Tocqueville, after all, did not write a more 'right-wing' history of the Revolution than Michelet. He wrote a *different* history of the Revolution, basing it upon a critique of revolutionary ideology and of what he saw as the French Revolution's illusion about itself.

Tocqueville's conceptual reversal of the accepted view of the French Revolution is not without analogies to the reversal that had marked his analysis of America. Before *Democracy in America*, European culture had conceived of America as the childhood of Europe, the image of its own beginnings, and had dwelt on the process of settling and clearing, on man's conquest of untamed nature. Tocqueville's book, proceeding by deduction, as it were, from the central hypothesis about equality, turned that image inside out like a glove. America, he told the Europeans, is not your childhood, it is your future. There, freed from the constraints of an aristocratic past, is opening out the democracy that will *also* be the

political and social future of old Europe. In the same way, although in
reverse, Tocqueville renewed his paradox twenty years later in discussing
the French Revolution, which had never – even and above all at the time
of the American 'detour' – ceased to be his central concern. 'So you think
that the French Revolution is a sudden break in our national history?', he
asked his contemporaries. In reality it is the fruition of our past. It has
completed the work of the monarchy. Far from being a break, it can be
understood only within and by historical continuity. It is the objective
achievement of that continuity, even though it was experienced subjectively as a radical break.

Thus, Tocqueville developed a radical critique of any history of the
French Revolution based only on the consciousness of the revolutionaries
themselves. His critique is all the more penetrating as it remains within
the political sphere – the relation between the French people and the
governing power – which is precisely the sphere that *seems* to have been
most profoundly transformed by the Revolution. Tocqueville is mainly
concerned with the domination of local communities and civil society by
the administrative power following the growth and extension of the
centralised State. The takeover of society by the administrative State was
more than the permanent feature linking the 'new' régime with the 'old',
Bonaparte with Louis XIV. It also explained the developments by which
'democratic' (i.e. egalitarian) ideology penetrated throughout traditional
French society. In other words, Tocqueville saw in the constitutive aspects
of the 'Revolution', that is, an administrative State ruling a society informed
by an egalitarian ideology, a work largely accomplished by the monarchy
before it was completed by the Jacobins and the Empire. And what is
called 'the French Revolution', an event later inventoried, dated, and
magnified as a new dawn, was but the acceleration of a prior political and
social trend. By destroying, not the aristocracy, but the aristocratic
principle in society, the Revolution put an end to the legitimacy of social
resistance against the central State. But it was Richelieu who set the
example, and so did Louis XIV.

I shall try to analyse, in one of the essays below, the difficulties raised
by that type of interpretation. If Tocqueville never wrote a real history of
the French Revolution it was, I believe, because he conceptualised only
one aspect of that history, namely its continuity. He presented the
Revolution in terms of its outcome, not as an event; as a process, not as a
break. At the time of his death, he was working on his second volume and
was confronting the problem of how to account for that break. But what
remains fundamental in the work of this deductive and abstract mind,

providentially wandering in a field suffused with the narrative method, is that it escaped the tyranny of the historical actors' own conception of their experience and the myth of origins. Tocqueville was not personally immersed in the choices that Necker, Louis XVI, Mirabeau or Robespierre had to make. He was a bystander. He was speaking of other things.

That is why his book is even more important for the method it suggests than for the thesis it advances. It seems to me that historians of the Revolution have, and always will have, to make a choice between Michelet and Tocqueville. By that I do not mean the choice between a republican and a conservative interpretation of the French Revolution, for those two kinds of history would still be linked together in a common definition of the problem, which is precisely what Tocqueville rejected. What separates Michelet and Tocqueville is something else: it is that Michelet brings the Revolution back to life from the inside, that he communes and commemorates, while Tocqueville constantly examines the discrepancy he discerns between the intentions of the actors and the historical rôle they played. Michelet installed himself in the visible or transparent Revolution; he celebrated the memorable coincidence between values, the people and men's action. Tocqueville not only questioned that transparency or coincidence, but felt that it actually masked the nearly unbridgeable gap between human action and its real meaning that characterised the French Revolution, owing to the rôle played by democratic ideology. For Tocqueville, there was a gulf between the Revolution's true outcome and the revolutionaries' intentions.

That is why, in my opinion, *L'Ancien Régime et la Révolution* remains the most important book of the entire historiography of the French Revolution. It is also why it has always been, for more than a century now, the stepchild of that historiography, more often cited than read, and more read than understood.[11] Whether of the Right or of the Left, royalist or republican, conservative or Jacobin, the historians of the French Revolution have taken the revolutionary discourse at face value because they themselves have remained locked into that discourse. They keep putting on the Revolution the different faces assumed by the event itself in

11. Georges Lefebvre's rather condescending introduction to *L'Ancien Régime et la Révolution* (Paris: Gallimard, 1952) is characteristic of that situation. Even so, Lefebvre was the only historian of the French Revolution to have read Tocqueville with some care. All my references to *L'Ancien Régime* are to the above-mentioned critical edition in two volumes, respectively vol. II:1 and II:2 of Tocqueville's *Oeuvres complètes* (J. P. Mayer, general editor): vol. I (1952; 2nd edn, 1964), contains the published text, with introductions by Lefebvre and J. P. Mayer; vol. 2 (1953), edited by André Jardin, contains Tocqueville's working notes and unfinished chapters.

an unending commentary on a conflict whose meaning, so they think, the Revolution itself has explained to us once and for all through the pronouncements of its heroes. They must therefore believe, since the Revolution says so, that it destroyed the nobility when it negated its principle; that the Revolution founded a new society when it asserted that it did; that the Revolution was a new beginning of history when it spoke of regenerating the human race. Into this game of mirrors, where the historian and the Revolution believe each other's words literally, and where the Revolution has become history's protagonist, the absolutely trustworthy Antigone of the new era, Tocqueville introduces a doubt that strikes at the very heart of the matter: what if that discourse about a radical break reflects no more than the illusion of change?

The answer to that question is not simple, nor would answering it take care of the whole history of the Revolution. Yet it is probably indispensable to a conceptualisation of that history. Its importance can be measured negatively: unless the historian comes to grips with it, he is bound to execrate or to celebrate, both of which are ways of commemorating.

II

If Tocqueville is a unique case in the historiography of the Revolution, it is because his book forces the reader to *take apart* the 'French Revolution' and try to conceptualise it. By means of explicit concepts, Tocqueville breaks up the chronological narrative: he treats a problem rather than a period. With him, the Revolution no longer speaks all by itself, in one sense or another, as if its meaning were clear from the outset and substantiated by the very course it took. Tocqueville, instead, subjects it to a systematic interpretation that isolates some of its elements, in particular, administrative centralisation during the Ancien Régime and its effect on what might be called the 'democratisation' of society. The very long time span studied by Tocqueville (he constantly calls upon, for example, the reign of Louis XIV to make his points) can be explained by the nature of the problem he has set for himself and by the interpretation he advances: the Revolution was in a direct line with the Ancien Régime.

I am not suggesting that every effort to conceptualise the 'French Revolution' must be set in a vast chronological framework. The two things are not connected, and the 'long term' is not the only analytical tool at the historian's disposal. I simply mean that every interpretation of the Revolution supposes some time frame, and that the historian who views the Revolution as continuity will naturally investigate a longer period than one who seeks to understand it as an 'event' or series of events. But the second approach is no less valid than the first, and equally conducive to a constructive interpretation. The only suspect approach is precisely that which characterises the historiography of the Revolution, and illustrates its analytical underdevelopment: writing the history of the same period over and over again, as if the story, being told, spoke for itself, regardless of the historian's implicit presuppositions.

Such a history could, of course, be explicitly conceived as a pure narrative designed to reconstruct the individual or collective experiences of the participants rather than to interpret the meaning or meanings of the events. However, I am not taking issue with Georges Lenôtre but with Mathiez. I am well aware that every history is implicitly, and in varying degrees, a mixture of narrative and analysis, and that 'scholarly' history is not exempt from that 'rule'. But what is peculiar to the historiography of the Revolution is the unvarying internal organisation of its discourse. The place of each genre within that history never changes. Analysis is restricted to the problem of 'origins' or causes, which are explanatory factors. Narrative begins with the 'events', in 1787 or 1789, and runs through to the end of the 'story', until 9 Thermidor or 18 Brumaire, as if, once the causes are set out, the play went on by itself, propelled by the initial upheaval.

That mingling of genres comes from confusing two objects of analysis: it fails to distinguish between the Revolution as a historical process, a set of causes and effects, and the Revolution as a mode of change, a specific dynamic of collective action. Those two objects cannot be dealt with in the same intellectual operation; even superficial examination shows that, for example, they involve two different chronological frames of reference. In examining the causes or the results of the Revolution, the observer must go back far beyond 1789 on the one hand, and far ahead beyond 1794 or 1799 on the other. Yet the 'story' of the Revolution is enclosed between 1789 and 1794 or 1799. If those who write it are not, in general, aware of those different levels of chronology, it is because they mentally telescope the different levels of analysis by resorting to the following implicit hypothesis: the course taken by the Revolution was inherent in its causes, since its participants had no choice but to do what they did, namely, to destroy the Ancien Régime and to replace it with a new order. Whether that new order turned out to be democracy, as in Michelet, or capitalism, as in Mathiez, is irrelevant, for in both cases it is the consciousness of the participants that retrospectively shapes the analysis of

their actions. The historian who wants to remain faithful to that consciousness without neglecting his duty to provide an explanation needs
only to justify the advent of the new order in terms of necessity. If he does
that, he actually has no need to concern himself with the outcome.

If it were true that objective reasons necessarily – and even inevitably –
compelled men to take collective action to shatter the 'Ancien' régime and
to install a new one, then there would be no need to distinguish between
the problem of the origins of the Revolution and the nature of the event
itself. For not only would historical necessity coincide with revolutionary
action, but there would also be a perfect 'fit' [*transparence*] between that
action and the general meaning attributed to it by the protagonists, who
felt that they were breaking with the past and founding a new history.

The postulate that 'what actually happened' did so of necessity is a
classic retrospective illusion of historical consciousness, which sees the past
as a field of possibilities within which 'what actually happened' appears *ex
post facto* as the only future for that past. But in the case of the French
Revolution, that postulate overlaps a second one, from which it is
inseparable: the illusion that 1789, or the period 1789–93, represents an
absolute chronological break in the history of France. Before 1789,
absolutism and the nobility held sway (as if those two features of the
Ancien Régime went hand in hand). After 1789, liberty and the bourgeoisie came into their own. Lastly, hidden away in the sound and fury of
the Revolution, were the promises of an early form of socialism. In
keeping with what the protagonists of the revolutionary break had said,
French history thus assumes the status of a new beginning, and the event
itself becomes a kind of crucible in which the past was abolished, the
present was constituted and the future was shaped. Not only was what
happened fore-ordained; it also contained the seeds of the future.

Now the dominant 'concept' of today's historiography of the Revolution,
'bourgeois revolution', seems to me to be used less as a concept than as a
mask concealing precisely these two presuppositions: that of the inevitability of the event and that of a radical break in time. And it is
indeed an opportune 'concept' or mask, for it reconciles all levels of
historical reality and every aspect of the French Revolution. After all, the
events of 1789–94 are supposed to have given birth, simultaneously, to
capitalism at the economic level, to the preponderance of the bourgeoisie
in the social and political order, and to the ideological values that are
assumed to go with those two developments. Moreover, those events
betoken the fundamental rôle of the bourgeoisie as a class in the
Revolution. Hence the confused notion of 'bourgeois revolution' in-

separably designates both a historical content and a historical agent, arising together out of the fore-ordained explosion of the last few years of eighteenth century. The allegedly inevitable 'work' of the Revolution is thus given a perfectly suitable agent. In its systematic application of the idea that there was a radical break between 'before' and 'after', the 'social' interpretation of the French Revolution enthrones a metaphysical system of essence and fate. It is therefore much more than an interpretation of the Revolution: since it includes in its subject the whole problem of origins, that is, all of French society before 1789, it is also a retrospective vision of the 'Ancien Régime', which it defines *a contrario* by the new. Was the French Revolution indeed inevitable? In order to view it as such, all one has to do is reconstitute the flow of the movement toward it and that of the resistance it encountered and then set up, precisely in 1789, the shock that resolved the contradiction. On one side one places a stupid monarchy and an egotistical nobility, linked by common interests as well as by reactionary policies and ideologies. On the other, the rest of civil society, led, indeed carried along, by a rich, ambitious and frustrated bourgeoisie. The first set of forces functions not only as a factor of resistance to the historian's idea of evolution, but also as a dynamic counter-current: that is the rôle assigned to the 'feudal reaction' (or 'seigneurial' reaction, since the two terms seem to be used more or less interchangeably), as is well indicated by the term 'reaction', borrowed from mechanics. That reaction, which is supposed to have covered the second half of the eighteenth century, would account both for peasant violence in the summer of 1789 and for bourgeois resentment; in other words, for the conditions that united the Third Estate against the nobility. Impeded not simply by the natural inertia of tradition and of the State but by institutions and social classes that were actively and almost malevolently engaged in reconstructing the past, the forces of progress were reduced to a single and inevitable recourse: revolution.

In the general pattern of those two class fronts advancing from opposite directions towards each other as if to join battle, it is not difficult to recognise the view that the militants of the revolutionary years had of the events they were experiencing, and their interpretation of those events. They were expressing the logic of revolutionary consciousness, which, by its very nature, tends to promote a Manichaean explanation and to personify social phenomena. At this point the historian's occupational disease, which forever compels him to reduce the potential outcomes of a situation to a single one, since it alone occurred, is compounded by the intellectual simplifications that accompany and justify political violence in modern times. Hence the powerful attraction of single-cause explanations at every level of argument: victory of the Enlightenment over obscurantism, of liberty over oppression, of equality over privilege; or the advent of capitalism on the ruins of feudalism; or, finally, the synthesis of all these factors in a kind of logical balance-sheet, where they are lined up face to face in a systematic accounting of the past and the future. All these explanations employ the same logical mechanism. The Marxian synthesis enlarges the content while making it more rigid; but the mechanism itself has been at work since 1789, for it is a constitutive feature of the revolutionary ideology.

Integrated into a history whose every aspect it tends to incorporate, that mechanism spins its wheels in a vacuum and is more interesting for the contradictions it raises than for the problems it solves, as I have tried to show in one of the essays below, devoted to a critique of the communist historiography of the Revolution. Caricaturing the elementary traits of the revolutionary consciousness, carrying them to the absurdity of an illusory rigor presented as conceptualisation, this historiography illustrates the hopeless crisis of a tradition. It has lost the attractiveness of the epic story, which it has placed in a strait-jacket without adding anything to its own power of explanation, since it reduces the story to nothing more than a disguise for the presuppositions underlying the narrative. Significantly, it is in one of the fields where the most notable progress has been made in recent years, the history of traditional French society, that that kind of historiography turns out to be most summary and most inexact. In the system of equivalences and opposites it has contrived in order to celebrate the inevitability of a new beginning, no feature stands up to scrutiny, whether it be the confusion between monarchical State and nobility, between nobility and feudalism or between bourgeoisie and capitalism, or the opposition between absolutism and reform, aristocracy and liberty, society of orders and Enlightenment thought.

I shall not enter here into the detail of my critique, which can be found below.[12] However, it is necessary to add to it a more general observation: the establishment of a logical (and almost always implicit) connection identifying the Revolution as an objective historical process with the Revolution as a set of events that 'actually happened' – the Revolution-as-content with the Revolution-as-mode – necessarily leads to deducing the first aspect from the second. Yet it seems to me that the wise thing to do is to see them separately, a course that is suggested not only by

12. Cf. below, p. 81ff.

chronology but also, after all, by that old axiom – bourgeois as well as Marxist – that men make history but do not know the history they are making.

A phenomenon like the French Revolution cannot be reduced to a simple cause-and-effect schema. The mere fact that the Revolution had causes does not mean that they are all there is to its history. Let us assume for a moment that these causes are better understood than they actually are, or that some day it will be possible to list them in a more functional order; the fact remains that the revolutionary event, *from the very outset*, totally transformed the existing situation and created a new mode of historical action that was not intrinsically a part of that situation. One could, for instance, explain the revolt of most of the deputies to the Estates General by the political crisis in the Ancien Régime; but the situation created in its wake by the vacancy of power and the ensuing insurrection added a totally unprecedented dimension to that crisis, with consequences that no one could have foreseen two months earlier. One could also explain the popular urban uprisings of June–July by the economic crisis, the price of bread, unemployment, the commercial treaty between England and France, and so forth; but that type of explanation does not account for the transition from the grain or tax riot – a relatively classic occurrence in towns under the Ancien Régime – to the revolutionary *journée*, governed by an altogether different dynamic. In other words, the debate about the causes of the Revolution does not cover the problem of the revolutionary phenomenon, which was largely independent of the situation that preceded it, and therefore had its own consequences. The main characteristic of the Revolution as an *event* is a specific mode of historical action; it is a dynamic that one may call political, ideological or cultural, for its enhanced power to activate men and to shape events arose from the fact that it meant many things to many people.

Here again, Tocqueville was the first to sense that central problem. For his approach centres on the examination of what I call the Revolution-as-process, in his case a process of continuity. Tocqueville contends that the Revolution extended, consolidated and brought to perfection the administrative State and the egalitarian society whose development was the main achievement of the old monarchy. Hence, he finds an absolute incompatibility between the objective history of the Revolution – its 'meaning' or end result – and the meaning attributed to their own actions by the revolutionaries. One of the essays below discusses the elements of Tocqueville's conceptual analysis. Setting out from Tocqueville's present – the Revolution's outcome – *L'Ancien Régime* goes on to analyse the origins of the Revolution. There the central rôle was played by the administrative monarchy, which had emptied the society of orders of its living substance and opened the way less to equality of condition than to egalitarianism as a value. But between the origins and the end result, between Louis XIV and Bonaparte, there is a blank page that Tocqueville never filled. It contains some questions that he raised but never clearly answered: why did the process of continuity between the old régime and the new involve a revolution? And what, in those circumstances, is the significance of the revolutionaries' political commitment?

It is true that Book 3 of *L'Ancien Régime* does contain some partial answers to those questions, such as the substitution of intellectuals for politicians in eighteenth-century France, or the spread to all classes of society of democratic attitudes. But the extraordinary vitality of egalitarian ideology between 1789 and 1793 remains for Tocqueville a kind of mystery of evil, a religion in reverse. Nowhere in his work does he establish a conceptual link between his theory of the French Revolution and revolutionary action as it was experienced by contemporaries and expressed in such characteristic phenomena of the period as Jacobinism. Tocqueville makes us wonder whether one can even establish such a link; he forces us to separate, at least temporarily, the two parts of the confused amalgam called the 'history of the Revolution', and to stop juxtaposing the analysis of causes with the description of events as if the two techniques were part of one homogeneous discourse, and as if one could be deduced from the other.

These 'events', being political and even ideological in nature, invalidate by definition a causal analysis based on economic and social 'contradictions'; moreover, such an analysis, even when it deals with the political system and its legitimacy, does not take into account the radically new dimension added by revolutionary momentum. There is something in the concept of revolution (used in the latter, 'radical' sense) that corresponds to its 'experienced' historical reality, and is not subservient to the logical sequence of cause and effect: the appearance on the stage of history of a practical and ideological mode of social action totally unrelated to anything that came before. A specific type of political crisis made it possible, but not inevitable; and revolt was not its model, since revolt was by definition a part of the old political and cultural system.

The French Revolution is thus the matrix of a new type of historical action and consciousness, related to, but not defined by, a specific situation. One must take stock of that entire complex in order to propose an interpretation, instead of proceeding as if revolutionary consciousness were the normal result of legitimate grievances and a perfectly natural phenomenon in human history. The Marxist vulgate of the French Revolution actually turns the world upside down: it makes the revolutionary break a matter of economic and social change, whereas nothing resembled French society under Louis XVI more than French society under Louis-Philippe. And since it fails to take any distance from the revolutionary consciousness whose illusions and values it shares, it is incapable of realising that it treats the most radically new and the most mysterious aspect of the French Revolution as no more than the normal result of circumstances and as a natural occurrence in the history of the oppressed. After all, neither capitalism nor the bourgeoisie needed revolutions to appear in and dominate the history of the major European nations in the nineteenth century. But France was the country that, through the Revolution, invented democratic culture, and revealed to the world one of the basic forms of historical consciousness of action.

Let us first consider the impact of the circumstances, not of misery or oppression but of society's independence from politics. If the Revolution invented new structures and upset the old ones, if it set in motion enough new forces to transform the traditional mechanisms of politics, it was because it took over an empty space, or, rather, proliferated within that once forbidden sphere of power that it so suddenly invaded. In the dialogue between societies and their States that is part of the underlying texture of history, the Revolution tipped the scales against the State and in favour of society. For the Revolution mobilized society and disarmed the State; it was an exceptional situation, which provided society with a space for development to which it does not normally have access. From 1787, the kingdom of France had been a society without a State. Louis XVI continued to rally the consensus of his subjects round himself, but behind that traditional façade lay panic and disorder; while royal authority was nominally still respected, its legitimacy no longer extended to the agents of the crown. The king, it was said, had bad ministers, perfidious advisers and nefarious *intendants*; but as yet no one realised that this old monarchist refrain for difficult times had ceased to exalt the authority to whom the people could turn as an ultimate recourse, and had become instead a call for citizen control. In other words, civil society, where examples filter down from top to bottom, was ridding itself of the symbolic powers of the State, along with the rules it imposed.

Then came 1789. Affecting everyone, from the noblest of nobles to the humblest of peasants, the 'revolution' was born of the convergence of very different series of events, since an economic crisis (a complex phenomenon in itself, involving agricultural, 'industrial', meteorological and social factors) took its place alongside the political crisis that had begun in 1787. This convergence of several heterogeneous series, surely a fortuitous situation, was to be transformed as early as the spring of 1789 by a retrospective illusion in which it was seen as the inevitable consequence of bad government and as the central issue in the struggle between patriots and aristocrats. For the revolutionary situation was not only characterised by the power vacuum that was filled by a rush of new forces and by the 'free' activity of society. (I shall come back to that freedom later.) It was also bound up with a kind of hypertrophy of historical consciousness and with a system of symbolic representations shared by the social actors. The revolutionary consciousness, from 1789 on, was informed by the illusion of defeating a State that had already ceased to exist, in the name of a coalition of good intentions and of forces that foreshadowed the future. From the very beginning it was ever ready to place ideas above actual history, as if it were called upon to restructure a fragmented society by means of its own concepts. Repression became intolerable only when it became ineffectual. The Revolution was the historical space that separated two powers, the embodiment of the idea that history is shaped by human action rather than by the combination of existing institutions and forces.

In that unforeseeable and accelerated drift, the idea of human action patterned its goals on the exact opposite of the traditional principles underlying the social order. The Ancien Régime had been in the hands of the king; the Revolution was the people's achievement. France had been a kingdom of subjects; it was now a nation of citizens. The old society had been based on privilege; the Revolution established equality. Thus was created the ideology of a radical break with the past, a tremendous cultural drive for equality. Henceforth everything – the economy, society and politics – yielded to the force of ideology and to the militants who embodied it; no coalition nor any institution could last under the on-slaught of that torrential advance.

Here I am using the term ideology to designate the two sets of beliefs that, to my mind, constitute the very bedrock of revolutionary conscious-ness. The first is that all personal problems and all moral or intellectual matters have become political; that there is no human misfortune not amenable to a political solution. The second is that, since everything can be known and changed, there is a perfect fit between action, knowledge and morality. That is why the revolutionary militants identified their private lives with their public ones and with the defence of their ideas. It was a formidable logic, which, in a laicised form, reproduced the psychological commitment that springs from religious beliefs. When politics becomes the realm of truth and falsehood, of good and evil, and when it is politics that separates the good from the wicked, we find ourselves in a historical universe whose dynamic is entirely new. As Marx realised in his early writings, the Revolution was the very incarnation of the *illusion of politics*: it transformed mere experience into conscious acts. It inaugurated a world that attributes every social change to known, classified and living forces; like mythical thought, it peoples the objective universe with subjective volitions, that is, as the case may be, with responsible leaders or scapegoats. In such a world, human action no longer encounters obstacles or limits, only adversaries, preferably traitors. The recurrence of that notion is a telling feature of the moral universe in which the revolutionary explosion took place.

No longer held together by the State, nor by the constraints that had been imposed by power and had masked its disintegration, society thus recomposed itself through ideology. Peopled by active volitions and recognising only faithful followers or adversaries, that new world had an incomparable capacity to integrate. It was the beginning of what has ever since been called 'politics', that is, a common yet contradictory language of debate and action around the central issue of power. The French Revolution, of course, did not 'invent' politics as an autonomous area of knowledge; to speak only of Christian Europe, the theory of political action as such dates back to Machiavelli, and the scholarly debate about the origin of society as an institution was well under way by the seventeenth century. But the example of the English Revolution shows that when it came to collective involvement and action, the fundamental frame of intellectual reference was still of a religious nature. What the French brought into being at the end of the eighteenth century was not politics as a laicised and distinct area of critical reflection but democratic politics as a national ideology. The secret of the success of 1789, its message and its lasting influence lie in that invention, which was unprecedented and whose legacy was to be so widespread. The English and French revolutions, though separated by more than a century, have many traits in common, none of which, however, was sufficient to bestow on the first the rôle of universal model that the second has played ever since it appeared on the stage of history. The reason is that Cromwell's Republic was too preoccupied with religious concerns and too intent upon its return to origins to develop the one notion that made Robespierre's language the prophecy of a new era: that democratic politics had come to decide the fate of individuals and peoples.

The term 'democratic politics' does not refer here to a set of rules or procedures designed to organise, on the basis of election results, the functioning of authority. Rather, it designates a system of beliefs that constitutes the new legitimacy born of the Revolution, and according to which the 'people', in order to establish the liberty and equality that are the objectives of collective action, must break its enemies' resistance. Having become the supreme means of putting values into action and the inevitable test of 'right' or 'wrong' will, politics could have only a public spokesman, in total harmony with those values, and enemies who remained concealed, since their designs could not be publicly admitted. The 'people' were defined by their aspirations, and as an indistinct aggregate of individual 'right' wills. By that expedient, which precluded representation, the revolutionary consciousness was able to reconstruct an imaginary social cohesion in the name and on the basis of individual wills. That was its way of resolving the eighteenth century's great dilemma, that of conceptualising society in terms of the individual. If indeed the individual was defined in his every aspect by the aims of his political action, a set of goals as simple as a moral code would permit the Revolution to found a new language as well as a new society. Or, rather, to found a new society through a new language: today we would call that a nation; at the time it was celebrated in the *fête de la Fédération*.

This type of analysis has the two-fold advantage of restoring to the French Revolution its most obvious dimension, the political one, and of focusing attention on the true break in continuity it wrought between 'before' and 'after', that is, a change in the ways of legitimating and representing historical action. The action of the *sans-culottes* of 1793 is important not because it involved a 'popular' social group (impossible, by the way, to define in socio-economic terms) but because it expresses in its chemically pure form, as it were, such revolutionary notions of political action as obsession with treason and plot, the refusal to be represented, the will to punish, and so forth. And there is no way, nor will there ever be one, to explain those notions by a social situation fraught with conflicting interests. The first task of the historiography ,of the French Revolution must be to rediscover the analysis of its political dimension. But the price to pay is two-fold: not only must we stop regarding revolutionary consciousness as a more or less 'natural' result of oppression and discontent; we must also develop a conceptual understanding of this strange offspring of '*philosophie*' (its offspring, at least, in a chronological sense).

It is here that I turn to the work of Augustin Cochin, to which one of the chapters of this book is devoted.[13] For Cochin's unfinished work, which, like Tocqueville's, was brought to a halt by death, also raises a series of questions. But before going any further, I should like to outline his major historical insight by way of acknowledging how much my own book is indebted to it.

III

Cochin was interested precisely in what Tocqueville had not, or had barely, treated: not the continuity between the Ancien Régime and the Revolution, but the revolutionary break; not the similarity between two societies and two types of administrative centralisation dominated through-out by the same process creating equality, but instead the rending of the political fabric, the vacuum of power, replaced by the reign of democratic rhetoric and domination by the 'philosophical societies' (*sociétés de pensée*)* in the name of the 'people'. In short, Cochin wanted to re-write Michelet in conceptual terms, to analyse what he had felt and to interpret what he had merely relived. In comparison with his two great predecessors, Michelet and Tocqueville, Cochin's paradox lies in the fact that, like Tocqueville, he mistrusted the outpourings of the heart and the impas-sioned writing that are Michelet's genius, but, like Michelet, he was interested in the French Revolution as a political and cultural discon-tinuity. In trying to analyse why democratic ideology – the growth of which Tocqueville ascribed to the long-term development of the adminis-trative monarchy – erupted with such torrential violence, he brought to bear Tocqueville's deductive spirit on Michelet's dishevelled material. He sought to formulate a theory of the revolutionary event itself on the basis of the new system of action it unveiled: for him, it was a matter of analysing Jacobinism, rather than reliving it.

One must stop to consider that ambition, for after sixty years it is still brand-new. No one had followed in Cochin's footsteps, even though political science has since become a highly respectable academic field. It is therefore best to start again from the question he raised and to make it the

* Cochin's term *société de pensée* has been rendered throughout as 'philosophical society'. (Translator's note.)
13. Cf. below, p. 164ff.

centre for the discussion, independent of the particular arguments and the partial answers he himself put forward (these will be examined later on).

If one agrees that Jacobinism was the classic form of revolutionary consciousness (at the height of its development and social impact), one must treat it as both an ideology and a form of power – a system of representations and a system of action. These two aspects, while analytically distinct, are closely intertwined in historical reality, because such a system of representations confines and contains the choices of action, especially in the case of modern ideology, which, since the end of the eighteenth century, has emphasized individual commitment and the sanction of history. The Jacobin creed was indeed founded on immanence in history, on the realisation of values in and by political action, so that those values were at stake in every conflict, were embodied by the actors, and were as discoverable and knowable as truth itself. But the analogy to the operations of knowing and perceiving is fallacious to the extent that there was, prior to any reasoning, a kind of spontaneous equivalence between the values of revolutionary consciousness – liberty and equality – the nation that embodied those values, and the individuals charged with implementing or defending them. Indeed, it was this equivalence that *ipso facto* transformed those isolated individuals into a collective entity, the people, making the people the supreme source of legitimacy and the Revolution's sole agent. Hence the need for the constant presence of people within action, which otherwise would *degenerate* and once again fall into the hands of the wicked. Hence too the central notion of popular vigilance, the counterpart of the aristocratic plot and the symbolic affirmation of the perfect fit between action, power and values; such vigilance precluded, discredited or confined within narrow limits the constitutional devices of legislative representation and of the delegation of executive power. By the same token it was always raising – especially whenever the Revolution took a new turn – the insoluble problem of what forms the Revolution should take; and of who was speaking in its name. Which group, which assembly, which meeting, which consensus was the trustee of the people's word? That issue, a matter of life and death, determined the course of events and the distribution of power.

Yet the revolutionary situation connected even more closely the two levels of Jacobin consciousness, by transforming the system of representations into a system of action. To be more precise, the revolutionary situation and the new political dynamic were created when the vacant sphere of power was invaded by this type of ideology. The system of representations that the event could set in motion already existed: it had been developed earlier, as a kind of sociological counterpoint to Enlightenment philosophy. It thus did have origins, that is, materials and spokesmen; but the materials and projects would not necessarily have come together in a revolution.

To list the materials would lead to an examination of eighteenth-century political philosophy, which lies beyond the scope of this essay. What can be said in more general terms, as a suggestion for further research, is that classic modern thought came into its own when it focused on the problem of the individual. In economic thought, the concept of the individual served to distinguish the agents of production from the agents of consumption; in political thought, it led to the notion that absolutism had separated the State – defined as holder of the monopoly of violence over individuals – from society, defined as an aggregation of 'private' individuals. But it assumed its most general form in the idea of natural *equality* among men, meaning not that all men are born equal in strength or intelligence, but that no one has the right to subject others, since every person is endowed with sufficient reason to obey only himself. And since that natural equality is a form of liberty, the individual is not only a concept but a value. That fundamental notion led to the critical issue of eighteenth-century political philosophy: what kind of society is commensurate with the individual seen as both concept and value?

French thought, by and large, eschewed the recourse to the notion that there is a final harmony of interests, and that particular conflicts will benefit the common good. Even in devising a liberal economic system such as physiocracy, it felt the need to embody society in a unified image – the rational authority of legal despotism – because it was constantly groping for a political vision of society and was always concerned with the question of origins and the legitimacy of the social contract. If power and the law are based exclusively on the consent of the individual, then what is a society? How does one reconcile the concept of the free individual with the alienation of his freedom in the State?

The most rigorous theoretical formulation of that problem was provided by Rousseau, who also elaborated the speculative solution at the level of political justice by advancing the notion of the general will. It is not by chance that the philosopher who experienced and theorised, with greater sensitivity and power than anyone, the autonomy of the self, should also have conceived of the image of a totally unified society. For the general will presupposes the atomisation of society into myriads of 'autarchic' individuals who communicate with each other only through the general will; the general will must also identify itself fully with each individual will, so that in obeying the general will each individual obeys only himself. That is why, at least in theory, there can be no intermediary structure, such as a representative body, to represent citizens, between the general will and the individual wills that compose it, for any such arrangement would create a layer of special interests that would break the equivalence between individual liberty and subordination to the law. The sovereignty of each citizen is inalienable, except precisely in the one act that constitutes society, that is, a nation; the act by which each individual citizen continually establishes the general will. 'Sovereignty, being but the exercise of the general will, can never be alienated.'[14] Since there is only one sovereignty, it resides both in each individual and, through him, in a free people.

Rousseau's merit is his rigour. Given the principle of equality among men, that is, the principle that the individual has rights, Rousseau sees only two possible forms of the social contract, as he explains in his famous letter to the elder Mirabeau (26 July 1767). One of these is the state of political justice, that is, of man freely obeying the law, achieved by the constant mirroring between individual wills and the general will. If that is impossible, the next best thing is still the rule of force, which places man above the law, since the citizens have given over their sovereignty to an absolute despot who will at least guarantee peace within society. 'I do not see any tolerable middle ground between the most austere democracy and the most perfect Hobbesian régime; for the conflict between men and laws brings unending internicine war into the State and is the worst of all political situations.'[15]

Rousseau may well have been the most far-sighted genius ever to appear in intellectual history, for he invented, or sensed, so many of the problems that were to obsess the nineteenth and twentieth centuries. His political thought set up well in advance the conceptual framework of what was to become Jacobinism and the language of the Revolution, both in his philosophical premises (the fulfilment of the individual through politics) and because the radical character of the new consciousness of historical action is in keeping with his rigorous theoretical analysis of the conditions necessary for the exercise of popular sovereignty. Rousseau is hardly 'responsible' for the French Revolution, yet he unwittingly assembled the cultural materials that went into revolutionary consciousness and practice. It is an ironic twist of history that at the very moment when the Revolution believed it was implementing Jean-Jacques' ideas, it demonstrated, on the contrary, the validity of Rousseau's pessimism, that is

14. *The Social Contract*, Book 2, ch. 1.
15. *Correspondance générale* (Paris, 1932), vol. 17, p. 157.

to say the infinite distance between the rule of law and the rule of force, democracy's inability to follow its own theory in practice. That discrepancy, which was repeatedly conjured up in words, gave rise to the most garrulous discourse of the contemporary world: what we have here is no longer the theory, but the ideology of what Rousseau called 'the most austere democracy'.

But there is more to our eighteenth century than Rousseau, and most political theorists, either because they lacked his theoretical genius or because they shied away from democratic radicalism, did not push the logic of equality to its extreme conclusions – although they shared it as one of the century's credos. The escape hatch from that logic is a perfectly simple device; it consists of nothing more than turning toward the empirical reality of history. Men are born equal in rights, but history has made them unequal; and since history also shapes the conditions of the social contract, the parties to that contract, which is the only basis of legitimate power, are no longer endowed with that original equality. That is why Boulainvilliers and Montesquieu were able, on the one hand, to reconcile natural equality with actual inequality and, on the other, to transform the inequalities born of history into individual and collective rights guaranteed by the contract between the king and his subjects.

Seen in that perspective, the social contract is grounded in history; nonetheless it fulfills the same functions as Rousseau's theoretical demonstration: both ensure that not only power, but also the relationship between individuals and the abstract community that makes them a people, will have a legitimacy based on the rights of those individuals. And here, more clearly than in Rousseau, that abstract community has a name: the nation. For the nation is precisely the matrix for history and for the social contract, an aggregate of imprescriptible individual rights whose cohesion and defence it alone can ensure. The nation is thus the trustee of the original relationship that gave rise to the monarchy and thereby to the original contract. History is a collective reminiscence, the only means by which the French people can reconquer the rights of the nation, that is, their own. That is why Boulainvilliers' or Mably's histories of France, so full of ever-repeated usurpations, of periods or actions that dealt disastrous blows to that reconquest, are nonetheless ultimately tinged with optimism: one need only return to Charlemagne and the 'Champs de mai' and all will be well.[16]

16. See François Furet and Mona Ozouf, 'Deux légitimations historiques de la société française au XVIIIᵉ siècle: Mably et Boulainvilliers', *Annales E.S.C.* (May–June 1979), 438–50.

The history of the nation thus develops, along with a constitutional theory of royal power from which it is inseparable, a definition of citizenship, that is of individuals endowed with imprescriptible (though not necessarily equal) rights in relation to that power. The nation is the homogeneous and unanimous group of citizens who have recovered their rights. Society is thus conceived of in terms of the nation: the multiplicity of individuals and of private interests is immediately cancelled out and reaggregated by the existence of a historical contract harking back to the nation's origins. There can be no society without that contract and without that origin.

Now, to conceive of society in terms of the nation is no longer, as in Rousseau, to reduce society to its founding principle; it is to celebrate the marriage between society and its myth. That is another cultural element that was to be used extensively in the revolutionary consciousness, which was quick to appropriate the benefits to be reaped by referring to origins. The Revolution only needed to shift that founding image onto itself in order to legitimate its claim to constitute the matrix of the social and national contract. Celebrated as a re-enactment of 14 July, the *fête de la Fédération* needed no other claim to found the nation. What had been perceived before 1789 as a future restoration had become the original contract.

One can gauge the widespread acceptance of the 'national' interpretation of society in Ancien-Régime France by the thousands of pre-revolutionary pamphlets[17] in which 'Germanic' freedoms, formerly a monopoly of the nobles, have become the mythic patrimony of the entire nation in its decisive struggle for *restoration*. More than half the pamphlets[18] include references to the history of France, which, when analysed in their context, amount in most cases to a genuine historical plea for the rights of the 'nation'. The powerful appeal of that new national awareness can also be read in the rejection of all foreign models, on the rare occasions when they are invoked. The authors of that literature invoke English, Swiss or Dutch institutions only to point out that they are inapplicable to France, given the country's special features (size of the population, extensive territory) and its tradition. But what is even more remarkable is that all the texts make the history of France begin with the Franks; there is no trace of the *abbé* Dubos's 'Romanist' thesis, which

---

17. Most of these pamphlets are in the Bibliothèque Nationale but the British Library and the New York Public Library hold a few hundred each.
18. This commentary is based on a sample of 230 pamphlets published between February 1787 and March 1789, representing one-tenth of those held at the Bibliothèque Nationale.

aimed, in the middle of the century, at defending the primacy of royal authority by linking it to the Romano-Byzantine *imperium*. Boulainvilliers and Mably had triumphed; France was indeed issued from a contract between the Franks and their king.[19]

France created kings just as kings created France. At the core of that notion is the king–nation pair, two powers defined not by a conflict, but as the two indispensable elements of legitimate authority bound together in a pattern of subordination. The king, whose historical calling is attested by lineage, is the embodiment of the State. The nation, a human community both historical and mythical, is the trustee of the social contract and embodies the general will arising out of the depth of the past, as well as a pledge to uphold the original promises. King and nation are tied by a bond of necessity, which also compels them to cooperate: the king is the head of the nation, yet derives his authority from the nation's consent, ruling legitimately only so long as he continues to respect the essential contract, also called the kingdom's constitution.

Should he fail to show such respect, it can only be because baneful but powerful forces are interfering with that cooperation and upsetting the harmonious relationship between him and his people. For French history is a play with three, not two actors. Between the king and the nation there are a number of distinct social forces, all of which are nonetheless defined with reference to the original contract. The nobility is the most important of them, but the *parlements*, the *robe* [magistrature], and the clergy can also function as intermediary bodies.

They may be a party to the contract as representatives of the people, and so invested with the legitimacy of origins. A minority of the texts of that period reflect the ideas of that history of France *à la Boulainvilliers*, which assigns a central rôle to the intermediary function of the kingdom's traditional *corps*, headed by the nobility; any failure by the king to respect that function is regarded as a violation of the 'constitution' and thus as despotic. The threat of that deviation, say the texts, has always been present and has been conspicuous since the days of Richelieu.

The intermediary *corps* may act instead as so many screens between the king and the nation; far from representing the people, they usurp its function. In that history of France *à la Mably*, by far the more widespread, the nefarious forces that periodically short-circuited the legitimate political communication between the king and the nation advance under a

19. One has only to recall that these historical themes were already used in the sixteenth century, notably by François Hotman, during the national crisis brought about by the religious wars to realise to what extent the cultural traits of the Ancien Régime were still dominant in the years immediately preceding the French Revolution.

mask, since they would be crushed if they showed their true faces; but one can name them in the abstract by a generic formula that covers an ever-recurring calamity: usurpation of power by the nobility. It is a phenomenon that existed throughout the Merovingian age, between the two blessed ages of Clovis and Charlemagne, and was responsible, in the period between Charlemagne and Philip Augustus, for the situation referred to in most of the second variety of texts as 'feudal anarchy'. Beginning with Philip the Fair, the rise of a power that was indissolubly royal and popular led to the emergence of a few great symbolic figures of kings as fathers of the people, such as Louis XII and Henry IV. But Richelieu, who is as nefarious a figure in this kind of history as in the one described above, marks the return to a tyranny that is both 'aristocratic' and 'ministerial' and was to be exemplified by Louis XIV and Louis XV.

Those two versions of the history of France are inspired by the same interpretation of origins and dominated by a vision of imminent restoration. The first includes a theory of representation, but it was unacceptable, as was aristocratic liberalism as a whole, because it was a vehicle and a plea for corporate interests. The second version, on the other hand, builds up a historico-political schema that foreshadows the dilemma of revolutionary democracy. The sovereign nation is conceived as the integrating embodiment of sovereign individuals and the matrix of rights and values. It constitutes both the people (the collective, unanimous and vigilant protagonist of a history received and transformed), and power (a power constantly threatened by the usurpation and the plots of enemies of the nation and of the people).[20] What is striking in this inextricably historico-sociological configuration is that the image of power it conveys through the king–nation pair should be one of absolute power. Even though the administrative monarchy was never (and certainly not at the end of the eighteenth century) an absolute power in the modern sense of the word, its own notion of the power it wielded and the image it

---

20. Perhaps the most typical example of the historico-political vision I am trying to reconstruct can be found in two consecutive *mémoires* written by d'Antraigues, the future royalist agent, on the subject of the Estates General. These *mémoires* appeared in late 1788 and early 1789. D'Antraigues's main idea is that the Estates General are the repository of national sovereignty (which had been usurped first by feudal tyranny, then by royal despotism); hence the elected representatives must serve in that body in strict accordance with the will of their constituents, so that they are 'not empowered to decide any question whatsoever without their [constituents'] orders, and obliged to sollicit them if unforeseen developments should call for a new decision' (first *mémoire*). The second text is devoted to the problem of representation: supporting his reasoning by references to the *Social Contract* and to Rousseau's modified view of the exercise of the general will put forward in his work on the Polish constitution, d'Antraigues recommends the idea of the binding mandate.

projected had both, in a way, become part of the national consciousness. Through the nation – and also through the general will – the French unwittingly recovered the mythical image of unlimited power, since such power could encompass and represent all of society. The slow drive of civil society toward *power* was carried out in the name of *this absolute* power, since it was seen as the very principle of all power: identical with the nation and the people, it even possessed its anti-principle, the plot.

Although French political thought thus developed specific cultural assumptions that were to be used or recast by revolutionary ideology, we have yet to understand why these assumptions – which precluded for example (at least in a form that could easily be implemented under the law) the English idea of representation – developed so rapidly in the last years of the Ancien Régime and by whom they were conveyed.

French society in the eighteenth century was desperately searching for responsible spokesmen. It was too highly 'developed', as we would say today, to be kept, as in the preceding century, in silent and obedient submission to the State. But in its search for political representation it was hampered by the legacy of Louis XIV, who had systematically closed off the channels of communication between society and the State (such as the Estates General, the remonstrances of the *parlements*, the municipalities and the town councils) yet also maintained and even consolidated the structure of the society of orders. It was only natural that after the death of Louis XIV, society should attempt to revive the traditional circuits of representation, especially the rôle of the *parlements*. But since these same *parlements*, throughout the century, gave repeated proof of their conservatism, since they condemned the *Encyclopédie*, and *Émile*, and the unfortunate Calas, they hardly constituted the best spokesmen for an 'enlightened' society. They could perpetuate the illusion of their representative character only so long as the monarchical State – before or after it yielded to them – fought them; but the illusion was short-lived.

That is why eighteenth-century society increasingly turned to other spokesmen, namely to the *philosophes* and men of letters. No one has understood and expressed that better than Tocqueville in the first chapter of Book 3 of *L'Ancien Régime*. He felt that, by abolishing the ancient 'liberties' and destroying the political function of the nobility without also permitting the formation of a new ruling class on a different basis, the monarchy unwittingly set up the writers as imaginary substitutes for that ruling class. Hence literature took on a political function:

Considering that this same French nation – so unfamiliar with the conduct of its own affairs, so deprived of experience, so hampered by its political institutions, and so powerless to improve them – was also at that time the most literate nation on earth and the one that cared most deeply about the things of the mind, one can easily understand how its writers came to be a political power and eventually became the foremost of these powers.

That confusion of rôles, in which men of letters assumed a function they could fulfil only in its imaginary aspects, that is, as opinion-makers who wielded no practical power whatsoever, was to shape political culture itself. The men of letters tended to substitute abstract right for the consideration of facts, principles for the weighing of means, values and goals for power and action. Thus the French, deprived as they were of true liberties, strove for abstract liberty; incapable of collective experience, lacking the means of testing the limits of action, they unwittingly moved toward the *illusion of politics*. Since there was no debate on how best to govern people and things, France came to discuss goals and values as the only content and the only foundation of public life.

Yet Tocqueville's brilliant analysis, which explains so much about the intellectuals' rôle in French political debate since the eighteenth century, is not sufficient to account for the sociological conditions that shaped the elements of what was to become the revolutionary consciousness. What is missing in his general intuition is an examination of the channels by which the new power of public opinion, existing side by side with power *tout court*, came to act upon society. For society produced, and maintained, alongside the traditional one, a new *political sociability*, waiting in the wings to take over the entire stage: that was Augustin Cochin's discovery.

By political sociability, I mean a specific mode of organising the relations between citizens (or subjects) and power, as well as among citizens (or subjects) themselves in relation to power. An 'absolute' monarchy implies and presents a type of political sociability in which all of society is arranged concentrically and hierarchically around the monarchy, which is the central organising force of social life. It occupies the summit of a hierarchical arrangement of *corps* and communities whose rights it guarantees and through which authority flows downward, while obedience (tempered by grievances, remonstrances, and negotiations) flows upward. Under the Ancien Régime, however, the circuits of the old political sociability were increasingly stripped of their traditional meaning and their symbolic content; the administrative monarchy dealt a severe blow to ranks and *corps* when it taxed them. To the very end it clung to the image of a society it had done its best to destroy; but nothing in that theoretical society allowed it to communicate any longer with real society. Everything, beginning with the court, had become a screen.

Yet real society did reconstruct, in other ways and other places, beyond the monarchy, a world of political sociability. This new world was based on individuals, and no longer on the institutional groups to which they belonged; it was founded on the confused notion called 'opinion' that came into being in cafés, salons, Masonic lodges and the so-called *sociétés de pensée*, or 'philosophical societies'. One can call it democratic sociability – even though its network did not extend to all of the people – simply to express the idea that its lines of communication were formed 'below' and ran horizontally in a disjointed society, where all individuals were equal. 'Opinion' was precisely the obscure way of expressing the idea that something new had emerged from the silence that had engulfed the pyramid of the king's traditional interlocutors. That 'something' was based on new principles, but nobody clearly understood what they were.

The reason is that while democratic sociability did indeed begin to reunify a disintegrating society – for it played, on a practical level, the same integrating rôle as ideologies of the 'nation' on the intellectual level – it remained in many respects, like its older counterpart, impenetrable. The new centres around which it took shape, such as the philosophical societies or the Masonic lodges, lay by definition outside the traditional institutions of the monarchy. They could not become 'corporate bodies' in the traditional pyramid since they were not only of a different, but indeed of an incompatible order. The elements they were made of did not exist prior to society, as so many indivisible nuclei that together might constitute a hierarchical organisation. They were, on the contrary, *products* of a society, albeit of a society emancipated from power and engaged in creating a new social and political fabric based on the individual. Such a principle could not be openly proclaimed and had, in fact, long been fought against by the kings of France, so that for a very long time those new centres of democratic sociability seemed suspect and were often secret or semi-secret.

The new circuit of sociability thus had no communication with the traditional one; it was totally unrelated to the network of relationships woven by the authorities. It produced opinion, not action – or, better, it produced opinion that had no effect on action. Its image of power was thus substitutive, yet patterned on the 'absolute' power of the monarch, simply inverted in favour of the people. The very fact that a philosophical society or club claimed to be speaking for the nation, or for the people, was sufficient to transform individual opinions into plain 'opinion' and opinion into imaginary absolute power, for in that kind of alchemy there was no room for either legitimate disagreement or legitimate representation. The two symmetrical and opposite images of undivided power furnished the ingredients for notions and reciprocal imputations of conspiracy: enlightened 'opinion' believed in a conspiracy of ministers or a plot to institute a ministerial despotism; the royal administration believed in a conspiracy among the grain merchants or the men of letters.

It is precisely in that sense that the eighteenth-century French monarchy was *absolute*, and not – as has been said again and again by republican historiography on the basis of what the Revolution asserted – because of the way it exercised its authority. Its power was weak, but it conceived of itself as undivided. That notion, which remained intact even after its actual content had eroded, was precisely the sufficient and necessary reason for the concealment of the political circuit. As society wrested – or reconquered – more and more power from the monarchy, the notion of absolutism proved so persuasive that it became necessary to refashion that power in an outwardly radically different manner and yet on the model of absolutism. The two circuits were incompatible precisely because they had so much in common. If they excluded any means of communicating with each other, it was because they shared the same idea of power. The French Revolution is inconceivable without that idea, or that phantasm, which was a legacy of the monarchy; but the Revolution anchored power in society instead of seeing it as a manifestation of God's will. The revolutionary consciousness took form as an attempt to recreate undivided power in a society free of contradictions. The new collectively shared image of politics was the exact reverse of that of the Ancien Régime.

It is clear that ever since the death of Louis XIV the idea of absolute monarchy had blocked all efforts at revamping the political system, in particular the attempt at establishing a representative régime. The *parlements*, being an integral part of the traditional structure, usurped rather than exercised a representative rôle. Yet when they too finally claimed to embody 'the nation', as in the famous episode of 1769–71,[21] they unwittingly based their stand on the system of fictive equivalences that was

---

21. I am referring to the series of remonstrances of the *Cour des aides* [tax court], many of which were written by Malesherbes himself, who was First President during these years of bitter conflict with Louis XV. The most explicit text is that of 18 February 1771. Written after the most active members of the *parlement* had been exiled and their offices confiscated, it protests against the 'destructive system that threatens the entire nation', and against the arbitrary royal power that 'deprives the nation of the most essential rights of a free people'.

just beginning to form the democratic texture of the philosophical societies. Nothing shows more clearly the identical though opposite character of the two sets of political assumptions, and the mutual exclusiveness this implied, than that oligarchy of privileged men who started speaking of the 'nation' and the 'people', and who could break out of the absolute monarchy only by espousing pure democracy.

Yet one must resist the temptation to rebuild our entire eighteenth century, or even its second half, in the light of 1789 or 1793. While it is true that the *materials* of the revolutionary consciousness to come existed in France in the 1770s or 1780s, there is no reason to conclude that a 'crystallisation' took place, or was inevitable. The two types of political sociability still coexisted peacefully in early 1789, when the French were called upon by Louis XVI to draw up their *Cahiers de doléances*, and to send their deputies to Versailles. It would be too much to say that they blended in harmony. The king juxtaposed them awkwardly in his summons when he mixed the ancient structure for expressing 'grievances', supposedly to be drawn up by an ascending sequence of unanimous assemblies, with an electoral procedure of a modern and democratic kind, at least within the Third Estate.[22] The incoherences of the 'Regulations' of January 1789 and the absence of public debate and of any organised contest of opinions made it possible to manipulate the assemblies; yet the immense task of writing the *Cahiers* produced a set of texts in which unanimity is far more frequent than disagreement, even among the three Orders, and in which there is nothing to foreshadow a brutal rending of the social and political fabric. The revolutionary actors emerged from the elections of 1789, but the language of the Revolution was not yet used in the *Cahiers*.

For the *Cahiers* did not speak the language of democracy, but that of the jurists of the Ancien Régime. It is not that they were more 'moderate' than the revolutionary texts that appeared later or already accompanied them in a few instances. But what they expressed was altogether different from the Revolution, for they amounted to the testament of the reform movement of the Ancien Régime, written in its own language. Quite clearly the substance of these thousands of texts, and especially, for the Third Estate, of the summaries drawn up at the *bailliage* level, was borrowed from the practices and the vocabulary of royal officials: that is what gave them their homogeneous tone, despite their having been drawn up on behalf of communities, corporate bodies or estates. Through the

22. Jacques Cadart, *Le Régime électoral des États généraux de 1789 et ses origines, 1302–1614*, Annales de l'Université de Lyon, 3rd series, 11 (Paris: Sirey, 1952).

voice of the *robe*, the old circuit of political sociability delivered its last message: *la nation, le roi, la loi.*

Yet the first hypothesis that comes to mind about the *Cahiers* is the exact opposite. The historian is spontaneously inclined to expect these texts, written in March or April, to contain a premonition of things to come and to read them as a foreshadowing of the events of June and July. His inclination is all the more 'natural' as these thousands of documents were drawn up and distributed according to the divisions within the old society, so that they seem to offer an ideal vantage point from which to discern the central antagonism between the Third Estate and the nobility, which was to be of such crucial importance. However, a term-by-term comparison between the *Cahiers* at the *bailliage* level of the Third Estate and those of the nobility does not bring to light anything of the kind; in fact the two groups of texts can be analysed far better in terms of what they have in common than in terms of contradictions or even simple differences.

The *Cahiers* of the nobility are on the whole somewhat more 'enlightened' than those of the Third Estate, in that they made greater use of the vocabulary of the Enlightenment and placed greater emphasis on such demands as personal freedom or the rights of man. The *Cahiers* of the Third Estate at the *bailliage* level were more or less obliged to take over the litany of rural demands, even though they owed their inspiration and content largely to urban texts, especially – and not by coincidence – those of 'free' inhabitants (that is, independent of the trade-guilds). Those *Cahiers* go into greater detail when enumerating needed reforms; and it is not surprising that a larger number of them call for voting by head.[23]

But those differences did not lead to antagonism among the kingdom's estates. The last consultation conducted by the monarchy, though organised upon largely new principles, still had the power to contain public opinion within traditional channels. Thus, contrary to what Tocqueville wrote about the *Cahiers*,[24] one finds in them almost no hint of the coming

23. In addition to my own research I am using here the unpublished work of an American historian, Sasha R. Weitman, 'Bureaucracy, Democracy, and the French Revolution' (Ph.D. thesis, Washington University, Saint Louis, 1968). His work is based on a systematic and quantitative analysis of the demands contained in the noble *Cahiers* and in those of the Third Estate at the *bailliage* level.

24. Cf. *L'Ancien Régime*, Book 2, part 1, p. 197: 'I am carefully reading the *Cahiers* ... I see that here they are demanding a change in the law, there in a custom, and I take note of the demands. I continue this immense labor to the end, and when I come to add up all these particular demands I realise with a kind of terror that what is called for is the simultaneous and systematic abolition of all laws and all customs governing the country; and it immediately becomes clear to me that this will be one of the most far-reaching and dangerous revolutions the world has ever seen.' (*To continue next page.*)

revolutionary ideology, nothing to foreshadow the character of the Revolution, nor even, in particular, a trace of the battle for the symbolic monopoly over the people's will that was to be at the centre of the great events to come. Even more important, that entire corpus of texts – a monument to the spirit of the *robe*[25] – is still imbued with a common reference to tradition. The very men who had for centuries made the French monarchy were determined to reform it, but according to its true principles. Of all the demands voiced by the *Cahiers* concerning power (and they are very homogeneous indeed), the most unanimous is surely for control of taxation by periodically convened Estates General. It is related to very old notions of the monarchy: the power to tax is seen as the royal prerogative *par excellence*, indeed as more crucial to the State than judicial power, yet it must be exercised within just limits and negotiated with the Estates General, which deliver the consent of the king's subjects. Many *Cahiers* demand wider powers for those Estates – provincial or general – to the detriment of the royal *intendants* and in the name of a constitution that must be not so much established as 'restored', indeed 'secured'. But, with rare exceptions,[26] those demands remain within the limits of traditional political legitimacy. There is no better proof than the frequency with which the *Cahiers* sound the theme of the good king and the bad ministers, a typical feature of the 'absolutist' notion of monarchy.

It is true that whenever the *Cahiers*, especially at *bailliage* level, show any 'learning' at all, they speak of 'the nation' in order to demand the restoration or the securing of its rights. But in so doing they by no means reject the notion of citizen representation. On the contrary, they base their demand on the old idea that there is a set of original rights predating

Tocqueville's analysis, or rather 'impression', seems to me excessive, and characteristic of a kind of teleological illusion to which every historian of the French Revolution is prone: since the Revolution did take place, everything must have foreshadowed it. In fact, a very painstaking study of several thousand *Cahiers* I have undertaken as part of a wider investigation, under the auspices of the Centre de Recherches Historiques at the École des Hautes Études en Sciences Sociales, has shown that most of the grievances voiced by those *Cahiers*, even at the *bailliage* level, concern the reform of taxation and of the judicial system; and that the demand for power as such rarely went beyond the 'constitutional' (in both the archaic and the modern sense of the word) frameworks analysed above. The American historian George V. Taylor comes to the same conclusion by a different approach and stresses the moderate character of the *Cahiers de doléances*. Cf. his 'Les Cahiers de 1789 sont-ils révolutionnaires?' *Annales E.S.C.* (November–December 1973), 1495–1514.

25. A. Dupront, 'Cahiers de doléances et mentalités collectives', *Actes du 89e Congrè's national des Sociétés savantes*, Lyons, 1964 (Paris: Imprimerie Nationale, 1964), vol. 1, pp. 375–7.

26. One of the exceptions is the *Cahier* of the Rouen merchants, which states: 'There is no need to delve into the depths of the past in order to ascertain the rights of the nation; the assembled people is everything; it alone holds sovereign power.'

the monarchy itself; in adapting the ingredients of a 'Germanist' historiography or notions of 'natural' equality to a modern theory of powers, they simultaneously transformed the structure of the Estates General into a representative system. That alchemy, which becomes visible in the ambiguity of the word 'constitution', did not yet involve the notions of popular will and direct democracy that were to be held by the revolutionary clubs. It laid the groundwork for the delegation of powers, but did not inaugurate the symbolic reign of the popular will as the substitute for society.

Thus, the *Cahiers* were well in the mainstream of the old power structure: the king consulted his people, and all the communities that composed it, indeed made it a people – responded. However, that consultation involved an election, which was not part of the traditional scenario. For, unlike in 1614, when the 'natural' delegates of the various communities, such as aldermen, were simply appointed, it gave rise to political competition, a clear sign that in addition to or beyond what was stated 'unanimously' in the *Cahiers*, there was power to be had and people willing to fight for it. It was precisely during that battle that revolutionary ideology came into being and assumed the function of sorting men into different categories, which the elaboration of grievances had failed to do.

Two conditions were thus necessary for the birth of revolutionary ideology. The first was the availability of power, which, having been vacated by the traditional authorities, was there for ideology to take over. That situation is denied by the *Cahiers*, which were imprisoned in what one might call their outmoded channels of communication with the monarchy, so that these thousands of texts speak with a voice that is genuine in every outward detail, yet hides the new political configuration. But for the Revolution to gain strength as an idea, it also needed the chance to appropriate for its own benefit the interpretation of what was meant by the 'people's will'. That chance came with the balloting of 1789, which provided only for a unanimous outcome, although it was set up as a true election. The future deputies therefore had no choice but to recast absolute power for their own benefit.

That is why revolutionary ideology was born not in the *Cahiers* but in the battles of the election itself: although seemingly marginal, they were in fact vitally important for excluding certain persons in relation to the people's will. Robespierre became Robespierre only when he had to win his seat as deputy for the Third Estate from Arras. It was then that the young conformist invented the discourse of equality. Similarly, what brought national attention to *Qu'est-ce que le Tiers État?* and a seat in the Third Estate of Paris to the *vicaire général* of Chartres was the fact that his famous pamphlet was both a discourse on exclusion and a discourse on origins. Sieyès's theory was that the nobility was not part of the national will, and he ostracised the order as a whole, setting it up as the enemy of the common weal and announcing the dawning of an age of a science of society and happiness for all:

In the dark ages of barbarism and feudalism it was possible to destroy true relations among men, to sow disorder in every nation, and to corrupt all justice; but now that daylight is rising, all Gothic absurdities must flee, all remnants of ancient ferocity must crumble and die. That much is certain. But will we only exchange one evil for another, or will true social order, in all its beauty, take the place of the old disorder?[27]

After that, it mattered little that Sieyès also developed a theory of representation, since what could be represented was precisely what the citizens had in common, that is, the will to found a nation in opposition to the nobility. With that staggering tautology the new political world was invented.

I have long thought that it might be intellectually useful to date the beginning of the French Revolution to the Assembly of Notables in early 1787, for that chronological transfer has the double advantage of dating the crisis of traditional authority more precisely and of integrating what has come to be called the 'aristocratic revolution' into the Revolution itself. For the absolute monarchy died, in theory and in practice, in the year when its *intendants* were made to share their responsibilities with elected assemblies in which the Third Estate was given twice as many representatives as in the past.[28] What foundered in the void created by the rapid collapse of the monarchy's authority was not only the 'aristocracy' or the *parlements*, but indeed political society as a whole. And the break that occurred in late 1788 between the *parlements*, which favoured a traditional summoning of the Estates, and the rest of that political society – which already called itself 'the nation' – was, as Cochin already realised, the first of the many schisms that were to divide the revolutionary camp.

In fact, Tocqueville dates what he calls the 'true spirit of the Revolution' from September 1788. He wrote long passages about it, but never put them into a definitive form, and they were published together with his working notes (*L'Ancien Régime*, vol. 2, Book 1, ch. 5). He defines that 'spirit' less exclusively than I do, tracing its various manifestations,

27. *Qu'est-ce que le Tiers État?*, ch. IV, section 3.
28. The basic book on this question is still P. Renouvin, *Les Assemblées provinciales de 1787* (Paris: Picard, 1921).

such as the abstract search for the perfect constitution to be established once the slate of the past has been wiped clean, or the will to transform 'the very foundation of society' (p. 106). Yet he comes close to the definition I am trying to develop when he characterises the evolution of ideas in late 1788 as follows:

At first people spoke only of working for a better adjustment in the relations between classes; soon they advanced, ran, rushed toward the idea of pure democracy. In the beginning they quoted and commented Montesquieu; in the end they talked of no one but Rousseau. He became and was to remain the only tutor of the Revolution in its youth (pp. 106–7).

I am not sure that the evolution of ideas was that simple. In order to find out, one would have to be able not only to read but to date all the pamphlets of the period, which are for the most part anonymous and undated. Tocqueville made extensive use of Sieyès's pamphlet, which he considered typical, while I feel that at that date it was prophetic and therefore exceptional. It was no doubt because he wanted to keep to his timetable of radicalisation that Tocqueville saw the *Cahiers* as a corpus of revolutionary texts. But I believe that in fact the current of traditional political ideas (or what I have called the old political sociability) lived on in the *Cahiers* and also in many political pamphlets, even those written after September 1788.

Yet the chronological break of September is important, and Tocqueville's intuition was fundamentally correct. The summoning of the Estates General, the appointment of Necker, the recall of the *parlements*, all in the summer of 1788, were so many acts of capitulation by Louis XVI that created a general power vacuum. They touched off a war among the classes who wanted that power, a war that was fought over the modes of representation in the Estates and thus opened up a vast field for the deployment of ideas and social passions. Here was the opening through which the ideology of pure democracy surged in, even though it did not gain full control until the spring of 1789.

If one defines the Revolution as the collective crystallisation of a certain number of cultural traits amounting to a new historical consciousness, the spring of 1789 is indeed the key period. For while power had been available for at least two years, the fact became fully apparent only at this point, with the victorious revolt of the 'Commons' against the king's orders. Until May, the old mode of political sociability, centred on the king of France at the summit of the social order, more or less held up – as the *Cahiers* indicate – for the area of power he had in fact relinquished had not yet been discovered. But all that changed with the events of May, June and July. The victory of the Third Estate over the king, the capitulation of the First and Second Estates, the taking of the Bastille, and the vast popular excitement that preceded and followed it clearly went beyond the framework of the old legitimacy. Thought and speech were liberated, not only from censorship and the police – as, in fact, they had been for some years – but from the internal inhibition created when voluntary consent is given to age-old institutions: the king was no longer the king, the nobility was no longer the nobility, the Church was no longer the Church. Moreover, once the masses had broken in on the stage of history, political education gained a vast new public, whose expectations called for completely new modes of social communication. Speeches, motions and newspapers ceased to be aimed at educated people, and were henceforth submitted to the judgment of the 'people'. The Revolution marks the beginning of a theatre in which language freed from all constraints seeks and finds a public characterised by its volatility. This two-fold shift in the functioning of the symbolic circuit that surrounds and protects power was the outstanding development in the spring of 1789.

That is why, in a sense, everything indeed 'began' here: 1789 opened a period when history was set *adrift*, once it was discovered that the actors in the theatre of the Ancien Régime were mere shadows. The Revolution is the gap that opened up between the language of the *Cahiers* and that of the *Ami du peuple* in the space of only a few months.[29] It must be seen as not so much a set of causes and consequences as the opening of a society to all its possibilities. It invented a type of political discourse and practice by which we have been living ever since.

IV

By the spring of 1789, then, it had become clear that power no longer resided in the royal Councils and *bureaux*, from which a steady stream of decisions, regulations and laws had been sent out for so many centuries. All of a sudden power had lost its moorings; it no longer resided in any institution, for those that the Assembly tried its best to reconstruct were bound to be swept away, rebuilt, and destroyed again, like so many sandcastles assaulted by the tide. How could the Ancien-Régime king accept them when everything about them expressed distrust of him and the will to dispossess him? And how, in any event, could so recent a creation, so new a State, rebuilt or rather reconceived on such precarious

---

29 The first issue of Marat's paper is dated 12 September 1789. Its definitive title appeared on the 16th.

ground, quickly produce a minimum of consensus? No one believed it, though everyone professed to do so, since everyone was speaking in the name of the people. Nor did anyone have the power to create that consensus, even among those who might be called the 'men of 1789', and who were in agreement about the society and the kind of political régime they wanted. There was an essential instability inherent in revolutionary politics, as a consequence of which the periodic professions of faith concerning the 'stabilisation' of the Revolution unfailingly led to renewed bursts of revolutionary activity.

Leaders and factions spent their time wanting to 'stop' the Revolution, always for their own benefit, at a time that suited them, and in opposition to others. Mounier and the *monarchiens*, spokesmen for a kind of French Whiggism, did so as early as August 1789. Mirabeau and Lafayette pursued the same aim throughout 1790, simultaneously, but each for his own ends. Finally, the Barnave–Duport–Lameth triumvirate was the last to rally, after Varennes, to the moderate politics of a constitutional monarchy. But each of these successive rallyings took place only after its leaders had taken the Revolution a step further in order to keep control of the mass movement and to discredit rival factions. Unable to attain the first objective, the moderates succeeded so well in the second that the weapon soon turned against them and against 'moderatism' of any kind. Thus, even during the apparently 'institutional' phase of the Revolution, when France had a rather widely accepted Constitution, every leader – from La Fayette to Robespierre – and every group took the risk of extending the Revolution in order to eliminate all competitors instead of uniting with them to build new national institutions. That seemingly suicidal behaviour was due to exceptional circumstances, which explain the blind determination of the protagonists. The *Constituants* of 1789, unlike those of 1848, were not primarily interested in bringing the Revolution to a 'close'. But then 1848 had its eyes riveted on 1789. There was no precedent for 1789. The politicians of that time had, as Mirabeau put it, 'far-reaching ideas'; but when it came to political action they had to improvise.

The reason is that they were caught up in a new system of action that severely constrained them. The characteristic feature of the Revolution was a situation in which power was perceived by everyone as vacant, as having become intellectually and practically available. In the old society exactly the opposite had been the case: power was occupied for all eternity by the king; it could not become available except at the price of an act that would be both heretical and criminal. Moreover, power had owned society, and decided what its goals should be. Yet now it had not only become available, it had become the property of society, which was called upon to take it over and subject it to its own laws. Since power was held responsible for all the ills of the Ancien Régime and considered the locus of arbitrariness and despotism, revolutionary society exorcised the curse that weighed upon it by reconsecrating it in a manner that was the very opposite of that of the Ancien Régime: henceforth it was the people that was power. But by the same token society forced itself to keep that equation alive through opinion alone. Language was substituted for power, for it was the sole guarantee that power would belong only to the people, that is, to nobody. Moreover, language – unlike power, which is afflicted with the disease of secrecy – is public, and hence directly subject to scrutiny by the people.

Democratic sociability, which had characterised one of the two systems of political relations coexisting in the eighteenth century, because, like two parallel lines, they could never meet, now took over the sphere of power. But it did so only with what it was able to produce, that is, the ordinarily soft and pliable thing we call opinion. In those special circumstances, however, that material suddenly became the object of the most meticulous attention, the core, indeed the stake, of the entire political struggle. Once it had become power, opinion had to be at one with the people; language must no longer serve to hide intrigues but reflect values as in a mirror. In the frenzied collective preoccupation with power that henceforth shaped the political battles of the Revolution, representation was ruled out or perpetually put under surveillance; as Rousseau had stated, the people cannot, by definition, alienate its rights to particular interests, for that would mean the instant loss of its freedom. Legitimacy (and victory) therefore belonged to those who symbolically embodied the people's will and were able to monopolise the appeal to it. It is the inevitable paradox of direct democracy that it replaces electoral representation with a system of abstract equivalences in which the people's will always coincides with power and in which political action is exactly identical with its legitimacy.

If the Revolution thus experienced, in its political practices, the theoretical contradictions of democracy, it was because it ushered in a world where mental representations of power governed all actions, and where a network of signs completely dominated political life. Politics was a matter of establishing just *who* represented the people, or equality, or the nation: victory was in the hands of those who were capable of occupying and keeping that symbolic position. The history of the Revolution between 1789 and 1794, in its period of development, can therefore be seen as the rapid drift from a compromise with the principle of representation toward the unconditional triumph of rule by opinion. It was a logical evolution, considering that the Revolution had from the outset made power out of opinion.

Most histories of the Revolution fail to assess the implications of that transformation; yet none of the leaders who successively dominated the revolutionary scene wielded power in the normal sense, by giving orders to an army of underlings and commanding a machinery set up to implement laws and regulations. Indeed, the régime set up between 1789 and 1791 made every effort to keep the members of the Assembly away from executive power, and even to protect them from any such contamination. The suspicion of ministerial ambitions under which Mirabeau had to labour until the very end and the parliamentary debate about the incompatibility between the functions of representative and minister are telling illustrations of that attitude.[30] It was related to more than political circumstance and the Assembly's distrust of Louis XVI. It was inherent in a specific idea of power, for the Revolution held that executive power was by its very nature corrupt and corrupting, being separate from the people, out of touch with it and hence without legitimacy.

In actual fact, however, that ideological disqualification simply led to a *displacement of power*. Since the people alone had the right to govern – or at least, when it could not do so, to reassert public authority continually – power was in the hands of those who spoke for the people. Therefore, not only did that power reside in the word, for the word, being public, was the means of unmasking forces that hoped to remain hidden and were thus nefarious; but also power was always at stake in the conflict between words, for power could only be appropriated through them, and so they had to compete for the conquest of that evanescent yet primordial entity, the people's will. The Revolution replaced the conflict of interests for power with a competition of discourses for the appropriation of legitimacy. Its leaders' 'job' was not to act; they were there to interpret action. The French Revolution was the set of new practices that added a new layer of symbolic meanings to politics.

Hence the spoken word, which occupied centre stage, was constantly under suspicion, for it was by nature ambiguous. It strove for power yet denounced the corruption power inevitably entailed. It continued to obey the Machiavellian rationality of politics yet identified only with the ends to be achieved: that contradiction lay at the very root of democracy, from

30. Debate of November 1789.

which it was inseparable, but the Revolution brought it to the highest degree of intensity, as if in a laboratory experiment. One only has to read Mirabeau's *Correspondance secrète*[31] to realise the extent to which revolutionary politics, when its protagonists had failed to assimilate its tenets like a credo, were conducted in a *two-fold language*. In offering his services to the king, Mirabeau did not become a traitor to his ideas; as his friend La Marck, who acted as his confidant and go-between with the king, put it: 'He takes payment, but he believes in the advice he gives.' In his secret notes to Louis XVI Mirabeau defends the same political aims as in his public speeches in the Assembly: a popular and national monarchy rallied to the Revolution, acting on behalf of the nation against the privileged *corps* of the Ancien Régime and all the stronger as it is henceforth called upon to reign only over individuals. But while his aims are stated clearly enough in his secret notes, they can only be glimpsed between the lines of his speeches, because in the Assembly, where his adversaries were watching his every move, where the gallery was looking on, and where he addressed himself to 'opinion', an entity that was nowhere and yet already everywhere, he had to speak the language of revolutionary consensus, in which power had dissolved itself in the people.[32] That language had its specialists and experts, those who produced it and so became the custodians of its legitimacy and its meaning: the militant revolutionaries of the *sections* and the clubs.

Revolutionary activity *par excellence* was the production of a maximalist language through the intermediary of unanimous assemblies mythically endowed with the general will. In that respect, the history of the Revolution is marked throughout by a fundamental dichotomy. The deputies made laws in the name of the people, whom they were presumed to *represent*; but the members of the *sections* and of the clubs acted as the *embodiment* of the people, as vigilant sentinels, duty-bound to track down and denounce any discrepancy between action and values and to reinstate the body politic at every moment. As regards domestic politics, the salient feature of the period between May-June 1789 and 9 Thermidor 1794 was not the conflict between Revolution and counter-revolution, but the struggle between the representatives of the successive Assemblies and the club militants for the dominant symbolic position, the people's will. For the conflict between Revolution and counter-revolution extended, with nearly unchanged features, far beyond 9 Thermidor, while the fall of

---

31. La Marck, *Correspondance entre le comte de Mirabeau et le comte de La Marck pendant les années 1789, 1790 et 1791*, 3 vols. (Paris, 1851).
32. This point is developed in my introduction to a selection of Mirabeau's *Discours* (Paris: Gallimard, 1973).

Robespierre marked the end of a politico-ideological system characterised by the dichotomy I am trying to analyse here.

One of the most frequent misunderstandings of the historiography of the French Revolution is its attempt to reduce that dichotomy to a social cleavage by granting in advance to one of the rival powers a status that was precisely the undefined and quite literally elusive stake in the conflict, namely the privilege of being the people's will. In substituting the opposition between the bourgeoisie and the people for the one between aristocratic plot and the people's will, that misunderstanding turns the 'public safety' period into the culminating though temporary episode in which the bourgeoisie and the people marched hand in hand in a kind of Popular Front.[33] That rationalisation of the political dynamic of the French Revolution has one major flaw, for in reifying revolutionary symbolism and in reducing political motivation to social concerns, it makes 'normal' and obliterates what calls for explanation: the fact that the Revolution placed that symbolic system at the centre of political action, and that it was that system, rather than class interest, which, for a time at least, was decisive in the struggle for power.

There is little need, therefore, to launch upon a critique of that type of interpretation and to point out its incoherences with respect to the strictly social aspects of the problem. Not only has that critique already been made, notably by the late Alfred Cobban,[34] but, more important, that type of interpretation is *irrelevant to the problem at hand*. Even if it were possible to show – and that is not the case – that, for instance, the conflict between the Girondins and the Montagnards had its roots in the contradictory class interests of the antagonists or, on the contrary, that the period dominated by the Committee of Public Safety was characterised by a compromise between 'bourgeois' and 'popular' interests, such a demonstration would still be altogether beside the point. The 'people' was not a datum or a concept that reflected existing society. Rather, it was the Revolution's claim to legitimacy, its very definition as it were; for henceforth all power, all political endeavour revolved around that founding principle, which it was nonetheless impossible to embody.

That is why the history of the French Revolution, in the narrow sense, is characterised throughout by violent clashes between the different versions of that legitimacy and by the struggle between the men and the groups who found ways to march under its banner. The successive

33. The expression was used by Georges Lefebvre.
34. Alfred Cobban's most important articles were collected in *Aspects of the French Revolution* (London: Jonathan Cape, 1968).

Assemblies embodied the legitimacy of representation, which, however, was from the very outset fought against by direct democracy, as supposedly expressed in the revolutionary *journées*. Moreover, in between *journées*, a vast range of organisations – newspapers, clubs and assemblies of all kinds – were contending for the right to express direct democracy, and so for power. That double system gradually came to be institutionalised in the Jacobin Club, which, as early as 1790, functioned as the symbolic image of the people controlling the Constituent Assembly and preparing its decisions. Its structure may have remained very diffuse – as diffuse, by definition, as direct democracy, since every *section*, every meeting, indeed every citizen was in a position to produce the people's will – but the fact remains that Jacobinism laid down the model and the working of direct democracy by dictating opinion in the first organised group to appropriate the Revolution's discourse on itself.

Augustin Cochin's fundamental contribution to the history of the French Revolution was to examine how that new phenomenon came into being through the production and manipulation of revolutionary ideology. But because his study sets out to show that the phenomenon worked in a nearly mechanical manner – as soon as the discourse of pure democracy, concealing an oligarchic power, had appropriated the consensus – it underestimates the cultural links that were also vitally necessary for that system. Although the exact congruity between revolutionary democracy – as proclaimed and practised by the club militants – and the 'people' was a fundamental and mythical image of the Revolution, it is nonetheless true that this notion gave rise to a special relationship between politics and a section of the popular masses: the tangible 'people' – a minority of the population to be sure, but very numerous compared to 'normal' times – who attended revolutionary meetings, took to the streets on important *journées* and provided visible evidence for the abstraction called 'the people'.

The birth of democratic politics, which is the only real 'advent' of those years, could not have occurred without a common cultural environment in which the world of action and the world of conflicting values overlapped. Such a congruity is not unprecedented: that was how the religious wars of the sixteenth century, for example, had mustered most of their recruits. What is new in the laicised version of revolutionary ideology – the foundation of modern politics – is that action totally encompassed the world of values, and thus became the very meaning of life. Not only was man conscious of the history he was making, but he also knew that he was saved or condemned in and by that history. That lay eschatology, which was destined to so great a future, was the most powerful driving force of the French Revolution. We have already noted its integrating function for a society in search of a new collective identity, as well as the extraordinary fascination it exerted by promoting the simple and powerful idea that the Revolution had no objective limits, only enemies. Those premises gave rise to an entire system of interpretation, which, strengthened by the first victories of the Revolution, became a credo whose acceptance or rejection separated the good from the wicked.

The central tenet of that credo was the idea of equality, experienced as the reverse of the old society and perceived as the condition and purpose of the new social compact. But the notion of equality did not directly produce revolutionary energy, which first had to pass, as it were, through a relay to which the idea of equality was directly connected. That relay was the opposite principle, which created conflict and justified the use of violence: the aristocratic plot.

To review the uses and acceptations of the idea of plot in revolutionary ideology would be an unending task, for it was truly a central and polymorphous notion that served as a reference point for organising and interpreting action. It was the notion that mobilised men's convictions and beliefs, and made it possible at every point to elaborate an interpretation and justification of what had happened. From the very first events of the French Revolution one can see it function in those two ways and observe how it gained currency at all cultural levels, thereby unifying them: during the 'Great Fear' (*Grande Peur*), the peasants armed themselves to forestall the conspiracy of the brigands; the Parisians stormed the Bastille and then Versailles to forestall the Court plot; the deputies to the Estates General gave legitimacy to the insurrection by invoking the plots it had foiled. The idea appealed not only to a religiously oriented moral sensibility that had always seen evil as the work of hidden forces, but also to the new democratic conviction that the general, or national, will could not be publicly opposed by special interests. Above all, it was marvellously suited to the workings of revolutionary consciousness, for it produced the characteristic perversion of the causal schema by which every historical fact can be reduced to a specific intention and to a subjective act of will; thus the crime was sure to be heinous, since it was unavowable, and crushing the plot became a laudable and purifying act. Moreover, there was no need to name the perpetrators of the crime and to present precise facts about their plans, since it was impossible to determine the agents of the plot, who were hidden, and its aims, which were abstract. In short, the plot came to be seen as the only adversary of sufficient stature to warrant concern, since it was patterned on the Revolution itself. Like the Revolution, it was abstract, omnipresent and pregnant with new developments; but it was secret whereas the Revolution was public, perverse whereas the Revolution was beneficial, nefarious whereas the Revolution brought happiness to society. It was its negative, its reverse, its anti-principle.

The idea of plot was cut from the same cloth as revolutionary consciousness because it was an essential aspect of the basic nature of that consciousness: an imaginary discourse on power. That discourse came into being, as we have seen, when the field of power, having become vacant, was taken over by the ideology of pure democracy, that is, by the idea that the people are power, or that power is the people. But the revolutionary consciousness believed in historical action: if its advent was made possible only by the intervention of the people, it was because it had been blocked and continued to be threatened by a counter-power potentially more powerful than power itself: the plot. Hence the plot revived the idea of absolute power, which had been renounced by democratic power. Once the transfer of legitimacy, the very hallmark of the Revolution, had been accomplished, that absolute power became a hidden though formidable threat, while the new one was supreme though fragile. Like the people's will, the plot was the figment of a frenzied preoccupation with power; they were the two facets of what one might call the collectively held image of democratic power.[35]

That figment turned out to be almost indefinitely expandable. It adapted itself to every situation, rationalised every form of conduct, and penetrated all sections of the public. It started out as a vision of power held by those who had been excluded from power and were free to express their vision once the existing power had become vacant. In the initial revolutionary situation the denunciations of the 'aristocratic plot' coalesced into a call for action. At a time when its opponents were still very weak and poorly organised – in 1789–90 – the Revolution invented formidable enemies for itself, for every Manichaean creed needs to overcome its share of eternal evil. The adjective 'aristocratic' brought to the idea of plot a definition of its content, referring no longer to the methods but to the nature of the adversary. In fact, it was a rather vague definition, since it very soon came to encompass not only the aristocracy

35. This analysis owes a great deal to the discussion in Pierre Nora's seminar at the École des Hautes Études en Sciences Sociales in 1977 about the idea of plot and the French Revolution. M. Gauchet and L. Theis in particular helped me refine the terms of my analysis.

but also royal authority, all the old society, the inertia of a world confronted with change, and impersonal as well as human resistance. But if the word was – as it had to be – obscure, since it was the abstract and expandable designation of a hidden enemy, it was perfectly clear about the values it celebrated *a contrario*: just as aristocracy was seen as the reverse of equality, so the plot was seen as a power directly opposed to that of the people. It stood for inequality, privilege, a society splintered into separate and rival 'bodies', and the entire universe of rank and difference. The nobility – less as an actual group than as a social principle – was seen as the symbol of that 'difference' in the old world and made to pay the full price of the reversal in values. Only its formal exclusion from society could lend legitimacy to the new national pact.

The 'aristocratic plot' thus became the lever of an egalitarian ideology that was both exclusionary and highly integrative. Here again, two complementary systems of symbols came into play: the nation was constituted by the patriots only in reaction to its adversaries, who were secretly manipulated by the aristocrats. The potential applications of that basic proposition were practically unlimited, since equality, being a value more than a state of society, could never be taken for granted, and since its enemies were not real, identifiable and circumscribed forces, but constantly renewed incarnations of its anti-values. The symbolic content of the revolutionary struggle was the most immediate reality to act on attitudes and behaviours. In that sense it is quite true that there was no break between the two revolutions that can be dated to 1789 and 1792. From the meeting of the Estates General to the dictatorship of the Committee of Public Safety, the same dynamic was at work; it was fully developed, though not yet supreme, as early as 1789. Considered from that angle, the history of the Revolution spans the years during which that dynamic came to fill the entire sphere of power, up to the fall of Robespierre.

The struggle against the aristocratic plot began as the discourse on power of revolutionary society as a whole, and became the means of conquering and preserving real power. That central notion for militant action, whose most systematic spokesman was perhaps Marat, was also the site of the power struggle among groups and individual leaders. Whoever controlled that site was in a dominant position so long as he could hold on to it. The power to govern legitimately was directly related to the ability to keep up the denunciation of the aristocrats' plot: the constant raising of the ideological stakes was the rule of the game in the new system. Obsession with conspiracy thus became a discourse common to all, to be heard on either side of power. Those who were excluded from it used the discourse to conquer power. Those who held power used it to warn the people of the constant and formidable threat posed by that other and less fragile power. So the Revolution eventually had to face a cynical version of the aristocratic plot in which those who wielded power might call for the unmasking of a conspiracy only in order to reinforce their own position. The tendency of ideology to slide toward manipulation was inherent in the nature of revolutionary power, which was set up and legitimised by opinion alone, without there being rules for expressing that opinion. Robespierre ruled thanks to that ambiguity.

Yet he was not the only one to have realised the fundamental pheno-menon that the *sites of power had shifted radically*. All the great leaders of the Revolution were aware of the shift, for they all owed their temporary ascendancy to it. All of them – Sieyès and Mirabeau, Barnave and Brissot, Danton and Robespierre, to name only the parliamentary leaders – successively embodied the one great revolutionary act that was tan-tamount to power: the discourse of equality. At the pinnacle of his influence, each wielded the mastery over communication that had become not just the lever of power, but its very essence. Yet Robespierre alone systematically turned that mastery into an ideology and a technique of power. Always placed at the strategic crossroad where the rhetoric of the streets and the clubs intersected with the rhetoric of the Assembly, always absent on the great revolutionary *journées*, yet always the first to give them a meaning, that alchemist of revolutionary opinion-making was able to transform all the logical quandaries of direct democracy into secret tools of domination.

Ever since Mathiez, republican historiography has explained Robespierre's public rôle by his moral virtues, making its own – here as elsewhere – the feelings and passions of the Jacobins and the *section* members.[36] The debate about Robespierre's integrity versus Danton's corruption is an academic remake of the trials of 1794: it once again sends Danton to the guillotine and reinstates the Incorruptible back in his legend, which portrays him as the embodiment of popular justice. The trouble is that showing us the totally upright existence of that delicate soul, from the Arras courts to the Committee of Public Safety, tells us nothing about the determining factors in his life. What intrigues us about Robespierre is not the simplicity of his life-style, but what gave him the strange privilege of becoming an *embodiment*. A mysterious connivance

36. Albert Mathiez, *Études sur Robespierre* (Paris: Éditions Sociales, 1958, repr. 1973).

between the Revolution and Robespierre surrounds him like a halo, more closely and more durably than with any other leader. He may have put the Revolution 'on ice' when he silenced the Parisian *sections* and instigated the trials of the spring of 1794; but it was when he died, in Thermidor, that the Revolution died. Moreover, his myth survived him like an independent offshoot of his life: Robespierre embarked upon a great posthumous career – promoted by his former friends turned 'Thermidorians' – as the eponymous hero of the Terror and of the Committee of Public Safety. He who had so skilfully handled the dialectic between the people and the conspiracy, carrying it to its logical and bloody conclusion, fell victim in his turn to that very dialectic. The mechanism was familiar enough, for the same boomerang-effect had already struck down Brissot, Danton, Hébert and many others; but for Robespierre, and for him alone, it conferred a permanent place in history. While he lived, he embodied the people for a longer time and with greater conviction than anyone else. Once he was dead, his former friends, who knew the score, assigned him the central rôle in the plot against the Republic, without understanding that they were thereby contributing to his legend.

For there was an essential difference between Thermidorian anti-Robespierre literature and the revolutionary ideology of the Year II described here. Although that ideology did not die with Robespierre, it ceased to decide the outcome of power struggles, as if he had taken its magic with him to the grave. The conspiracy against liberty and the Revolution he was alleged to have masterminded with his accomplices Saint-Just and Couthon was a different matter from the common belief that a constant and hidden menace was threatening the indispensable unity between power and the people. It was a rationalisation of the past by which the ex-terrorists of the Year II sought to interpret and to justify their own rôle. The image of Robespierre as an unmasked plotter no longer served to stimulate a revolutionary dynamic, but was an answer to (as well as a shield against) the major question after Thermidor: how to interpret the Terror. The Incorruptible had become the scapegoat for the guillotine.

So the plot theme now worked within a different discourse. It was aimed no longer at establishing an imaginary communication between the people and its government, but at justifying the conduct of a ruling class produced by the revolutionary events. Utilitarian and cynical, it 'covered up' the notorious 'even-handed' policy pursued by the syndicate of Thermidorians, who felt that it was unsafe to adhere to the rules of a true representative system. They struck against both Right and Left, against both the royalist and the Jacobin plots, depicted as equivalent threats, not so much against the people as against those who represented it. In its new form, the plot theme not only failed to damage Robespierre's legend, but actually *created it*, for it clearly opened the way for the counter-revolutionary ideology of the revolutionary – and more specifically Jacobin – plot: the *abbé* Barruel had only to follow in the Thermidorians' footsteps to arrive at his global interpretation of the Revolution as a plot by the *philosophes* and freemasons.[37] Sullied by a mere act of rationalisation by his adversaries – who had explicitly designed it to serve not the people but its unworthy representatives – and used in the end to vilify the Revolution itself, Robespierre's image became available again, a few months after Thermidor, for those who hankered after the Year II, and for a kind of posthumous fidelity to itself, beyond the life and the death of one ephemeral individual.[38] Henceforth it no longer served to nurture the charismatic appeal of power by the people, but to fuel the pretended or real opposition to the usurpation of that power by those who used the Revolution for their own ends.

That is why 9 Thermidor is such a sharp break in the history of the Revolution and indeed in French history as a whole and why, arriving at that date, the Jacobin historian often succumbs to a strange listlessness, which he is at a loss to explain clearly. Thermidor marked the end of the Revolution because it was the victory of representative over revolutionary legitimacy, the exercise of power to control the revolutionary ideology of power, and, as Marx said,[39] the reassertion of real society over the *illusion of politics*. If that is indeed the meaning of Robespierre's death, the reason is not that he was honest while the Thermidorians were corrupt, but that he, more than anyone, had embodied the Revolution in power.

That trait is paradoxical in the opposite sense that Mirabeau's rôle was; for if the life of the deputy from Aix-en-Provence did not measure up to his genius, the destiny of the lawyer from Arras cannot be explained by his talents. At the time when Robespierre lived with his sister and his aunts, spoiled by 'all the small attentions of which only women are capable', as Charlotte was to write in her memoirs,[40] Mirabeau experien-

---

37. *Abbé* Barruel, *Mémoires pour servir à l'histoire du jacobinisme*, 4 vols. (1797–8).
38. It was to be fundamental – more than the idea of 'communism' – in Babeuf's conspiracy.
39. Karl Marx, *La Sainte Famille* [The Holy Family], (1st edn, 1845) (Paris: Éditions Sociales, 1959), pp. 149–79.
40. Charlotte Robespierre's memoirs were published during the July Monarchy by Albert Laponneraye, in vol. 2 of his edition of Robespierre's *Oeuvres* (Paris, 1840). On the same subject one can also consult H. Fleischmann, *Charlotte Robespierre et ses Mémoires* (Paris, 1910).

ced revolt, scandal, exile and prison. Robespierre made no choices but espoused a typical Ancien-Régime future: the women of his family, a tailor-made job (helped along by some string-pulling at the bishopric), trite speeches before the bar, the Academy of Arras, pretty verses for the ladies – nothing in that life, until the revolutionary crisis, distinguished it. Whatever came to him without his choosing – Latin studies at the *collège*, his life with Charlotte, the profession that ran in the family, the milieu of that profession – he not only accepted but actually cultivated.

Indeed, it was probably that passion for conformity that made him the ideal choice for conveying revolutionary ideology. He had been defined by the Ancien Régime. The Revolution would speak through him. It is idle to probe his 'psychology', for psychology deals with a field of realities that has nothing to do with the factors that shaped his destiny. Before 1789 he had embodied the beliefs of his time and his world, the extolling of morality, the cult of virtue, the love of humanity and equality, and respect for the Creator. As soon as revolutionary ideology appeared, he was totally won over by it.

What is unusual in his case is that he was unable to wield anything but the priestly language of that ideology; he was totally unfamiliar with the art of playing on a double keyboard that is part and parcel of what we now call 'politics', an art that had, a little earlier, been so brilliantly exemplified by Mirabeau. While Mirabeau and Danton – another virtuoso of revolutionary language – were conscious practitioners of political art, able to speak well in two languages, Robespierre was a prophet. He believed everything he said and expressed it in the language of the Revolution; none of his contemporaries assimilated as he did the ideological coding of the revolutionary phenomenon. For him there was no difference between the struggle for power and the struggle on behalf of the people, since they were one by definition. The historian who 'decodes' his speeches in order to lay bare their momentary political motivation is often impressed with his skill as a parliamentary manoeuvrer. But that separation would have made no sense to him, for in his prose, which was totally bound up with action, the defence of equality, virtue or the people was the same thing as the conquest or the exercise of power.

Today, thanks to the work of Guérin and Soboul,[41] we know quite well to what extent, as far as rational tactics are concerned, the victorious Robespierre of 1793–4 was a politician torn between allegiance to the

41. D. Guérin, *La Lutte de classes sous la Première République. Bourgeois et 'bras nus', 1793–1797*, 2 vols. (Paris: Gallimard, 1st edn, 1946, 2nd edn, 1968); A. Soboul, *Les Sans-culottes parisiens en l'an II, histoire politique et sociale des sections de Paris, 2 juin 1793–9 Thermidor an II* (La Roche-sur-Yon, 1958).

Convention and to the *sections*; at least we know that he can be objectively described in these terms. He based his reign of opinion squarely upon the defeat of the principle of representation when he gave his blessing to the exclusion of the Girondins from the Convention and to the violent *coup* of the Parisian *sections* on 31 May – 2 June 1793. But his approval of the *coup* was not motivated by the same vision of the people and of revolutionary power. For the staunch Rousseauist was unfaithful to the *Social Contract* in one essential respect: he identified popular sovereignty with that of the Convention (from which he drew his own sovereignty). He thus embodied an extraordinary syncretism between the two forms of democratic legitimacy. He was the idol of the Jacobins, yet he did not become involved in any of the intrigues designed to break up the national representative body, neither after Varennes, nor on 20 June, nor on 10 August 1792. He was swept into power by the violent anti-parliamentary coup of 31 May – 2 June 1793, yet he remained the man of the Convention. He was worshipped by the members of the Parisian *sections*, yet it was he who silenced them. That was possible because he alone mythically reconciled direct democracy with the principle of representation, by occupying the summit of a pyramid of equivalences whose continued existence was guaranteed, day after day, by his word. He *was* the people to the *sections*, he was the people to the Jacobin Club, he was the people to the national representative body; it was continually necessary to establish, control and restore the perfect fit between the people and the various assemblies that claimed to speak in its name (above all the Convention), for without that perfect fit there could be no legitimate power, and the first duty of power was to maintain it: that was the function of Terror.

Hence the problem is not to find out whether Robespierre had a tender soul, a sympathetic heart or, on the contrary, a passionate desire for revenge. Robespierre's relation to the Terror is not psychological. The guillotine fed on his preachments about the good and the wicked, and the prisons were filled because his sermons gave him the tremendous power to decide who was included in 'the people'. Thus his own consecration, the Festival of the Supreme Being – which for a long time was more shocking than the guillotine to republican historians – nevertheless fulfilled the same function as the Terror. The discourse on equality and virtue that gave meaning to the people's action was based on the assumption that the guilty must be put to death; but at the same time it made that dread necessity acceptable through the solemn assertion of a providential sanction.

There are two ways of totally misunderstanding Robespierre as a historical figure: one is to detest the man, the other is to make too much of him. It is absurd, of course, to see the lawyer from Arras as a monstrous usurper, the recluse as a demagogue, the moderate as a bloodthirsty tyrant, the democrat as a dictator. On the other hand, what is explained about his destiny once it is proved that he really was the Incorruptible? The misconception common to both schools arises from the fact that they attribute to the psychological traits of the man the historical rôle into which he was thrust by events and the language he borrowed from them. Robespierre is an immortal figure not because he reigned supreme over the Revolution for a few months, but because he was the mouthpiece of its purest and most tragic discourse.

V

In so deducing the Terror from revolutionary discourse one lays oneself open to the objection that one is disregarding 'circumstances', that godsend of historical causality. For republican historiography, called upon to plead the entire case before the prosecutors representing counter-revolutionary history – and in any case unable to accept without humanitarian misgivings the bloody acts of repression that marked the Jacobin period – has developed by way of explanation a theory of circumstances strongly reminiscent of what we would now call 'extenuating circumstances'.[42] It has shown in detail that those repressive acts took many different forms, ranging from open civil war to sporadic assassinations, from spontaneous massacres perpetrated by revolutionary crowds to organised government Terror. But it has included all those acts of violence in a single tally of assets and liabilities, explaining and finally justifying them by the objective conditions of the struggle in which the Revolution itself became embroiled. And since the Terror reached its most memorable episodes and its 'classic' forms only between September 1792 and July 1794, when the Revolution was at war with Europe, that school has found an additional – indeed exonerating – excuse in the notion of national interest. If the 'circumstances' were no longer simply the hostility and the intrigues of the Court and the nobility, but an armed conflict with foreign powers who had prepared and precipitated it, so that the enemies of the Revolution were no longer citizens bound to the Ancien Régime by self-

42. Developed or borrowed? The doctrine of public safety can be found in the absolutist theoreticians of Richelieu's time, who claimed that 'circumstances' (domestic or foreign) can justify the temporary suspension of 'natural' laws and of the fundamental laws of the realm.

interest or prejudice, but Frenchmen who had betrayed their country in wartime, then the historian can 'explain' the Terror in a way that will satisfy not only the Jacobin tradition, by echoing its assertions, but also the liberal school of thought, for the explanation involves the overriding consideration of national survival. The doctrine of public safety, developed by the revolutionaries themselves, makes it possible to treat the republican historians' plea on behalf of the Terror as a single unit, for it was current in both the nineteenth and the twentieth centuries.

Aside from the values and emotions it carries, however, it is logically only the most general variant of the doctrine of 'circumstances', whose implications must be examined here. To see an event like the French Revolution as the response to a series of ever greater perils that threatened it after its inception and to explain its development and its radicalisation between 1789 and 1794 by the intrigues of its enemies just misses the problem at hand. In the first place, one repeats yet again the type of interpretation current at the time of the events themselves, by presenting a free-floating version of the plot theory, in which more blame is attached to impersonal forces than to people. But above all, one defines the Revolution by factors external to it, and one treats it as an escalating series of popular reactions to events that thwarted or besieged it. Therefore the theory of 'circumstances' transfers historical initiative to the forces hostile to the Revolution: that is the price to be paid for relieving the Revolution of responsibility for the Terror. No one would mind, were it not that this operation totally obscures – and that is precisely its function – the very things we need to understand. Situations of extreme national peril do not invariably bring a people to revolutionary Terror. And while the revolutionary Terror that gripped France at war with the European monarchies always conjured up that peril to justify its existence, it actually raged independently of the military situation: the 'spontaneous' massacres of September 1792 took place after the fall of Longwy, but the 'Great Terror' conducted in the spring of 1794 by the government and by Robespierre made heads roll after the military situation had improved.

The truth is that the Terror was an integral part of revolutionary ideology, which, just as it shaped action and political endeavour during that period, gave its own meaning to 'circumstances' that were largely of its own making. There were no revolutionary circumstances; there was a Revolution that fed on circumstances. The mechanism of interpretation, action and power I have attempted to describe above was fully operative from 1789. There is no difference in kind between Marat in 1789 and

Marat in 1793. Nor were the murders of Foulon and Berthier fundamentally different from the massacres of September 1792, any more than Mirabeau's aborted trial after the October Days of 1789 was different from the sentencing of the Dantonists in the spring of 1793. As Georges Lefebvre noted in an article in 1932,[43] the aristocratic plot was, as early as 1789, the outstanding feature of what he called the 'collective revolutionary mentality'; indeed I regard the plot as central to the system of notions and actions that constituted the revolutionary phenomenon itself.

Nonetheless, there is no doubt that the 'circumstances' provided the ground upon which that system grew and came to occupy the sphere of power. In that sense, they are indeed the underlying fabric of events for the history of the Revolution. Narrative history must treat them as a chronological unit developing like a crescendo until 9 Thermidor, because there was behind that crescendo of events something never clearly conceptualised, unrelated to the circumstances, existing apart from them, though evolving with and through them. That force, which the historian usually calls an increasingly 'popular' power, because it *manifested itself* in that form, had no objective existence at the social level, it was but a *mental representation of the social sphere* that permeated and dominated the field of politics. Its decisions were made in a strictly oligarchical manner, yet the legitimacy that covered those decisions and alone gave them their validity was derived from the will of the people itself.

Every history of the Revolution must therefore deal not only with the impact of 'circumstances' on the successive political crises but also, and above all, with the manner in which those 'circumstances' were planned for, prepared, arranged and used in the symbolic universe of the Revolution and in the various power struggles. Defining the revolutionary 'collective mentality' in its own terms and in its social manifestation is only the first step in the investigation, for that 'mentality' was of such crucial importance only because it was the lever and the locus of the new power. To that extent, the 'circumstances' that propelled the Revolution forward were those that seemed to fit naturally into the pattern of revolutionary expectations: having in this sense been 'anticipated' by the revolutionary consciousness, they were quickly given the necessary and appropriate meaning. The banquet held by the officers of the *gardes du corps* and of the Flanders regiment on 1 October 1789 was no more than an inept demonstration of loyalty to the royal family; but it became the proof of a plot and triggered the *journées* of 4 and 5 October. Poorly

43. G. Lefebvre, 'Foules révolutionnaires', in *Études sur la Révolution française*.

planned and organised, the flight to Varennes turned out to be catastrophic for Louis XVI; but it was seen as proof that Marat had been right
all along and that the Ancien-Régime king had never ceased to make
secret preparations for a counter-revolutionary bloodbath. That episode
was crucially important for the Revolution, not because it changed
anything – when it was over, Louis XVI remained, as before, a powerless
constitutional monarch – but because of its symbolic impact. The return
of the captive king, flanked all along his route by the silent rows of his
erstwhile subjects, was more than a coronation in reverse, the final
undoing of what had been done at Reims. It was also the national
consecration of the aristocratic plot.

The unsuccessful flight of the king also marked a turning-point for
revolutionary ideology. Although it had crystallised very early, separating
by the spring of 1789 the 'patriots' from the 'aristocrats', and the 'nation'
from what it excluded, revolutionary ideology was not, at first, war-
mongering or chauvinistic. The early wave of emigration had fuelled a
distrust of all things foreign, but foreign countries were not uppermost in
patriots' minds. For example, the arrest and subsequent release in
February 1790 of Mesdames, the king's aunts, at Arnay-le-Duc, on their
way to Rome, shows that it was more a matter of keeping potential
hostages than of preventing them from arming potential adversaries. But
the obstreperous collusion between the *émigrés* and the European monarchs, and above all the Varennes episode, which showed up the complicity of a potential invader, created a situation which, though it did not
change the basic tenets of revolutionary consciousness, did add substance
and breadth to its content and to its cast of characters: the 'aristocratic
plot' took on a European dimension, and the revolutionary construct a
universal significance. Against an internationale of kings, only the internationale of peoples could ensure the lasting victory of the Revolution.
Nothing could stop that widening of the original schema, which made
room for notions of war and crusade.

For the war that began in the spring of 1792 was not, by its nature or
its inherent open-endedness, bound to ensue from either 'bourgeois'
interests on the French side or from a counter-revolutionary system
devised by European monarchs. To be sure, the war might be seen as the
climax of the old commercial rivalry between France and England. But
there is a considerable difference between recognising that aspect of the
conflict and making it the main issue and the 'objective' cause of the
unending war; indeed, no historian of the Revolution, aside from Daniel

Guérin,[44] has gone that far. As for the European monarchies, it is true
that they felt threatened by the French Revolution; but for all that they
did not forget old quarrels and earlier decisions, nor give up traditional
calculations and sacrifice conflicting ambitions to a supposedly overriding
need for a counter-revolutionary crusade. Despite the pressures brought to
bear by the *émigrés* and the French monarchy, the war was agreed to
rather than launched by the European powers. As Jean Jaurès realised, it
was for domestic political reasons that France embarked upon the awesome adventure that began in 1792. But what were these reasons?

If the Girondins, from late 1791, were the most eloquent advocates of
war with the Austrian Emperor, it was because they were convinced that
it was the only way they could come to power. Louis XVI too, albeit in a
diametrically opposite perspective, counted on the war to reassert his
authority. At that point, the leaders of the Mountain – Danton,
Desmoulins and Marat – were quick to withdraw their support from
Robespierre, who was temporarily isolated because of his opposition to
the war. They thus shared at least one project with the Girondins when
they launched the Revolution on a foreign adventure that would radicalise it through the exaltation of a Jacobin brand of patriotism. The
political currents that led France to war in 1792 cannot therefore be
dissociated from the calculations of leaders and groups who wanted to
conquer, preserve or reconquer power. Louis XVI's calculations turned
out to be a suicidal mistake, while Brissot and Danton proved correct,
although they failed to foresee one crucially important development: the
fact that the radicalisation of the Revolution would succeed so well that
they, too, would end up on the guillotine.

Robespierre, it is true, was the one Montagnard leader to oppose the
war. Hence the exceptional lucidity with which he dismissed as illusions
the military and moral arguments of Jacobin rhetoric: no, he told Brissot,
the war would not be easy; French troops, even if victorious, would not be
welcomed as liberators; and victory itself would saddle the Revolution
with unruly generals. But his lucidity went hand in hand with an equally
exceptional blindness concerning the nature of the revolutionary dynamic, for Robespierre failed to realise that the war would open up a vast
field of action for his Manichaean genius. He had no inkling of the
explosive force that would be released in the first convergence of a lay
eschatology and nationalism. He rejected, or denied, the circumstances
that shaped the discourse he and his friends were to use better than

44. D. Guérin, *La Lutte de classes*, vol. 2, p. 501.

anyone, the very discourse that would carry him to the crest of the wave. He took that stance because he embodied ideology in its purest form better than his rivals did, and because his extreme suspiciousness enabled him to perceive the slightest hint of *duplicity* in their discourse: the ambition for power lurking behind the assertion of values. If Brissot, like Louis XVI, wanted war, what could they possibly have in common but that ambition? The constant denunciation of power was one of the ways in which revolutionary ideology wielded power; and in the winter of 1791–2 the circumstances were such that, in speaking through Robespierre, that discourse became a discourse against the war, for he continued to speak the unbroken language of suspicion.

In fact the arguments advanced by Brissot (who made the best speeches in favour of the war) showed signs of a split that were not lost on Robespierre's expert ear: on the one hand, Brissot spoke the pure language of the Revolution, the two-dimensional world where nothing existed but patriotism and treason, the people and aristocratic plots, a world that, enlarged to include all of Europe, would justify a military offensive by the French Revolution.

Yes, we shall either prevail over all of them, nobles, priests, and prince-electors, and establish our public credibility and our prosperity, or we shall be defeated and betrayed ... the traitors will be convicted in the end, they will be punished, and we shall finally be able to get rid of everything that prevents France from becoming a great nation. I admit, gentlemen, to only one fear, namely, that we may not be betrayed ... We need great acts of treason: therein lies our salvation ... Great acts of treason will be fatal only to those who perpetrate them; they will serve mankind.[45]

On the other hand, the Girondin orator opened himself to charges of collusion with the Court and the ministry, that is, with the very embodiment, in revolutionary consciousness, of the old power against which the people had risen. Those who extolled the war presented it as a means of unmasking the plots of hostile powers, but for Robespierre it was a diabolical machination by those same powers, a trap set for the patriots and a ploy designed to push the 'innumerable fraction' of the 'undecided party' into the aristocratic camp. So far as he was concerned, the war existed only as a means to gain power in the Revolution. In the confrontation with Brissot, his forceful analysis and his keen insight into the illusions of Brissot's bellicose rhetoric were not derived from any particular lucidity, but from the fact that he never went beyond the

45. Speech of 30 December 1791 at the Jacobin Club, from the printed text, n.d., in the Bibliothèque Nationale, Paris (call. no. Lb. 4° 666).

confines of the Manichaean language of conspiracy, hence of suspicion:

It was your destiny to defend liberty without distrusting anyone, without displeasing its enemies, without offending either the Court or the ministers or the moderates. What an easy and pleasant road to patriotism you have discovered.[46]

If, as Robespierre believed, the heart of the conspiracy against liberty was not at Koblenz but in France, 'in our midst', it was more than ever the patriots' duty to be on their guard, to denounce, to unmask, and to keep up suspicion. Robespierre, who was not at the time a member of the Assembly, fulfilled that paramount duty on behalf of the people more vigorously than ever through the Jacobin Club. As soon as Brissot had warned the patriots that 'great acts of treason' were in store, Robespierre pointed out that such a warning was in itself suspect, for treason by definition never came out into the open but worked in cunning, improbable and unexpected ways:

No, the Court and those who serve it will never betray you in a gross and obvious manner, that is, so clumsily that you will realise it, so early that you will still be able to undo the damage they will have inflicted upon you. Rather, they will deceive you, they will lull you to sleep, they will exhaust you; they will lead you step by step to the last phase of your political agony; they will betray you with skill, moderation and patriotism; they will betray you slowly and constitutionally, as they have done all along; they will even win the war if necessary, the more thoroughly to betray you afterward.[47]

Robespierre, unlike Brissot, did not see treason as a *possible side-effect* of the war, as a kind of choice to be made by the enemy within. To him, it was consubstantial with that enemy, the very core of his existence, and all the more dangerous when it was least apparent and spoke with the voice of patriotism. Brissot had argued, in his last great speech for the war,[48] that it was impossible to foresee the turn of events and that human intentions and the course of history were two separate matters. If the Court and the Austrian Emperor appeared to want war, although they only intended to frighten the patriots, their undertaking, whatever its real motives, was liable to turn against them:

When Louis XVI called the Assembly of Notables, did he foresee the fall of the Bastille? ... once again, only a spark is needed to set off a universal explosion. Patriotism has nothing to fear from the consequences; war is a threat only to the thrones of kings.

But the reference to a kind of historical objectivity, which made it possible

46. Speech of 11 January 1792 at the Jacobin Club, in M. Robespierre, *Textes choisis*, ed. Jean Poperen, 3 vols. (Paris: Éditions Sociales, 1974), vol. 1, p. 126.
47. Speech of 25 January 1792 at the Jacobin Club, *ibid.*, vol. 1, p. 144.
48. Speech of 20 January 1792 at the Jacobin Club, from the printed text, n.d., Bibliothèque Nationale, Paris (call. no. Lb. 4° 675).

to disregard the possibility – indeed, in this case, the probability – that evil intentions were at work, was by definition totally alien to Robespierre's political universe, in which it was implicitly assumed that intentions are perfectly coherent with the actions they prompt and the effects they aim at. Robespierre therefore believed that the Court and the ministers wanted war not because it might provide them with a chance to betray the Revolution, but because they had been betraying it all along and would continue to do so, since that was their only function. And if Brissot had joined his voice to theirs, it was because he had become ensnared in the tentacles of their intrigue.

In such a universe, action never had unforeseeable consequences, nor was power ever innocent. Like the Revolution itself, Robespierre recognised only the good and the wicked, patriots and offenders, the public expression of vigilance and the hidden conspiracy of the ministers. By casting suspicion from the outset on Brissot, along with Narbonne and Louis XVI, Robespierre pushed his rival into the very trap Brissot had baited for Louis XVI and his advisers. The hapless Girondin, who had called for 'great acts of treason' to unmask the king and give impetus to the Revolution, was implicated in advance in those acts as an accomplice of the ministers. The Girondins were, as has so often been said, 'light-weight' not so much in their failure to implement their policies (for revolutionary politics were not concerned with means) as in their half-hearted use of the language of the Revolution. Robespierre, who identified completely with that language, could dispatch them in advance to a guillotine of their own making.

The issue of revolutionary power thus continued to be paramount in the debate about the war, until the war itself not only created the objective conditions for strengthening that power, but also brought an essential element of legitimacy to the discourse of the Terror. It is paradoxical that the Girondins, who, in calling for and obtaining a declaration of war, only followed the pre-existing pattern of inflated revolutionary rhetoric, could be denounced for aspiring to a ministerial power reminiscent of the Ancien Régime. It is equally paradoxical that Robespierre, who, in the name of an apparent realism, demolished the rhetoric that advocated a war of 'liberation', was nonetheless able to give ever wider scope to the mythology of popular power. Thus he eventually benefited from both the temporary success of his adversaries and his intuitive denunciation of their ambitions. The war was to carry him to power; not to the ministerial power of which Mirabeau or Brissot may have dreamt, but to the mastery over opinion that was inseparable from the Terror.

For the war unequivocally identified the new values with the nation that embodied them and branded as criminals all Frenchmen suspected of not cherishing them. From the very beginning of the Revolution, of course, the pursuit of 'patriotic' objectives had been the badge of good citizens, the supporters of the new social order, and the unanimous demonstrators at the *fête de la Fédération*. Although the men and the groups allegedly hostile to the new France, but hidden from view as conspirators, were excluded from that national integration, which defined itself in opposition to them, they were originally subjected to no more than abstract suspicion and sporadic, unauthorised violence. The war was to turn them into full-fledged traitors and hand them over to popular justice. By substantiating the enormity of the crime, the war made it possible to name the conspirators; indeed the revolutionary discourse came to consider it a sacred obligation to do so. The denunciation of traitors thus became a mechanical reaction that could strike anyone at any time. Working from the grass roots upward, from the *sections* to the committees, it gradually excluded more and more individuals from the ranks of true patriots.

The exponents of what I have called the 'theory of circumstances' would like to confine that mechanical reaction to periods of distress and defeat, precisely in order to use 'circumstances' as its basic explanation. After all, a state of extreme national emergency provides a semblance of rational justification for believing in an enemy plot, and for violent repression. In fact, as is shown by the first two major *journées* of terrorism, in August 1792 and in the summer of 1793, that type of situation is indeed a particularly favourable breeding-ground for the denunciation of the enemy within and demands for punitive action. But such a situation by no means provides a basic explanation. One only has to read the *Ami du peuple* to realise that the dialectic between people and plot had existed as early as the summer of 1789, when the counter-revolution was still in limbo, and at any rate without serious support from outside. The dialectic grew until it came to dominate the entire political history of France in the spring of 1794: by then the 'factions' had been eliminated, the dictatorship of the Robespierrist group was at its height, the military situation was dramatically improving, the Vendée rebellion had been crushed and no foreign army was threatening French territory or the achievements of the Revolution. Robespierre's egalitarian and moralising metaphysics then held full sway over a Revolution that was finally living up to its principle. The Festival of the Supreme Being and the Great Terror had an identical purpose: they were to bring about the reign of virtue. The guillotine was the means of separating the good from the wicked.

Thus, each successive political group pursued the same objective: to radicalise the Revolution, by making it consistent with its discourse. The pursuit of that aim was the decisive factor in every political struggle, and through it the purest form of that discourse was eventually brought to power. Robespierrist metaphysics was therefore not a parenthesis in the history of the Revolution, but a type of public authority that the revolutionary phenomenon alone made possible and logical. Starting out as the site of power struggles, a way of differentiating political groups and of integrating the masses into the new State, ideology became, for a few months, coextensive with government itself. Hence debate lost its *raison d'être*, for there was no longer any gap to be filled between the idea and power, nor any room for politics except in consensus or death.

In that sense, the victory of the Thermidorians closed off one of the directions of the Revolution, namely, the objective that had shaped France's entire political life between 1789 and 1794, and thanks to which the ideology of pure democracy, having become the real power of the Revolution, ended up as the only true government the Revolution ever had. When the men who brought down Robespierre attempted to restore the legitimacy of representative government – which they themselves were unable to respect – they rediscovered the independence and the inertia of society, the need for political trade-offs, and the compromises demanded by the interplay of means and ends. They did more than stop the Terror; they discredited it as a type of power and dissociated it from the people's will. Like reformed drinkers, they occasionally resorted to it, in particular after 18 Fructidor; but they did so shamefacedly and as an expedient rather than on principle.

In fact, they were no longer able even to think in terms of the Terror. They were not so much divided by their plans for the future as torn apart by their own past. On 31 May 1793, they had agreed to the proscription of the Girondin deputies and to the amputation of the national representative body. How could they suddenly reincarnate the representative principle, which was once again indispensable to republican legitimacy? They had voted for the stringent terrorist measures of 1793–4 and often personally conducted brutal purges. How could they justify their own rôle, now that they had toppled Robespierre in the name of liberty and restored to society the right to detest the guillotine? The terrorist ideology, which until yesterday had seemed to them to be consubstantial with the Revolution, had been stripped of its apparent rationality by the events of

9 Thermidor. The crime was no longer in the same camp. That is why the Thermidorians, if they wanted to stay in power, had to do more than keep the ex-terrorists in command positions. They also, and at the same time, had to exorcise the Terror by dissociating it from their power, that is, to assign the entire responsibility for it to Robespierre and his inner circle. Having once been the Revolution itself, the Terror now became the result of a plot or the expedient of one man's tyranny. Babeuf, writing in the first months after 9 Thermidor, simply said that it was the counter-revolution. Thibaudeau, who wrote his memoirs with greater hindsight, was to advance a rationalisation that did not go quite so far, but was based on the same dissociation between Terror and Revolution:

The Terror of 1793 was not a necessary consequence of the Revolution, but an unfortunate deviation from it. It did more harm than good to the Republic, because it exceeded all limits, led to atrocious suffering, sacrificed friend and foe alike, could not be avowed by anyone, and provoked a reaction that dealt a fatal blow not only to the terrorists but to freedom and its defenders.[49]

When it abandoned the Terror, revolutionary ideology ceased to be co-extensive with the government of the Republic and to fill the entire sphere of power. Henceforth, it was a rationalisation of power rather than a means of achieving it, a consensus rather than a principle of legitimacy. But if ideology restored independence to society, if it gave back to political life an autonomy and a rationality of its own, it nonetheless remained a shaping force in republican opinion, and the common reference by which the Thermidorian syndicate still addressed the people in the language of the Revolution. Ideology was no longer the only power, nor the government, nor, therefore, the Terror. But that change only served to attach the values it conveyed – liberty and equality – all the more firmly to the symbolic image of the Republic pitted against counter-revolutionary Europe. Of the two Jacobin legacies, the Terror and the war, the Thermidorians liquidated the first but remained prisoners of the second. They had wrested power from Robespierre by destroying his ideological instrument, which had been equality through the guillotine. Their own power could be preserved only through a shift in ideological commitment: equality through a crusade.

The war thus remained the last criterion of fidelity to the Revolution. To make peace would be to give in to an implacable enemy, to take a first step toward the restoration of the Ancien Régime. That reasoning was a posthumous victory of the Girondins, and it impeded the Thermidorians as much as it had impeded the Montagnards: in that respect 9 Thermidor

49. Antoine-Clair Thibaudeau, *Mémoires*, 2 vols. (Paris, 1824), vol. 1, pp. 57–8.

had not changed anything. Neither the Feuillants, nor Danton, nor Robespierre were able to negotiate with the enemy, though all of them had envisaged doing so. Nor was the syndicate of regicides that succeeded them able to conclude more than a series of truces, each followed by a flare-up of the conflict and a raising of the stakes – at the very time when the war was preparing the conditions for their overthrow by Bonaparte. For the war was not grounded in the rational balancing of means against ends that had made Ancien-Régime wars limited conflicts over negotiable stakes. Because it had become the very meaning of the Revolution, the first democratic war of the modern era could have no other outcome than total victory or total defeat.

The war ended up as the common denominator of the Revolution, straddling as it were its different phases and in a sense reconciling the Montagnard dictatorship with the Thermidorian Republic. Yet 9 Thermidor marks a break, by separating the time when the war was only an enlarged form of the aristocratic plot – the anti-power of revolutionary power – from the time when it had become not just an ideological commitment, but a social and political one as well. When society was restored to its rights by the fall of Robespierre, it also regained its unwieldiness and its conflicting interests; mental representations of action no longer completely concealed the interplay of social forces and the existence of political conflicts. By the same token, the Thermidorian war reveals a fact that the Montagnard war had hidden, namely, that it made use of certain age-old tendencies of French society, albeit in a somewhat different guise. It revitalised the crusading spirit in one of the oldest countries of Christendom. It reinforced, or recreated, the authority of officialdom and of central power, both of which were achievements of the monarchy. It gave the people access to military careers and military glory, which had for so long been the preserve and pride of the nobility.[50] If the banner of equality put the entire nation on its colours, it was not only because it was new. Under its aegis the French had rid themselves of the injustices of their past, yet it also gave them back their historical ambitions, purified by democracy.

Thermidor thus marks not the end of *the* Revolution, but that of its purest form. By making society once again independent from ideology, Robespierre's death takes us from Cochin to Tocqueville.

50. Speaking of the Empire, George Sand remarked: 'At that time [1812] the French imbibed pride of victory with their milk. The chimera of nobility had expanded and affected all classes. To be born French was a great distinction, a title of nobility. The eagle was the coat of arms of the entire nation.' *Histoire de ma vie*, in *Oeuvres autobiographiques*, Pléiade edn, vol. 1 (Paris: Gallimard, 1970), p. 736.

VI

Thermidor separates not only two phases, but two concepts of the Revolution. It marks the end of Cochin's Revolution, and brings to light Tocqueville's Revolution. That chronological turning point is also an intellectual dividing line. It brings out different interpretations within an apparently continuous tradition.

Cochin fits in with left-wing academic historiography of the twentieth century, for he too was primarily interested in the Jacobin phenomenon. He therefore decided for intellectual reasons to analyse the period that left-wing historians have favoured out of an implicit preference, and to focus on the period that ended with Robespierre's fall. The only difference – but a crucial one – is that Jacobin historiography takes Jacobin discourse about itself quite literally and therefore makes popular partici-pation in government the outstanding characteristic of the period. Cochin, by contrast, sees Jacobinism as an imaginary discourse of power (the people's will) assuming absolute control over society. Yet in both views it was indeed a system of power that was destroyed on 9 Thermidor.

Even by the implicit standards of left-wing historiography, however, that chronological divide is becoming increasingly incompatible with the known facts, since Daniel Guérin and Albert Soboul, each in his own way, have shown in their studies that the Robespierrist dictatorship was established only through the repression of the Parisian *sections*, especially in the autumn of 1793 and the spring of 1794;[51] hence the 'popular' character of the power that fell in Thermidor is becoming increasingly questionable, even for the most 'Robespierrist' historiography, by which I mean Soboul. If that tradition nevertheless continues to regard 9 Thermidor as a decisive turning point, it is because the date conveys its existential truth, which is far more powerful than any progress of scholar-ship. For the tradition holds that there was a revolutionary mystique that died with Robespierre, after having survived Jacques Roux's arrest and Hébert's execution. Cochin gives us the key to that mystique when he defines the Revolution by the Jacobin phenomenon, and the Jacobin phenomenon by the symbolic appropriation of the people's will.

For what disappeared on 9 Thermidor was not the participation of the masses in the government of the Republic. Their participation was totally non-existent during the months of actual Robespierrist dictatorship (April to July 1794), and had, in any case, been confiscated throughout the so-called public safety phase by militant oligarchies – the clubs, *sections* and

51. Cf. below, p. 200.

committees – who were vying with the Convention for the right to be the image of the people. Robespierre was but the final incarnation of that mythical identity. It was that system of power that was overthrown by the Thermidorean conspirators. Their action did not simply involve substituting one power for another – as in a *coup d'état* or in a change of majority – but substituting one *type* of power for another. In that sense, but in that sense alone, Thermidor was the end of the Revolution.

In fact, revolutionary power depends for its survival on the constant projection of an image that shows it to be wholly consubstantial with, indeed equivalent to the 'people'; if ejected from that symbolic position, it yields to the group or the leader who, in denouncing it, restores the consubstantiality and equivalence that have been endangered. The Revolution has no legality, only a legitimacy. Its very existence is bound up with a multifaceted yet single discourse of democratic legitimacy.

After the fall of Robespierre it lost its legitimacy; all it had left was its legality (even when it violated it). Its very existence was confined within the dead-ends of republican legality.

Revolutionary ideology had thus ceased to embody both political power and civil society and to take their place in the name of popular sovereignty. That such a break had occurred was shown in the aftermath of Thermidor by the exuberant rejoicing of all sections of society and by the general expression of loathing for the Terror. For the immediate and most obvious result of Robespierre's fall was society's recovery of its independence at every level, whether in everyday life, in mores and habits, or in the expression of passions and interests. That new-found freedom was essentially society's revenge on ideology, and so it conveys to the observer an impression of prosaic heaviness that offends the admirers of the Incorruptible. Thermidor brought to light not a *'reaction'*, but *another Revolution* that had been obscured by the preceding one, from which it is distinct – because it succeeded it – but inseparable, because it could not have occurred without it: the Revolution of special interests.

The peasants had acquired national property, the bourgeoisie was engaged in business and doing well, soldiers were making money and a career out of the war. 'France', wrote Tocqueville 'no longer loved the Republic but remained deeply attached to the Revolution.'[52] He meant that if anything was still 'revolutionary' in French society after Thermidor, it was the pursuit of personal interest, rather than of political

52. Tocqueville, *L'Ancien Régime*, vol. 2, p. 282. This statement occurs at the beginning of the unfinished second chapter on the Directory (1852), entitled 'How the nation ceased to be republican yet continued to be revolutionary.'

aims, and that society was intent on defending or preserving the benefits it had acquired, rather than on giving a new start to the history of mankind. Having ceased to be an advent, the Revolution had become a record of acquisitions. Re-conquered and once again taken in hand by civil society, it became visible as a balance-sheet of losses and gains. Tocqueville, who studied the Revolution a half-century later from such a point of view, was to show just how much the final balance also owed to the Ancien Régime.

Yet the French after Thermidor 'no longer loved the Republic'. Tocqueville meant that the political régime of the period had neither the support of public opinion, nor a constitutional focus, nor even any real power. He noted that when the Terror 'had become impossible, and public spirit flagged, the entire apparatus of power collapsed at once'.[53] But since he had not developed a theory of the Terror, he was also unable to explain just why the Terror had become impossible. Imprisoned in his concept of the Revolution-as-continuity, he had to treat as an extensive parenthesis the study of the various political forms engendered by the French Revolution between 1789 and the Consulate.

In fact, the Terror was 'impossible' after 9 Thermidor because society had recovered its independence from politics. But that recovery itself had become possible only because revolutionary ideology was no longer co-extensive with power. Henceforth, ideological notions were subordinated to pragmatic action. Moreover, now the values behind action were distinct from the actors themselves. Men began to use those values to justify themselves, now that values had ceased to identify men. To defend the Republic against the internal royalist offensive of 1798, the Thermidorians had no need to assert that they were 'the people'. That is the essential difference between Robespierrist Terror and the one that followed the 18 Fructidor *coup*. The first was an act of legitimation, while the second was no more than an operational measure. By the same token the first, a lasting and bloody phenomenon, was an act of the Revolution, while the second, soon halted by the resistance of society, was simply an expedient that sealed the downfall of Thermidorean power. This power, no longer upheld by the Terror, but not yet upheld by an administrative network, lacked the strength of the Revolution and legal force.

It would not be difficult to show, from the laborious prescriptions issued by the successive administrations under the Directory on the way republican ceremonies should be held, how revolutionary ideology degenerated into a mere rationalisation for specific policies. Not that it was less needed now than during the Jacobin period: in a sense, the need was

53. Tocqueville, *L'Ancien Régime*, vol. 2, p. 274 (note b).

even greater, since the Thermidorian government was unable to conform
to the legality it had imposed on itself. But revolutionary ideology now
fulfilled a different function; its very nature had changed. Now that power
was based on successive delegations of sovereignty, ideology no longer
served to define it or to bring it into conformity with the people's will.
Ideology was a help to power, because it provided for the republican
education of the citizenry. It was a tool to be used, because it taught
equality. It gave voice to the will and the interests of power, but no longer
conferred authority. The functioning of the Directorial régime precluded
revolutionary ideology as a principle yet counted on it as a means to its
ends.

Little does it matter that in fact the régime experienced an ever greater
need for revolutionary ideology as it lost the support of public opinion
and became more casual about the legality of its actions. The crisis in
which it had become embroiled only makes this trait stand out more
clearly, without changing its nature. Revolutionary ideology had been
transformed from a fundamental principle to a subordinate technique,
from the discourse of legitimacy to republican propaganda. Under the
régime of pure democracy, it had been the locus of power. The modern
representative State was to use it as a mere tool.

Yet revolutionary ideology played a deeper rôle than the purely
instrumental use to which it was put, in keeping with Thermidorian
cynicism, would make one believe. For it carried over from the very
recent period of its origin the awesome dignity of having been the
Revolution itself, and it also continued to embody the image of the
Revolution for its enemies, both foreign and domestic. That is why it was
more than a disguise for bourgeois interests or a simple means of
preserving the revolutionary legacy by uniting regicide deputies, newly
rich landowners, and peasant–soldiers. In conjunction and in mutual
dependence with the war, it was all that remained alive of the Revolution
and constituted the inseparable union of democracy and the nation. This
sediment was a blend of special interests and powerful egalitarian ideas,
and the representative Republic was both too oligarchical and too weak
to safeguard it for any length of time. It was Bonaparte who paid the full
price of such a history: a strong State and permanent war.

Thus revolutionary ideology, which, in its chemically pure form of
1792–3, had engendered the Terror and the war, was still, albeit in a
degenerate form – part opinion and part legitimacy – the key to the new
power that was taking shape in 1799. The bourgeoisie of Brumaire had
been looking for a liberal military figure to head a representative system.

Popular feeling incited a victorious general to set up an absolute State. As Marx explains,[54] it was an administrative variant of the Terror that put an end to the French Revolution.

Clearly Tocqueville, who interpreted the Revolution in terms of its final balance, was doubly correct in judging that this balance was mainly political and cultural (in the widest sense of the word) and that its most salient feature was the new strength of the administrative State, which no longer had to contend with the social and administrative networks of the Ancien Régime. What Tocqueville, in his last book, called 'democracy' was an egalitarian culture far more than a state of society. That culture had spread throughout society thanks to the development of the absolute monarchy, which had destroyed yet also congealed the traditional hierarchies by simultaneously emptying them of their content and perpetuating them in the law. In the triumph of that culture, and of a central administration that was both its cause and its effect, Louis XIV linked up with Napoleon. For Tocqueville, that was the meaning of the French Revolution.

But what is missing in his history, as I shall try to show,[55] is an analysis of the routes that triumph took, above all the most important and most improbable among them, the Revolution itself. For the question that must be answered is how the apparently relentless continuity of a phenomenon could come to light through the apparently radical discontinuity of a Revolution.

Obviously the Revolution removed – indeed destroyed – many of the obstacles to the exercise of authority by a central administration. But my aim here is to go beyond that negative finding: for in democratic culture – the real innovation of the French Revolution – and in the transfer of legitimacy – its very essence – the traditional image of absolute power was somehow reconstituted. Between 1789 and 9 Thermidor 1794, revolutionary France used the paradox of democracy, explored by Rousseau, as the sole source of power. Society and the State were fused in the discourse of the people's will; and the ultimate manifestations of that obsession with legitimacy were the Terror and the war, both of which were inherent in the ever-escalating rhetoric of the various groups competing for the exclusive right to embody the democratic principle. The Terror refashioned, in a revolutionary mode, a kind of divine right of public authority.

That configuration was broken on 9 Thermidor, when society re-

54. Marx, *La Sainte Famille* [The Holy Family], pp. 149–50.
55. Cf. below, pp. 160ff.

asserted its independence. Re-emerging with all its unwieldiness, its conflicting interests and its divisions, it attempted to re-establish a law based on the elective representation of the people. In a sense, the Revolution was over, for it had renounced its language and admitted that there were specific interests it had to defend. And yet a part of it continued to speak after Thermidor. That part of it was the war, which survived the Terror and constituted the last refuge of revolutionary legitimacy. Although it burdened the Directory – like the old monarchy before it – with all the administrative constraints entailed by mobilising resources and men, the war nevertheless was the voice with which the genius of the Revolution still murmured to the French the messianic words of the early days. The logical outcome of that ambiguity was Bonaparte, that is, a king of the Revolution who combined the ancient image of power with the new legitimacy.

Taking Tocqueville on such a detour by way of Augustin Cochin – with some disregard for chronology – yields a French Revolution whose *nature* can be defined as dialectic between actual power and a symbolic representation of it, and whose chief *outcome*, ten years after it broke out, was the establishment, with Napoleon, of a democratically based monarchy [*une royauté de la démocratie*]. The Revolution was a collectively shared symbolic image of power, which broke continuity and drifted toward pure democracy only the better to appropriate, albeit at a different level, the absolutist tradition. That is how French society fashioned a new political legitmacy along with a new central administrative power. Augustin Cochin helps us understand how democratic legitimacy came to replace the former divine-right legitimacy, how it came to fill the space left vacant by the latter, a vast, indeed unlimited space, since it contained by definition the entire political and social order. The democratic legitimacy of the Revolution was both its mirror image and its reverse, because it occupied the same space, which it refused to subdivide in any way, and because it was just as determined to make all of society conform to one founding principle. The difference lies in the new principle, which was the people's will.

No 'liberal' bourgeoisie, in the early years, was able to embody or interpret that legitimacy. No representative parliamentary body was ever able to transform the new citizens' rights and duties into lasting laws. Pure democracy culminated in government by the Terror. Bonaparte could only 'close' the Revolution because he embodied a plebiscitary version of it. Society was thus finally able to set up a government that, while deriving all its power from society, remained independent of it, even above it, just like the Terror. At the same time, however, that government provided the conditions in which a new king could establish a democratic administration, a goal society had pursued in vain – because it was a contradiction in terms – ever since 1789. The Revolution was over, since France had returned to its history or, rather, reconciled its two histories.

To understand that, one must be willing to concentrate on the conceptual core of the Revolution, without diluting it with vague notions of linear development designed to add a layer of dignity to the virtues of its protagonists. Modern France was special not because it had gone from an absolute monarchy to a representative régime or from a world of noble privilege to a bourgeois society. After all, the rest of Europe went through the same process without a revolution and without Jacobins, even though events in France may have hastened that evolution here and there and spawned some imitators. What sets the French Revolution apart is that it was not a transition but a beginning and a haunting vision of that beginning. Its historical importance lies in the one trait that was unique to it, especially since this 'unique' trait was to become universal: it was the first experiment with democracy.

Loan Receipt

Library Services
Liverpool John Moores University

Borrower: Harvey, Sam HSSSHARV

Loaned today:

Interpreting the French Revolution /
31111006054942
Due Date: 03/01/2024 23:59:00 GMT

Total items loaned today: 1

Library charges: £0 00 GBP
Overdue items: 0
Total items on loan: 1

16/12/2023 17:22

Please keep your receipt in case of dispute.

Part II

Three approaches to the history of the French Revolution

1. The Revolutionary catechism*

The tragedy of the French, and of the working class as a whole, is that they are caught up in their memories of a momentous past. Events must put an end, once and for all, to this reactionary cult of the past.

Marx, Letter to César de Paepe, 14 September 1870

I

Are we fighting, once again, the battles of the good old days? Is the spectre of the counter-revolution threatening the achievements of our great ancestors? One might believe it, despite the rather drab calm of our public life, when reading a little book recently published by Claude Mazauric,[1] with a preface by Albert Soboul. Its author solemnly denounces a history of the French Revolution, written for the general public, which I brought out five years ago with Denis Richet.[2] Our book is suspected of running counter to the particular brand of Marxist interpretation that Albert Soboul and his disciples have adopted, and thereby also to the writings of great predecessors from Jean Jaurès to Georges Lefebvre, whom these Marxist historians monopolise for their own ends with the good conscience of true believers. By the same token – for this reasoning proceeds with its own Manichaean logic – Richet and I

---

* This chapter originally appeared as an article in *Annales E.S.C.* (March-April 1971): 255–89. I have added here a section on the State in the Ancien Régime (pp. 108–13).

1. Claude Mazauric, *Sur la Révolution française* (Paris: Éditions Sociales, 1970).
2. François Furet and Denis Richet, *La Révolution française* (Paris: Hachette, 1965–6), 2 vols. A less expensive one-volume edition was published in hardback by Fayard (Paris) in 1973 and in paperback by Marabout (Verviers [Belgium]) in 1979.

are accused of playing the 'ideologically bourgeois' game, which led to launching our book with a 'powerful advertising campaign in the press, by radio and television'. Moved by courage alone, Claude Mazauric does not hesitate to modify for his own purpose the commonly understood rules of scientific endeavour. His unprecedented manoeuvre consists of appealing to his readers' patriotism, the better to stigmatise what he calls the 'anti-national bias' of his opponents, who are suspected of a lukewarm attitude toward the expansionist policies of the Jacobins. 'I must say frankly what I think', he states, moved to search his own motives after this display of jingoistic boldness. At the end, having treated us to a lengthy exposé, the intrepid scholar lets us in on the secret of his perspicacity: 'The historian's method, thus, is theoretically identical to that of the Leninist Workers' Party.' That is how he sets down the principles to be followed in the trial of a book suspected of heresy on two counts. The preosecutor is draped at once in our national glories and in Leninist theory. No one will be surprised that the verdict is not lenient. Truly, the defendants had been asking for it.

By now the reader will have understood that, as political theatre, this debate is actually a farce, or indeed shadow-boxing. In the political arena of present-day France, nothing nor anyone is threatening the achievements of the French Revolution, for the Right has ceased, ever since the defeat of fascism, to define itself in opposition to the Revolution of 1789–94 and to the Republic. In the academic world, Marxist historiography (which I prefer to call 'Jacobin') is today, more than ever, in a dominant position. It has its ancestors, its traditions, its canons and its vulgate; and it can hardly be said to cultivate a taste for impertinence and non-conformism. In short, the French Revolution is in power in society and its institutions, especially in academia. By this I mean simply that no historical debate about the Revolution any longer involves real political stakes.

Nonetheless, if certain historians continue to believe that it does, it is because they need to believe it. After all, imaginary participation in political battles is the more satisfying to one in an ivory tower the more illusory it is, for that is how it returns the most psychological satisfaction for a minimum of trouble. But if, in turn, that illusion is felt to be reality, it is because, through the history of the French Revolution, intellectuals share or glorify values that are still very much alive. Because they are the very foundation of our political civilisation, those values remain powerful sources of inspiration. The mere fact that they are no longer at issue in any real struggle does not mean that they have been erased from men's memories. That is because the national memory, on which so much pedagogical solicitude has been lavished, usually lags behind current social events, and especially because it has an almost boundless elasticity. For it is obvious that, starting with the French Revolution, every revolution, and above all the French Revolution itself, has tended to perceive itself as an absolute beginning, as ground zero of history, pregnant with all the future accomplishments contained in the universality of its principles. Thus it is particularly difficult for societies that claim a revolutionary 'founding', especially if it is relatively recent, to write their contemporary history.[3] Any such history is bound to be a commemoration of origins, and the magic of the birthday celebration depends on the fidelity of the heirs, not on the critical evaluation of the legacy.

In that sense, it is perhaps inevitable that any history of the French Revolution should be, up to a point, a commemoration. It can be a royalist commemoration, where one weeps over the misfortunes of the king and lost legitimacy. We have also seen 'bourgeois' commemorations, which celebrate the founding of a national contract. Or it can be a revolutionary commemoration, which emphasises the dynamism of the founding event and its promises for the future. From that point of view, any historiography of the French Revolution can legitimately be related to the evolution of the political and social circumstances of the nineteenth and twentieth centuries.[4] The result is rather odd, a kind of residual history that at each stage derives its distinct character from the part that the present plays in the different interpretations of the past. Such an exercise is undeniably useful, even salutary, for it makes us aware of the ambiguity in which historical questions are rooted and of the ways in which they become entangled in current issues. But lest it lead to complete historical relativism, to a concept of history as subservient to the demands of society, an illusory anchor amidst uncontrollable drift, it must do more than simply state the rôle of the present in the history of the Revolution; it must also be accompanied by an expertise, as precise as possible, of the constraints imposed by *our own* present.

The Revolution, past or present?

It is clear that those constraints are by no means all equally fruitful or sterile. The counter-revolutionary bias, for example – despite the fact that it underlies some histories of the Revolution of considerable interest, like

3. Cf. the article by Mona Ozouf, 'De Thermidor à Brumaire: le discours de la Révolution sur elle-même', *Revue Historique* (January–March 1970), 31–66.
4. Cf. Alice Gérard, *La Révolution française, mythes et interprétations, 1789–1970* (Paris: Flammarion, 'Questions d'histoire' series, 1970).

Taine's *Origines* – is the most detrimental of all to an understanding of the phenomenon, for it constantly tends to reduce its scope or even to deny it altogether. Moreover, it almost naturally leads to moralistic explanations (providence, plot, and so on) unsuited – and purposely so – to account for events and periods characterised by exceptional activity on the part of the masses. To understand the Revolution, one must somehow 'accept' it. But it is precisely 'how' one accepts it that makes the difference. The greatest historians in the first half of the nineteenth century were still hypnotised by the event that dominated their lives; but, for all that, not one of them, not Guizot, nor Michelet, nor of course Tocqueville, felt entitled to consider it familiar, 'normal', or easy to understand. Quite to the contrary, it was amazement at the *strangeness* of the phenomenon that shaped the existential purpose of their work as historians. They all split up the great event, decomposing it into elements and periods, which they then refitted into a long-term evolution in order to conceptualise its meaning or meanings. Indeed, every truly historical analysis of the Revolution begins with an – at least implicit – critique of the way it was perceived when it happened, namely as the break between the old and the new that lies at the core of revolutionary ideology. In that respect, Tocqueville went intellectually further than anyone when he inverted the idea that the revolutionaries had of themselves and their action and showed that, far from being the agents of a radical break with the past, the revolutionaries in fact put the finishing touches to the centralised bureaucratic State begun by the kings of France. As for Guizot, it was his political conservatism that liberated him from the mythology of the founding event. He felt that the Revolution had to be an end-result, not a beginning. Michelet, of the three historians, was the one who most thoroughly assimilated the revolutionary ideology. But he came to the history of the Revolution after he had covered the entire history of France; and his passion for the past for its own sake, together with the extraordinarily varied nature of his analysis of the Revolution, freed him from a teleological view. For the Revolution, if it was to be a foreshadowing and a foundation of the future, would have to be, to use the term current during the Third Republic, a single thing, a 'block'.

What reinforced the spontaneous ideology of the Revolution-as-mother was the struggles of the early years of the Third Republic and, above all, the development of the socialist movement. For this movement was the potential agent of a second revolution, destined to negate dialectically the conditions created by the first and to fulfil its promises at last. Thus was born that bizarre configuration, that naive ideology, that linear schema by which the twentieth century reinvested the Revolution-as-mother[5] with the same meaning of a founding event that its participants had assigned it in the heat of the moment. But now that meaning is different, excised as it were of much of its empiric richness, now drawn on and conceived selectively. The French Revolution is no longer seen as a total upheaval of values, a remaking of the bases of social pre-eminence and leadership that, between Mirabeau and Napoleon, had installed a new State and contemporary French society. Henceforth labelled 'bourgeois', that revolution is imagined to have stopped, on 9 Thermidor, at the very moment when its non-'bourgeois' phase actually came to an end. From then its core has been the Jacobin period, that is, the time when in fact the moralistic and utopian ideology most effectively masked the real historical process, the real relations between civil society and the State. Naive emotional commitment to those values and to that ideology by historians enables them to turn the illusions of the revolutionaries of the Years I and II to their own ends; they quickly credit the Revolution with a kind of two-fold founding power that gives it not just national, but universal validity. When Albert Soboul speaks of 'our common mother', I fear that this classic reference[6] does little to clarify the discussion; but at least, as a cry from the heart, it does throw light on the depths of his passion.

After 1917, the French Revolution became more than just the matrix of probabilities that could and would engender another permanently liberating revolution, more than just the realm of possible developments that Jaurès had discovered and described in all of its richness. It had become the mother of an actual event, and its offspring had a name: October 1917, and more generally, the Russian Revolution. As early as 1920, Mathiez wrote a pamphlet[7] stressing the kinship between the government of the Montagnards from June 1793 to July 1794, and the Bolshevik dictatorship during the civil war years: 'Jacobinism and Bolshevism are dictatorships of the same kind; both are born of civil and foreign war, both are class dictatorships, both use the same means – terror, requisitioning, and control of prices – and both ultimately pursue the same goal, namely, the transformation of society, that is, not just Russian or French, but society in general' (pp. 3–4). Moreover, as Mathiez pointed out, the

---

5. It would be interesting to find out why the English Revolution never plays the mother-rôle in European revolutions from the eighteenth to the twentieth centuries.
6. Cf. in particular D. Guérin, 'Bataille autour de notre mère', vol. 2 of the new edition of *La Lutte de classes sous le Première République* (Paris: Gallimard, 1968) pp. 489–513. This 'maternal' reference was quite common in the nineteenth century: it can be found in particular in the writings of Michelet and Kropotkin.
7. *Le Bolchévisme et le Jacobinisme* (Paris: Librairie de 'L'Humanité', 1920).

Bolsheviks always had their minds fixed on the example of the French Revolution, especially in its Jacobin phase. As early as 1903, when the Russian Social Democrats split into Bolsheviks and Mensheviks, Lenin pleaded his case by invoking the Jacobin example: 'A Jacobin firmly committed to *organising* a proletariat that has become conscious of its *class interest* is precisely what a *revolutionary social democrat* is.'[8] This reference nourished a full-scale polemic with Trotsky, who at that time had Menshevik leanings. In a too little-known work, recently republished, Trotsky stressed the anachronistic nature of Lenin's analysis.[9] He pointed out that either 'the Jacobin ... by being committed to organising a proletariat now conscious of its class interest' is no longer a Jacobin;[10] or else ... he *is* a Jacobin, that is, radically different from a revolutionary social democrat: 'Two worlds, two doctrines, two tactics, two mentalities separated by an abyss',[11] he stated in concluding a long historical analysis of the dead ends and ideological excesses of Jacobin terrorism. That call to intellectual order, however much informed by impeccable Marxist orthodoxy, did not prevent the constant telescoping of the two revolutions in the consciousness of the Russian revolutionaries. We know, for instance, that after Lenin's death, when the spectre of 'Thermidor' haunted the leadership, Stalin entered into a tactical alliance with Zinoviev and Kamenev because all feared a new Bonaparte, who was none other than Trotsky, the ex-commander of the Red Army.

That overlap between the two revolutions has not only bedevilled those who have made history in the twentieth century; it also exists in the minds of the historians of the French Revolution, the more so since the historiography of the latter, at least in France, has been mainly left-wing. In fact, the 'displacement' of interest within the French Revolution by the Russian Revolution, shifting the emphasis and curiosity from 1789 to 1793, has yielded some positive results for scholarship: the shift has been a powerful incentive to study more closely the rôle of the urban popular classes in the revolutionary process, and important books like Mathiez's *Le Vie chère*,[12] Daniel Guérin's *Les Bras nus*[13], and Albert Soboul's *Sans-*

8. Lenin, 'Un pas en avant, deux pas en arrière' [One step forward, two steps back], French trans., *Oeuvres choisies* (Moscow, 1954), vol. 1, p. 617. The italics are Lenin's.
9. L. Trotsky, *Nos Tâches politiques* [Our political tasks] (Paris: Pierre Belfond, 1970). Trotsky deliberately turned his back on this book, which had appeared in August 1904. After he had rallied to the Bolsheviks in 1917 he did not want to tarnish his political image by this 'rightist' opposition to Lenin.
10. *Ibid.*, p. 184.
11. *Ibid.*, p. 189.
12. A. Mathiez, *La Vie chère et le mouvement social sous la Terreur* (Paris: Payot, 1927 and reprint, 2 vols., 1973).
13. D. Guérin, *La Lutte de classes sous la Première République*.

culottes[14] probably owe their conception to that new interest.[15] In fact, it is clear, as many examples from Tocqueville to Max Weber show, that questioning the present can be helpful in interpreting the past.

For it to be useful, however, the scrutiny of the present must remain just that, a questioning and a series of new hypotheses, not a mechanical and impassioned projection of the present onto the past. But the interpretation of the French Revolution has gained neither in richness nor in depth for being accompanied, as in a minor key, by a second, implicit discourse on the Russian Revolution; that second and latent discourse has proliferated like a cancer inside the historical analysis to the point of destroying its complexity and its very significance. One can note at least three expressions of this phenomenon. First, the search within the French Revolution for precedents justifying the revolution and post-revolutionary period in Russia.[16] Take the example of the purges within the revolutionary leadership, which characterise the histories of both revolutions; Stalin, like Robespierre, liquidated his former associates in the name of the struggle against counter-revolution. On the strength of that, the interpretations of the two purges as 'spontaneous' – the French example coming to the rescue of the Russian one – reinforced each other and crystallized around the idea that counter-revolution is intrinsic to revolution, from which it must be flushed out. A genuine and possibly even fruitful comparison, on the other hand, would have consisted in examining in both cases – and they are of course quite different – the workings of the admittedly identical process of division and liquidation within the initial leadership group. Instead of that, what we see deployed is a mechanism that justifies the present by the past, which is the hallmark of teleological history.

The second development is the substitution of an extraordinarily simplified and simplistic Marxism for the few and sometimes contradictory analyses of the French Revolution that Marx and Engels left us.[17] It

14. A. Soboul, *Les Sans-culottes parisiens en l'an II* (La Roche-sur-Yon, 1958).
15. One might add to this list the important studies by the English school, notably those by Eric Hobsbawm and George Rudé. Less concerned with Marxism, Richard Cobb seems to me to have adopted a different intellectual approach.
16. In 'Leninist' historiography, the Russian Revolution occupies a special place precisely by virtue of its open-endedness: it is never completed.
17. Writing this article has led me to reread Marx and Engels. What they wrote about the French Revolution is fascinating, but nearly always allusive, and at times contradictory. These texts certainly deserve a systematic catalogue and analysis. I shall limit myself here to showing, by means of a necessarily eclectic use of Marx's and Engels's writings, just how inaccurate Mazauric's interpretation of them is. For those of Marx's and Engels's texts that have not yet been translated into French, my references are to the German edition of their collected works: Marx–Engels, *Werke*, 39 vols. (Berlin: Dietz, 1961–8).

amounts to a kind of simple, linear schema of history, in which the bourgeois revolution, uniting the peasantry and urban masses behind it, achieves the breakthrough from the feudal to the capitalist mode of production. The Montagnard dictatorship, which is given star billing as the most 'popular' episode of the whole process, also assumes the most 'progressive' significance, for it not only went 'all the way' – to war and terror – in carrying out the tasks assigned in advance to the bourgeois revolution, but also foreshadowed other liberations, notably and specifically the October Revolution of 1917. Such a view progressively cuts the Revolution loose from its true chronology, first drawing it away from 1789 toward 1793, and then suddenly interrupting it in July 1794, at the very time when it was setting all of Europe ablaze and was being firmly established in France itself. Necessarily that also blurs the concept of 'bourgeois revolution', which becomes much too big for comprehending a chronological process thus shrunk at both ends.

If 'Marxist' historians (in the sense defined above) are not disturbed by that obvious contradiction, it is because they are less Marxists than neo-Jacobins. For them, the Marxist schema conveyed by the Soviet Revolution is but a veneer superimposed on a far more powerful political and emotional commitment to the French Revolution's self-interpretation, its perception of itself as both the fountain-head of the *grande nation* and the universal liberator of society, in other words, as 'Jacobin' much more than as 'Constituent'. What they love about the Soviet Revolution is what Mathiez, who was not a Marxist, saw as early as 1920: the superimposing of one image of liberation on another; over the fabric of our contemporary history seen as a religion of progress is placed the image of the Soviet Union now assigned the rôle played earlier by France. Little does it matter that recent history has dealt such blows to that construct that it should not have survived; but then, it is precisely the function of ideology to mask reality and so outlive it. The neo-Jacobin historian, intoxicated by the idea of a nation entrusted with the rôle of enlightening humanity, balks at the idea of coming out from under his oxygen tent. Listen to him, speaking through the voice of Albert Soboul, as he once again expounds the 'lessons' of a history that teaches progress, and as he speaks of 1793 in the present tense: 'Who can fail to recognise that some of the problems the revolutionary movement is faced with today were already, in somewhat different form, at the heart of the complex and violent interplay of social and political forces of the Year II?'[18]

The interpretation of the French Revolution has thus produced a kind

18. A. Soboul's preface to Mazauric's *Sur la Revolution française*, p. 2.

of Lenino-populist vulgate. Soboul's *Précis*[19] is probably its best example, and its canons seem to be all the more firmly established as they appropriate the entire 'left-wing' historiography of the French Revolution, from Jaurès to Georges Lefebvre.[20] Woe to those who deviate from that vulgate, for instantly they become traitors to Danton and Jaurès, Robespierre and Mathiez, Jacques Roux and Soboul. In that extravagant medley, which is only slightly exaggerated, one recognises the Manichaean, sectarian and conservative spirit of a historiography that substitutes value judgments for concepts, final ends for causality, argument from authorities for open discussion. The new Teilhard de Chardins of the Jacobin Revolution, fountain-head of two revolutions, are once again ensconced in their old cradle, the two-dimensional imaginary world of politics that has named them the defenders of the people, and so they embody, not only as a heritage, but for the present and for the future, the alternative between revolution and counter-revolution, which they have the obligation to expound and transmit through a history that is at once communion and pedagogy. Any *other* history of the Revolution, that is, any history that attempts to break away from the mechanism of spontaneous identification with precisely that object and those values it is supposed to make explicit, is *ipso facto* branded as counter-revolutionary, even anti-national. The 'logic' of that reasoning is impeccable, except that it is not really a reasoning at all, but rather a ritual, always renewed and by now sclerotic, of commemoration. It is the tomb of the Unknown Soldier, the one who died not in the battle of the Marne but at Fleurus.

II

Albert Soboul's latest book[21] is a perfect illustration of that type of history; in this respect it is not as inconsequential as its casual mode of composition would suggest.[22] For the very simplicity of its architecture lays

19. A. Soboul, *Précis d'histoire de la Révolution française* (Paris: Éditions Sociales, 1962). A somewhat caricatural instance of this canonical interpretation of the Revolution can be found in the same author's afterword, entitled 'La Révolution française dans l'histoire du monde contemporain', to the recent reprint of Georges Lefebvre's *Quatre-vingt-neuf* (Paris: Éditions Sociales, 1970).
20. I shall return presently to the importance and the significance of Georges Lefebvre's work, which seems to me to have been misappropriated, even as regards his general interpretation, by Albert Soboul and his followers.
21. A. Soboul, *La Civilisation et la Révolution française*, vol. 1, *La Crise de l'Ancien Régime* (Paris: Arthaud, 1970).
22. Cf. the clarification of this matter in *Annales E.S.C.* (September–October 1970), 1494–6.

bare all the secrets of the commemorative and teleological historical consciousness just described.

The historian of the French Revolution has chosen a promising title borrowed from the programme of the series[23] in which the book appeared: *La Civilisation et la Révolution française.* Failing to live up to this enticing announcement, which promises to lead us all over the world in search of a vast cultural legacy, he gives us a rather more classical 'Crisis of the Ancien Régime', in fact an overview of eighteenth-century France. From the very first pages it becomes clear that the entire century was one great crisis; that all the elements of the analysis, at every level, converge on 1789 as if they were being sucked toward the inevitable climax that set them up *a posteriori*: 'Philosophy, an integral part of the general course of history, in accordance with economic and social trends, contributed to that slow maturing process which, in sudden mutation, became a revolution that crowned the century of the Enlightenment' (p. 22).

Somewhat taken aback by that exordium, which does not give him a chance to 'warm up' and bombards him at one go with a slew of metaphysical propositions, the reader frantically turns to the table of contents, wondering whether he should go on! There, another surprise is in store: the organisation of the book. There are four parts: the peasants, the aristocracy, the bourgeoisie and the 'fourth estate', that is, the urban lower classes. To be sure, any arrangement is arbitrary and by definition imposes intellectual constraints. But this one positively calls for acrobatics on the part of the historian of the eighteenth century. He is obliged to treat such topics as demography, economic trends, politics and culture piecemeal by social categories and must, for instance, deal with the 'Enlightenment' in the second part, devoted to the aristocracy, but with the *philosophes* only in the third, in connection with the bourgeoisie. He can introduce the absolute State only in treating the aristocracy, almost as an aside, only through the monarchy's relations with the nobility. Imperturbably Albert Soboul goes about his neo-Aristotelian surgery, in which social classes function as metaphysical categories.

One would like to believe that he accepted the risks involved in so artificial a division not only because he did not feel like rearranging the material he had already taught in this conceptual framework, though under a different and more appropriate title.[24] But the real reason must be that for him every history of eighteenth-century France, whatever its formal title, implicitly rests upon two basic propositions: (1) that the

23. *Les Grandes Civilisations*, Arthaud.
24. A. Soboul, *La Société française dans la seconde moitié du XVIIIe siècle* (Paris: C.D.U., 1969).

eighteenth century was characterised by a general crisis of the Ancien Régime, a crisis signposted by concomitant trends at all levels of historical reality; (2) that this crisis was essentially social and must be analysed in terms of class conflict. Now, of the two propositions, the first is either tautological, or teleological, or both. At any rate, its total lack of precision makes it impervious to any rational evaluation. The second is a historical hypothesis; and it is interesting that it should be the same one that the French Revolution had adopted to account for itself, at the time of the event and even just before its outbreak. Soboul's eighteenth century is that of Sieyès and his pamphlet, *Qu'est-ce que le Tiers Etat?*; it is a century totally preoccupied and determined by the social conflict between the aristocracy and the Third Estate. Never has the tyrannical hold of the revolutionary event over eighteenth-century history been more naively displayed. In fact, one wonders whether after one hundred and eighty years of research and interpretation, and after so many detailed studies and general analyses, it is a great intellectual achievement for a historian to share the particular image of the past that was held by the actors in the Revolution themselves, and whether it is not a rather paradoxical performance for an allegedly Marxist historiography to take its bearings from the prevailing ideological consciousness of the period it sets out to explain. For Soboul as for Sieyès, the Revolution was not one of the possible futures in store for the eighteenth century; it was its only future, its crowning glory, its purpose, its very meaning. Like Bernardin de Saint-Pierre's melon, which was created to be eaten at the family table, so Soboul's eighteenth century is sliced up to be savoured in 1789. But what is left of it?

The author, I imagine, must have had some misgivings, for at the last moment he did superimpose on his sociological division a concluding chapter, whose title quite simply repeats that of the book: 'The Crisis of the Ancien Régime'. However, it is not really a conclusion, but another, and quite classical, exposé of the immediate causes of the Revolution. Here we are told about the final inter-cyclical economic depression as described by Labrousse, the social crisis, the waning of the 'Enlightenment', the impotence of the State, and the revolt of the aristocracy. Where, then, should we look for the 'crisis' of the Ancien Régime? In the 1780s, which Soboul describes in his conclusion, or in the long-term social contradictions of the century? None of that is ever made clear to the reader, but the answer, at least implicitly, seems to be: in both places. The century accumulated the combustible pile, and the 1780s provided the spark that set it afire. Thus the last-minute introduction of a time-element into the analysis of social stratification modifies neither the conceptual classification nor the teleological philosophy of the analysis. On the contrary, it is brought in to confirm both. It is the new theologian's new Providence.

In that Procrustean bed, what becomes of our poor eighteenth century? It is a vast area of latent social contradictions, prefigurations of the future assigned to them, that is, of the class fronts drawn from 1789 to 1793 – the bourgeoisie and its allies in the lower classes; the peasants and the urban 'fourth estate', all on one side, and the aristocracy on the other.

The problem of seigneurial rights and the 'feudal reaction'

In Soboul's analysis, the peasants have the lion's share and occupy almost half of the book. Two hundred pages are devoted to them, in my opinion the best part of the volume. Albert Soboul gives us a synthesis of the many studies on the peasantry under the Ancien Régime, and produces a very full analysis of the various aspects of rural life, including the social setting, technology, demography, everyday working habits, cultures and beliefs.

These pages, in conveying a concrete sympathy for the world of the countryside and an insight into the life of humble people, have a very special flavour. Yet when it comes to the basic interpretation, the analysis raises one immense problem, with which it deals rather too summarily: seigneurial rights and the burden of feudalism in the French countryside of the eighteenth century.

Soboul has made up his mind. On the conceptual level, although he is evidently aware of the distinction between 'feudal' and 'seigneurial', just as were the jurists of the Revolution,[25] he constantly mixes the two notions in exactly the same way revolutionary ideology did. Thus, in his historical analysis, he can speak of a 'feudal complex' or 'régime' as defining what was essential in the economic and social relationships of the countryside. At the price of a constant confusion of words, between 'feudal', 'seigneurial' and 'aristocratic', the historian, here again, takes his bearings from the contemporary perceptions of the event he describes[26] and once more he is imprisoned in the sharp division made in 1789 between 'old' and 'new', a division in which 'old' meant 'feudal'. Suddenly there he is,

25. Cf. Merlin de Douai (whom Soboul cites on p. 67) and his reports to the Constituent Assembly on behalf of the *Comité féodal* (Committee on feudalism) on 4 September 1789 and 8 February 1790.
26. Mazauric proceeds in the same manner in *Sur la Révolution*, pp. 118–34. 'Marxism' is reduced to a device for justifying the contemporary consciousness of the event.

forced to charge to 'feudalism' all the negative and in the end 'explosive' aspects of rural life, from the exploitation of the peasantry and its misery to the obstacles to agricultural productivity and the slow pace of capitalist development. But since by the eighteenth century that 'feudal régime' had been under heavy attack for some four or five centuries, the old idea of an 'aristocratic reaction'[27] is brought in to rescue the threatened concept. From Soboul's language and ideas, the reader almost feels as if he were participating in the meeting held on the famous night of 4 August 1789.

As everyone knows, the facts and figures for an analysis on a national scale of the relative weight of seigneurial dues in the total landed revenue – and in the incomes of peasants and nobles – do not exist. Nor will they exist very soon, because the dues were incredibly diverse, the sources are scattered, and the data to be gathered from the *terriers* [seigneurial rent rolls] do not lend themselves to being grouped into statistical series. Soboul writes (p. 44): 'Landed income, *for the most part of a feudal nature*, was the main consideration in agricultural life.' This statement, in the part I have italicised, is patently false for eighteenth-century France, where leases, sharecropping and direct management unquestionably produced more income than seigneurial dues. And one is surprised to hear a specialist making it. The degree of his inexactness is what is important here. But just how wrong is he? The many monographs at our disposal testify to a wide variety of situations. Le Roy Ladurie's peasants in their relatively 'unfeudalised' *Midi* seem to have rid themselves of seigneurial payments quite early, that is, by the beginning of the sixteenth century.[28] In Paul Bois's Sarthe,[29] the level of seigneurial dues seems to have been very low, amounting to a tiny fraction of the total landed income in comparison with the income from leases. Nor did the revision of the *terriers* in the seventeeth century bring to light any supplementary dues. 'It is only slightly exaggerated to say', concludes P. Bois, 'that the matter of seigneurial dues did not concern the peasant.' The same goes for Abel Poitrineau's Auvergne,[30] where seigneurial dues do not seem to have represented more than ten per cent of net landed income, although here they did rise in the course of the century. By contrast, in Jean Meyer's

---

27. Here as elsewhere Soboul does not distinguish between aristocratic, seigneurial and feudal.
28. Emmanuel Le Roy Ladurie, *Les Paysans de Languedoc* (Paris: S.E.V.P.E.N., 1966), cf. vol. 1, pp. 291–2.
29. Paul Bois, *Paysans de l'Ouest* (Paris and The Hague: Mouton, 1960), cf. pp. 382ff.
30. Abel Poitrineau, *La Vie rurale en Basse-Auvergne au XVIIIe siècle, 1726–1789* (Paris and The Hague: Mouton, 1965), cf. vol. 1, pp. 342ff.

Brittany[31] and in Pierre de Saint-Jacob's Burgundy,[32] to which a new study was recently devoted by Régine Robin,[33] the seigneur's share deducted from the net yield of the land remained high, especially when it involved payments in kind. The *champart* levied in Burgundy and the rights attached to the *domaine congéable* in Brittany seem to have been, in the economic sense, truly burdensome seigneurial rights.

Given the present state of our knowledge, it is therefore impossible to speak of a 'feudal reaction' in the eighteenth century as if it were an objective process within the economy and rural society. It is not even sure that landed dues (*droits réels*), which were above all a burden to the landowner – since, like the Church tithe (*dîme*), they were usually deducted from the owner's share – appreciably affected the standard of living of the poorest of the peasants, those who worked a small plot. But even if the opposite were true, even if a growth in seigneurial levies as a share of agricultural output did cause a pauperisation of the peasantry at the end of the eighteenth century, it would still not follow that this trend was aristocratic and 'feudal' (by which Soboul means both noble and anti-capitalist). Abel Poitrineau published in his work a very interesting curve showing the increasing commercialisation of the *seigneuries* of Auvergne in the second half of the century, as well as their growing involvement in the market.[34] In the case of mid-eighteenth-century Burgundy, Pierre de Saint-Jacob – who, incidentally, seems to use the term 'seigneurial reaction' with a certain reserve[35] – has shown how the *seigneurie*, through its dues collectors, who invested their receipts, took part in what he calls the 'physiocratic revolution', that is, the development of rural capitalism.[36] Perhaps we would be well advised to speak, as Alfred Cobban suggested,[37] not of an 'aristocratic reaction' but of an *embourgeoisement* of the *seigneurie*. Seen in this light, the peasant's resistance against the *seigneurie* may well have been not anti-aristocratic or 'anti-feudal', but anti-bourgeois and anti-capitalist. Hence the enthusiasm of the night of 4 August would not be that of a battle-front rallying all classes of society to

31. Jean Meyer, *La Noblesse bretonne au XVIIIe siècle* (Paris: S.E.V.P.E.N., 1966). See in particular vol. 2. Meyer found relatively burdensome seigneurial levies in Brittany; yet he concluded that 'seigneurial rights in the narrow sense, high though they were, represented a relatively small percentage of the nobles' income' (p. 1248).
32. Pierre de Saint-Jacob, *Les Paysans de la Bourgogne du Nord au dernier siècle de l'Ancien Régime* (Paris: Les Belles Lettres, 1960).
33. Régine Robin, *La Société française en 1789: Semur-en-Auxois* (Paris: Plon, 1970).
34. Poitrineau, *La Vie rurale*, vol. 2, p. 123.
35. Saint-Jacob, *Les Paysans de la Bourgogne*, p. 434.
36. *Ibid.* pp. 469–72.
37. Alfred Cobban, *The Social Interpretation of the French Revolution* (Cambridge: C.U.P., 1964), p. 47.

the common interest, but the means to gloss over a disagreement or at least a radical misunderstanding. Indeed, it is only too obvious that the abolition of seigneurial rights and dues did not dispel the subsequent resistance in French rural society to the development of capitalism. As P. Bois's book suggests, the peasant's hostility toward the *seigneurie* may simply have been the archaic form of his opposition to economic change.

In this connection, a recent German article[38] suggests an interesting hypothesis, based on a comparison between Bavaria and France. It shows the very different situation that existed in the German territories west of the Elbe, where the clergy and the nobility, while keeping their seigneurial rights (*propriété éminente*), had ceded all the old domain lands to perpetual leaseholders (*paysans tenanciers*), who thus had become virtual owners of 80–90 per cent of the income-producing land. In France, by contrast, the outstanding trait of the *seigneurie* was the retention of title to domain lands by seigneurs who 'farmed out' those lands under a renewable money-lease, a practice that became increasingly widespread between the sixteenth and the eighteenth century. In France this was more important than the quit-rent (*censive*), which the nobles detested because fixed payments did not keep pace with inflation and the devaluation of the currency. By the end of the eighteenth century, perpetual leaseholders in France held little more than a third of the soil, far less, therefore, than what has been generally believed. This comparative analysis of the evolution of the seigneurial system in France and western Germany has the advantage of explaining pauperisation in the French countryside on the eve of the Revolution, and the presence of a vast peasant proletariat without equivalent on the other side of the Rhine, where 90 per cent of the land was permanently in the hands of owner-occupiers. But it also underscores the fact that in France the development of rural capitalism was linked to the practice of 'farming out' domain lands. Far from standing in its way, the *seigneurie*, with its stewards (*régisseurs*) and bourgeois middlemen, was the vehicle of that development.[39] And Paul Bois is quite probably correct when he claims that in protesting against residual and secondary seigneurial rights, which were psychologically all the more irritating as they represented a marginal drain on an already

---

38. Eberhard Weis, 'Ergebnisse eines Vergleichs der grundherrshaftlichen Strukturen Deutschlands und Frankreichs vom 13. bis zum Ausgang des 18. Jahrhunderts', *Vierteljahrschrift für Sozial- und Wirtschaftsgeschichte* (1970) 1–14.
39. Some remarkable examples of this fact can be found in Georges Lefebvre's *Etudes orléanaises*, 2 vols. (Paris: Bibliothèque Nationale, 1962–3), vol. 1, ch. 1, 'Les campagnes orléanaises'.

marginal operation, French peasants of the late eighteenth century were really attacking the spread of landed capitalism.

Yet if the hazy notion of an aristocratic reaction, characterised by an increased emphasis on seigneurial rights, has been accepted by historians for so long, it can only be because it fits perfectly into the simplistic vision of class struggle and alliances related to it. It also enables Albert Soboul to fall back on an elementary textbook Marxism and to write that 'the changeover to a capitalist form of agriculture demanded the abolition of feudalism and privilege' (p. 89). Above all, that notion holds sway because it rests upon a series of eighteenth-century literary documents, foremost among them the *Cahiers* of the Estates General. It should be recalled that the debate about the documentary value of the *Cahiers* – and Heaven knows that this debate has been animated since the beginning of the century – has so far turned essentially on whether and to what extent the writers of each *Cahier* faithfully expressed the true wishes of their respective communities. Supposing that the question can be answered in the affirmative – and it can, in most cases – a second and probably more fundamental problem must be solved before the *Cahiers* can be used. Should they be read as statements describing the actual situation or as documents reflecting the political climate and ideology prevailing in French society in 1789? I am inclined to opt for the second type of reading, along with R. Robin who, on this point, has opened a new perspective.[40] At the very least, the second question must be dealt with before the first; the content of the *Cahiers* at every sociological level must be described before they can be related to the real social circumstances from which they were issued.

It is true that the peasant *Cahiers* are often filled with grievances against seigneurial rights. Yet those grievances were expressed less frequently, it seems, than those against the tithe (*dîme*) and the royal income or property tax (*taille*), which together were the true bane of the rural community. Among the various seigneurial rights, the peasant *Cahiers* were often less opposed to landed dues (*droits réels*) than to personal rights, such as monopolies over mills and ovens (*banalités*), and hunting rights. The notion that these rights had become more onerous in the recent past can also be found, especially in the form of hostility toward the experts who brought the seigneur's *terriers* up to date. But even supposing – and this supposition is certainly unwarranted in this form – that the peasant *Cahiers* were unanimous in their complaints about a recent increase in the seigneur's share, what would that prove? Virtually nothing at all.

40. Robin, *La Société française*, pp. 255–343.

It is quite likely, for example, that if a consultation on the 1789 model, calling for written statements of grievances, were conducted in rural France today, these modern *Cahiers* would be unanimous against taxation, even though French farmers have been notoriously under-taxed for the last hundred and fifty years. It is in the very nature of a political text and of any political consciousness, however rudimentary, to place the blame for evil on men rather than on things; that is what Ernest Labrousse,[41] who is still the leading Marxist historian of the origins of the French Revolution, very aptly calls 'placing the blame on politics'. The pervasive poverty of the late eighteenth century, for which we have a great deal of undeniable evidence, may have been due to demographic growth; after all, the extra five or six million subjects of the king of France had to find a little niche for themselves somewhere. That poverty is also inscribed in Labrousse's admirable graphs, in which the price of leases, that is, landed income in its most 'bourgeois' form, climbs ever so much faster than wages and even prices.[42] But how would the peasants, and even the local *notaire*, know that? How could they fail to turn, almost spontaneously, against the château and its retainers, who represented the image of power at the local level? As R. Robin pointed out in connection with the *Cahiers* from the region of Auxerre,[43] the grievances of the rural community were not a matter of historical and economic analysis but of concrete everyday life: taxes, tithes, hunting; the things that were taken away and those that were no longer permitted. Moreover, the consultation took place in the spring of 1789, at the height of a short-term crisis. It was perfectly natural for the immense masses of poor peasants to seek reasons for their difficulties in the recent past and in increased deductions from the pay for their labours.

That the seigneur or, in the case of the tithe, the clergy was made to play the rôle of scapegoat for the crisis has been shown most convincingly by Paul Bois, who examines the case – a limited one to be sure – of the department of the Sarthe in the chapter of his book devoted to the analysis of the local *Cahiers*.[44] He demonstrates that there was simply no correlation between three things – the intensity of the peasants' objection

41. Ernest Labrousse, *La Crise de l'économie française à la fin de l'Ancien Régime et au début de la Révolution* (Paris: P.U.F., 1943), Introduction, p. 47.
42. Ernest Labrousse, *Esquisse du mouvement des prix et des revenus en France au XVIIIe siècle* (Paris: Dalloz, 1932), see Book 7, ch. 2. In fact, Labrousse clearly suggests, in *La Crise de l'économie française*, the idea I am developing here, i.e. that the 'seigneurial reaction' was, economically speaking, essentially a matter of the increasing price of leaseholds in terms of their real value, that is, their net yield (Introduction, p. 45).
43. Robin, *La Société française*, pp. 298–313.
44. Bois, *Paysans de l'Ouest*, pp. 165–219.

to abuses by the privileged orders, the actual burden of deductions by the seigneur or the *dîme*, and the political behaviour of the communities studied. Far to the contrary, the attacks on the privileged orders, and especially on the clergy,[45] were harshest in the *Cahiers* of the western part of the department, even though no objective reasons for this hostility, such as a particularly large proportion of Church land or a particularly onerous tithe, can be found there. Moreover, that part of the department was later to be an area of counter-revolutionary activity (*chouannerie*), while the south-eastern part, whose *Cahiers* were particularly moderate with respect to the privileged, was to become a stronghold of republican loyalty. In other words, it is a mistake to seek to unlock the secrets of the peasants' frame of mind and their behaviour by setting up, *ex post facto*, an imaginary 'anti-feudal' class front consolidated by a hypothetical 'feudal reaction'.

What, then, was the reason for the diffuse but fundamental and very intense frustration that eighteenth-century French society felt toward the nobility and the privileged orders? It seems to me that the 'aristocratic reaction' was a psychological, social and political reality far more than a fact of economic life. The eighteenth century witnessed a kind of exacerbation of noble snobbery,[46] which as a backlash produced the exacerbation of *differences* all along the social spectrum. In one of the footnotes to his thesis, Jean Meyer cites a very amusing text that makes this point.[47] It is an anonymous pamphlet against the *présidents à mortier* of the *Parlement* of Brittany, purporting to be a manual of etiquette for *présidents à mortier*:

Since there are very few of us, we cannot always be together. We must learn how to be alone and to be bored in a dignified manner; we are working hard at learning it, but one does eventually develop the habit, and I now prefer the honour of being bored by myself or in the company of another *président* to the pleasure I might derive from the company of a few councillors or *gentilshommes*. That degree of perfection is attained only by the long practice of being a *président*.

There is no doubt that among nobles of the *robe*, finance and the sword – but these distinctions within the nobility became less and less meaningful with time, as if they were muted in order to emphasise the real distinction, the great social gulf between noble and non-noble status – a real exacerbation of noble 'racism' had taken place. But the nobility's compulsive preoccupation with protocol and the trappings of power did

45. On the whole, the *Cahiers* of what was to become the department of the Sarthe were not particularly anti-noble.
46. Cf. in particular the article by Marcel Reinhard, 'Élite et noblesse dans la seconde moitié du XVIIIe siècle', *Revue d'histoire moderne et contemporaine* 3 (1956), 5–37.
47. Meyer, *La Noblesse bretonne*, vol. 2, p. 961.

not necessarily go hand in hand with increased economic demands on the peasantry. On the contrary, one can argue that the nobles, deprived of power by the absolutist State – or believing that they were so deprived, which in practice amounts to the same thing – harped on the outward signs of domination and the rituals of separation to the point of caricature.[48] Following the nobles' example, a whole society played out the psychodrama of dominance and subservience, setting nobles against non-nobles, great nobles against lesser nobles, rich against poor, Parisians against provincials, urban against rural dwellers. The problem thus involved not so much economic property as social dominance. As Tocqueville already realised,[49] eighteenth-century French society was a world that had been *deprived of its cohesion* by the centralisation of the monarchical State and the concomitant rise of individualism. Seen in this perspective, the Revolution can be considered a vast process of socio-cultural integration, achieved through the 'anti-feudal' patriotism of 1789 and the Jacobin ideology that succeeded it. Egalitarianism was the

48. *Ibid.* vol. 1. p. 793, one finds the following assessment by the Estates of Brittany in 1772 of 'feudal rights': 'Although feudal rights are not usually very considerable with respect to their financial benefits, they are sweet and precious with respect to adornment and respectability.'
49. Tocqueville, *L'Ancien Régime et la Révolution*, Book 2, ch. 9.
    I must parenthetically note here that Soboul's references to Tocqueville are no more than pious gestures and almost always incorrect. For example: in support of his analysis of the burden of feudal rights and the 'feudal system' on French rural life in the eighteenth century, he uses (p. 64) a page of *L'Ancien Régime* taken from chapter 1 of Book 2 devoted to the peasants' resentment of feudal rights. He thus repeats the misinterpretation he had already stated in an article published in *Annales historiques de la Révolution française* [(July–September 1958), 294–7], entitled 'La Révolution française et la féodalité'. For it must be clear to any attentive reader of *L'Ancien Régime* that Tocqueville's thesis was the following:
    (a) 'Feudal' rights were less burdensome to the French peasant turned landowner than to his neighbours in continental Europe, many of whom were still subject to labour services (*corvées*). If the rural population was strongly opposed to feudal rights, it was not because they were particularly burdensome, but because they were *vestigial* and no longer accompanied by their natural counterpart: local and 'paternal' administration by the seigneur.
    (b) If the French peasant was 'sometimes' worse off in the eighteenth century than in the thirteenth, it was because the eighteenth-century peasant was at the mercy of arbitrary measures by the monarchy, especially with respect to taxation, and yet no longer able to count on the seigneur's mediation (Book 2, ch. 12).
    (c) As in Marx's early writings (cf. especially *The Jewish Question*), feudalism is for Tocqueville a political as well as a civil and socio-economic institution: one of the causes of the Revolution was that the institution had ceased to exist politically, for it had been destroyed by the monarchy, and that it nonetheless survived in a vestigial and *therefore* intolerable form in civil society.
    Much could also be said about the use of certain passages from Tocqueville, carefully removed from their context, in Soboul's afterword to Georges Lefebvre's *Quatre-vingt-neuf* (Paris, 1970), pp. 260, 263 and 283. Only on the basis of a careless reading of Tocqueville or a total indifference to the meaning of these texts is it possible to suggest that *L'Ancien Régime et la Révolution* can lead to the kind of interpretation that is proposed by Soboul. Exactly the opposite is the case.

opposite side of humiliation, 'republican' togetherness the opposite of 'monarchical' isolation. Given those convictions, it is only natural that the nobility was made to pay the full price of national integration.

The dominant classes of the eighteenth century

That long excursion brings us back to Albert Soboul's book and to his analysis of the nobility and the bourgeoisie, which is the central yet most distressing part of the book. Is this because the attentive sympathy with which as an historian he had examined the rural world, its 'works' and 'days', disappears when he looks elsewhere? Or is it because he has moved out of his habitual sphere of investigation? Whatever the reason, the tone is lowered by a notch, the description becomes dry, and the interpretation more and more schematic. It is here that the arbitrary organisation of the book does the most serious violence to historical reality. The clergy, for instance, is treated together with the nobility in so far as it is 'high', and with the bourgeoisie in so far as it is not, and so characteristic a socio-cultural institution of the Ancien Régime is thereby lost to sociological surgery. In addition to deriving its income from the tithe and attracting general hostility or jealousy – and not only on the part of the peasantry, as the debates following the night of 4 August 1789 were to show – the church also played an active rôle in the cultural dislocation of the Ancien Régime. There is no hint of that in Soboul's analysis, except for the Richerism of the lower clergy. But where in this populist history are Groethuysen's[50] preachers, who propagated the 'bourgeois spirit'; where bourgeoisie'. To begin with, that is double misapprehension. 'Finance' where are the Jansenists and, even, more important where is Jansenism, the fundamental and undoubtedly decisive crisis that shook Catholic France? De minimis non curat praetor.

Another problem: the world of 'finance' is taken up, at the end of the chapters devoted to the bourgeoisie, together with the 'entrepreneurial bourgeoisie'. To begin with, that is a double misapprehension. 'Finance' had nothing to do with either entrepreneurship or banking, from which it was more and more carefully distinguished,[52] and with which it was

50. Bernard Groethuysen, *Origines de l'esprit bourgeois en France* (Paris: Gallimard, 1927).
51. Père François de Dainville, *La Naissance de l'humanisme moderne* (Paris: Beauchesne, 1940).
52. Herbert Lüthy, *La Banque protestante en France*, 2 vols. (Paris: S.E.V.P.E.N., 1959–61), reviewed by J. Bouvier in *Annales historiques de la Révolution française* (July–September 1962), 370–1. Cf. also Guy Chaussinand-Nogaret, *Les Financiers de Languedoc au XVIIIe siècle* (Paris: S.E.V.P.E.N., 1970) and, by the same author, 'Capital et structure sociale sous l'Ancien Régime', *Annales E.S.C.* (March–April 1970), 463–76.

moreover in competition, even if the two activities occasionally over-lapped. 'Finance', a privileged and closed form of capitalism, which lived on the financial management of an agricultural kingdom, was the very opposite of entrepreneurial capitalism of the Schumpeterian type; and the involvement of private banks in State 'finance' as a possible means of salvaging the royal finances – an involvement symbolised by Necker's appointment as finance minister – is one of the important signs of the crisis besetting the social structures of government at the end of the Ancien Régime. Moreover, the world of 'finance' was not uniformly 'bourgeois'. On the contrary, in the eighteenth century it was the cross-over point *par excellence* on the fateful line dividing noble from non-noble status. The upper crust of the financiers, the farmers-general, treasurers-general and receivers-general bought offices of *secrétaire du roi*, made their sons magistrates of the *parlements* and married their daughters to dukes. If Soboul were not locked into his framework requiring a 'feudal' aristocracy – which is belied even by the types of aristocratic income he himself cites on pp. 220–4[53] – he would have taken a look at the composition of the fortunes of the great financial officers as suggested in G. Chaussinand-Nogaret's studies,[54] which show that investments in offices and public bonds of all kinds predominated in those fortunes to an overwhelming extent. The purchase of a *seigneurie* was no more than the indulgence of snobbery, the racing-stable of the period. It was the symbol of status and dominance, not the real source of wealth.

In fact, the most sensitive point of the Ancien Régime was that zone of transition – or non-transition, depending on the circumstances and the period – between what one might call the upper bourgeoisie and the upper nobility. Indeed, it was more difficult in this society of orders to pass from the lesser nobility into the great nobility than to leave one's non-noble status and enter the ruling aristocracy by amassing a large non-noble fortune and thereby gaining access to key positions in government. Soboul's rigid and strictly vertical sociology, taken from both reactionary and revolutionary ideologues, from Boulainvilliers as well as from Sieyès, masks and overlooks that crucial fact, which I consider to be at the root of the crisis besetting the ruling classes of the eighteenth-century French monarchy. It is true that, to come to grips with it, it would have been necessary, at the very least, to examine the rôle of the monarchical State in society and its crisis. Yet in this weighty book of almost 500 pages, the

53. The sums derived from seigneurial rights certainly do not constitute the bulk, nor even a very large share, of the incomes he describes.
54. Chaussinand-Nogaret, 'Capital et structure sociale'.

tyranny of sociological thinking is such that not one chapter is devoted to the workings of absolutism. Actually, Soboul does give us, on p. 253, the key to his amazing silence. So far as he is concerned, the monarchical State had been, ever since Louis XIV, a mere appendage of the 'aristocracy' (which in his consistently imprecise vocabulary is another word for nobility). Any proof? Why yes, it is 1789, the later hopes for a counter-revolution, then Varennes, and finally the secret manoeuvres to start an unwinnable war. In short, the old tautological proof that deduces causes from results.

It is amusing to note that Soboul thereby abandons one of Marx's main ideas about the French Ancien Régime and the history of France in general,[55] namely, the idea that the State of the Ancien Régime was relatively independent from the nobility and the bourgeoisie. This idea, which belonged quite distinctively to Tocqueville, who considered it fundamental,[56] was also so clearly part of Marx's and Engels's thought that their most notable heir, Kautsky (in his 1889 phase), devoted the first chapter of his analysis of the French Revolution to it.[57] Interestingly enough, that chapter is preceded by a warning against any 'sociological' simplification of Marxism, a warning that seems most appropriate to the

55. Scattered throughout Marx's and Engels's works there are many texts concerning the independence of the absolute State from the bourgeoisie and the nobility. The most important are the following: Marx, *Critique de la philosophie hégélienne de l'État* [Critique of Hegel's philosophy of the State] (1842–3) (Paris: Costes, 1948), pp. 71–3 and 166–7; Marx, *L'Idéologie allemande* [The German Ideology] (Paris: Costes, 1948), pp. 184–5; Engels, letter to Kautsky, 20 February 1889, *Werke*, vol. 37, p. 154; Engels, letter to Conrad Schmidt, 27 October 1890, in *Études philosophiques* (Paris: Éditions Sociales, 1951), p. 131; Engels, 1891 preface to Marx's *The Civil War in France*, *Werke*, vol. 7, p. 624. These texts invalidate Mazauric's contention (*Sur la Révolution*, p. 89) that Marx and Engels, in later years, abandoned the idea of the absolute State as arbiter between the bourgeoisie and the nobility. In fact the idea is still found in their later writings, notably in the Engels–Kautsky correspondence, at the time when Kautsky, who was working on his book on the class struggle in France in 1789, turned to Engels for advice.

On the other hand, there is not, to my knowledge, the trace of an allusion to the Ancien-Régime State in *The Civil War in France*, or in the *Critique of the Gotha and Erfurt Programme*, which Mazauric cites as proof that Marx had developed a new thesis on the subject. The fact is that Mazauric is confused on two counts: he attributes to Marx a theory of the Ancien-Régime State that is in reality Lenin's theory of the bourgeois State (just as, on p. 211, he attributes to Lenin a famous quote from Marx's *The Poverty of Philosophy*: 'It is the bad side that moves history forward').

This confusion is characteristic of Mazauric's pervasive ignorance of Marx's and Engels's writings. I should never have thought of mentioning this, were it not that he claims, precisely, to represent Marx while in fact he reflects both Sieyès's and Lenin's thought, which is quite a different matter.

56. Marx carefully read *Democracy in America*, which he cited as early as 1843 (in *The Jewish Question*).

57. K. Kautsky, *La Lutte des classes en France en 1789*, trans. from the German (Paris, 1901). Kautsky discussed this book at length with Engels; cf. their correspondence between 1889 and 1895 (*Werke*, vols. 37–9).

case of Albert Soboul:

By attempting to reduce all historical development to a class struggle, one is only too prone to see but two causes, two classes locked in struggle, two compact, homogeneous masses, the one revolutionary and the other reactionary, those below and those on top. Within that framework nothing is easier than writing history. But, in reality, relations within society are not so simple.[58]

The truth is that the French monarchy had for centuries played an active rôle in the dislocation of the society of orders and continued to play it, more forcefully than ever, in the eighteenth century. Involved in the development of commercial productivity, hostile to local authorities, and vested with the power of the nation, the monarchy was, in conjunction with money, indeed more than money, the decisive factor in social mobility. It gradually undermined, chipped away at, and destroyed the vertical solidarity of the various orders, especially of the nobility, both socially and culturally. Socially, it created, notably through its offices, another nobility, which was different from that of the feudal period and by the eighteenth century constituted the majority of the nobility as a whole. Culturally, it attempted to imbue the kingdom's ruling classes, henceforth united under its aegis, with a new system of values, no longer based on personal honour but on the fatherland and on the State. In short, as purveyor of the means for social advancement, the monarchical State became a magnet attracting money. As it did so, and even while retaining the legacy of the society of orders, it created a social structure that paralleled and contradicted the traditional one. It created a new élite or ruling class. The king of France, still the first seigneur of the realm, was above all the head of all the *bureaux* of Versailles.

By the eighteenth century it was clear that there was no political solidarity within the nobility as an order. The Revolution was to recreate a solidarity of misfortune, an image it bequeathed to historians. But the period before the Revolution was filled with conflicts within the nobility, and it was resentment of the minor nobles toward the great nobles, even more than their shared contempt for the non-nobles, that led to Ségur's *règlement* of 1781.[59] Among the poorer nobility of the sword, the hostility toward money, parvenus and social mobility was tantamount to hostility toward the ruling class that the monarchy had created. As a testimony to that hostility, the book by the Chevalier d'Arc[60] is one of the most interesting documents of the age.

58. Kautsky, *La Lutte des classes*, p. 9.
59. The essential book on this conflict between the poor nobility 'of the sword' and the high nobility 'of finance' is Émile G. Léonard's *L'Armée au XVIIIe siècle* (Paris: Plon, 1958).
60. *La Noblesse militaire ou le patriote français* (1756).

But neither was there in the eighteenth century any solidarity within what one should call not the great nobility but the ruling nobility or aristocracy in the proper sense of the word; for this group, owing to the way it had been formed and to the functions it fulfilled, included a number of very disparate elements: very old 'feudal' families who constituted the historical reference point and set the tone of the social hierarchy, high military nobility hoping to reconquer the terrain lost under Louis XIV, bishops attached to the Court, renegade magistrates who had passed over into the service of the king, parvenu financiers allied by marriage to the greatest families, royal *intendants* and members of the high bureaucracy of Versailles – in short, those who were lumped together as 'Court nobility' and thereby aroused the hostility of the rest of the order[61] – were in reality broken up into clans and coteries that one would try in vain to define in terms of material interest. In the same manner, the members of the high *robe* nobility, who, unless they were called to high office at Versailles, did not live at Court and dominated a flourishing social life, devoted all their efforts to the cause of *parlementaire* opposition, which was their weapon in the struggle against the men who ruled from Versailles and their local representative, the *intendant*. And yet, nine times out of ten, that *intendant* had a *parlementaire* background.[62]

It is therefore undeniable that the political and cultural attitudes of the eighteenth-century French aristocracy, whose revenues, as we have seen, were mainly landed (which does not mean 'feudal'), were not uniform expressions of homogeneous social or economic groups defined by being already capitalist, or still feudal, or simply landowning. What does permit us to analyse this political and social élite is its attitude toward, or ambition for power and, by the same token, toward the mechanism of social mobility provided by the State. Through office-holding, ennoblement and a centralised administration, the State was swallowing up the entire civil society; all of the wealth of the bourgeoisie was, as it were, drawn into its coffers in exchange for ennoblement. Louis XIV had most carefully devised this system of 'competing élites', to borrow Louis Bergeron's term,[63] but his death gave the signal for a battle that was all

61. Cf. in Jean Meyer's *La Noblesse bretonne*, p. 908, a quote from Loz de Beaucours, the last *avocat-général* of the *Parlement* of Brittany: 'Comte de Buat has pointed out that the Court nobility has always been the most outspoken and the most dangerous enemy of the other nobles.'
62. Cf. Meyer, *La Noblesse bretonne*, p. 987. Also Vivian Gruder, *Royal Provincial Intendants: A Governing Elite in Eighteenth-Century France* (Ithaca: Cornell Univ. Press, 1968).
63. Louis Bergeron, 'Points de vue sur la Révolution française', *La Quinzaine* (December 1970). Cf. also the same author's subtle and intelligent analysis of the problem of French élites at the end of the eighteenth century: *Les Révolutions européennes et le partage du monde* (Paris: Bordas-Laffont, vol. 7 of the 'Le Monde et son histoire' series, 1968), pp. 269–77.

the more intense for involving stakes that were at once political, social and economic. If the monarchical State drew off the wealth of the realm, it also redistributed it.

Seen in this perspective, and so far as power is concerned, the eighteenth century undeniably appears to be a period of 'aristocratic reaction', provided that the term 'aristocracy' is used in its true sense: a ruling political élite. Indeed, a great deal of literary evidence for such a reaction can be found in contemporary memoirs, correspondence and administrative documents. Nonetheless, the phenomenon can be made to refer to real situations that were very different from that.

Take the alleged closing of ranks among the nobility against the entry into it by the upper strata of the Third Estate, leading to a kind of monopoly of the great offices of the State by the nobility, which thereby became once more what it had ceased to be under Louis XIV, an aristocracy. That is the traditional hypothesis,[64] and it does have the advantage of accounting for the frustration of bourgeois ambitions in the late eighteenth century. But, so far as we can judge today,[65] it is not backed by statistical evidence; the sales of offices of *secrétaire du roi*, which had declined sharply between the death of Louis XIV and the 1750s, rose to new heights in the second half of the century with the financial needs of the State. As for the magistrates of the *parlements*, neither the studies of F. Bluche[66] nor those of J. Égret[67] suggest any major changes in their recruitment in comparison with the seventeenth century. According to J. Égret, in the last two decades of the Ancien Régime 426 of the 757 members of the thirteen *parlements* and the two sovereign councils were newcomers; of that total almost one hundred came from a non-noble background, while many others were of very recent nobility. In order to be absolutely conclusive, those figures should be compared to others obtained from a longer time-span; but even so they do indicate that there is no proof of any social sclerosis in the recruitment of the members of the *parlements*. The same finding applies to the royal *intendants*. The data recently presented by Vivian Gruder[68] indeed show that the selection of

---

64. Cf. in particular Elinor G. Barber, *The Bourgeoisie in Eighteenth-Century France* (Princeton Univ. Press, 1955).
65. I am using here an unfortunately still unpublished article, entitled 'Social mobility in eighteenth-century France', by my friend Professor David D. Bien, of the University of Michigan. Parts of this study have appeared in his 'La réaction aristocratique avant 1789: l'exemple de l'armée', *Annales E.S.C.* (1974), 23–48; 505–34.
66. In particular, *L'Origine des magistrats du parlement de Paris au XVIIIe siècle, 1715–1771* (Paris: Klincksieck, 1956) and *Les Magistrats du parlement de Paris au XVIIIe siècle, 1715–1771* (Paris: Les Belles Lettres, 1960).
67. In particular, 'L'Aristocratie parlementaire à la fin de l'Ancien Régime', *Revue historique* (July–September 1952), 1–14.
68. Gruder, *Provincial Intendants*, part 2.

intendants was restricted to nobles (although there was considerable variation in the number of generations of nobility they possessed); but if anything the exclusivism diminished in the eighteenth century, as the number of *intendants* from the milieu of 'finance' (that is to say, recent nobility) increased. What about the recruitment of bishops? Ninety per cent of them were indeed nobles in the period 1774–90, but the figure had already been 84 per cent in the period 1682–1700.[69] The same pattern is true for the ministers of State: just about all those of Louis XIV and Louis XV had been nobles,[70] but so were those of Louis XIV, notwithstanding Saint-Simon, whose testimony Soboul innocently invokes (p. 250). Finally, the army, that preserve of noble exclusivism; but before the Revolution and the Empire, the army had never been an important channel of social advancement for the bourgeoisie; among the generals of Louis XIV examined by A. Corvisier,[71] very few were of non-noble origin. According to Émile Léonard,[72] however, an invasion of the high military grades by the sons of financiers began toward the end of Louis XIV's reign, when the interminable wars against all of Europe had wrought financial disaster. That trend continued in the eighteenth century, aided and abetted by the high cost of purchasing and above all maintaining a regiment. It did arouse the hostility of the 'old' nobility against the 'counting-house colonels', but also against the Court nobility, which was not necessarily old either. The attacks were directed, however, not so much against non-nobles as such, but against money, wealth and the complicity of the State in that process. Under conflicting pressures from these fissures within the nobility, the monarchy responded with the measures of 1718 and 1729, which reaffirmed the nobility's monopoly over military grades, but also with the edict of November 1750, which decreed that ennoblement could be granted on the basis of real service rendered by families and individuals. It was the *Legion d'honneur* anticipated by more than a half century.

Thus, there is no proof – until more information comes to light – of any social tightening of the ranks by the nobility itself. The monarchy,

69. According to D. Bien's tables in 'Social Mobility'. Cf. also Norman Ravitch, *Mitre and Sword* (Paris and The Hague: Mouton, 1966), a book that stresses, it is true, the advancement of the sons of the old 'nobility of the sword' to the detriment of other categories of nobles.
70. François Bluche, 'L'Origine sociale du personnel ministériel français au XVIIIe siècle', *Bulletin de la Société d'Histoire moderne* (1957), 9–13.
71. André Corvisier, 'Les Généraux de Louis XIV et leur origine sociale', *Bulletin du XVIIe siècle* (1959), 23–53.
72. Léonard, *L'Armée au XVIIIe siècle*, ch. 9: 'La Question sociale et l'argent dans l'armée. Le rêve d'une noblesse militaire'.

increasingly pressed by its financial needs, continued to ennoble more *secrétaires du roi*, new members of the *parlements*, and more non-noble military men who had given a lifetime of service, while the old nobility married its sons to the daughters of financiers. Verifiable processes, such as the accelerating rate of sales of *seigneuries*, also point to a continual integration of the upper strata of the Third Estate into the nobility. It is possible, indeed probable, although difficult to prove, that this integration did not proceed rapidly enough to accommodate the growth of bourgeois fortunes and bourgeois ambition. That is the impression conveyed by J. Meyer's study,[73] which contrasts the economic vitality of the bourgeois élites of Brittany to the relatively restricted number of ennoblements over the course of the century. Even supposing that was true on a national scale, that is one more reason for not isolating the study of the Ancien Régime's dominant classes from the areas in which nobility and non-nobility came into contact, no matter whether passage from the one to the other was easy or whether one blocked the other. It is probable that by the eighteenth century that magic line of demarcation in social ascent had become too rigid to satisfy a growing demand, yet too flexible and too venal to be worth defending.[74]

There is no doubt, however, that ennoblement by the king and by money gave rise, throughout the whole eighteenth century, to unending protests on the part of the 'old' nobility, which was free to express its deepest feelings after the death of Louis XIV. But in fact, the phenomenon that historians call the 'aristocratic reaction' may well have been nothing more than a fierce struggle within the élites of the Ancien Régime between old and new nobles, the expression of the resistance mounted by a relatively ancient and often impoverished nobility against the attempt to create a new ruling class by State fiat and money. As D. Bien points out, the famous *règlement* of 1781 was directed not against the commoners but against nobles who did not have four degrees of nobility. It is in the nature of societies of orders to foster the cult of difference; hence the major question for eighteenth-century élites was not only: bourgeois or noble? but: noble or ennobled? and even: ennobled, but since when? In any case, these two phenomena – on the one hand, a heavy bourgeois pressure to enter an increasingly crowded and perhaps proportionally more selective field and, on the other, beyond the dividing line, the conflict among the

73. Meyer, *La Noblesse bretonne*, see in particular vol. 1, pp. 331–442.
74. Demand was also stimulated by the fact that the very large generation born between 1750 and 1770 was reaching maturity at that time. Cf. B. Panagiotopoulos, 'Les Structures d'âge du personnel de l'Empire', *Revue d'histoire moderne et contemporaine* (July–September 1970), 442ff.

different segments of the nobility – do not contradict but complement each other. Both were caused by the increasing inadequacy of the relatively narrow mechanism of social mobility developed by the absolutist State within the framework of the society of orders. To begin with, of course, the mechanism was quantitatively inadequate, considering the century's prosperity. But it was also qualitatively inadequate to the extent that the only avenue open to non-noble fortunes was integration into the State, its Court, its bureaucracy, its army and its magistracy. No wonder that in those circumstances all dominant groups were primarily interested in power, and that in this respect the conflicts within the nobility over the control of the State – especially the conflict between the *parlements* and the royal administration – set the tone of the entire political life, amounting to a prolonged dress rehearsal for the huge crisis that was the come at the end of the century. The absolutist State itself had created those who would destroy it.

I therefore do not believe that either a hypothetical closing of the ranks by the nobility or its hostility toward the bourgeoisie as a whole, both grounded in an imaginary 'feudality', is the key to the social and political crisis of the eighteenth century. On the contrary, the essential factor was the opening in the ranks of the nobility, which was too wide to preserve the cohesion of the order, and yet too narrow to accommodate the century's prosperity. The two great legacies of the history of France, the society of orders and absolutism, had entered into a conflict to which there was no solution.

For what the late eighteenth century perceived as 'despotic' was in reality the *advance of the administrative monarchy*. Ever since the end of the Middle Ages the French kings had, through foreign wars and the institution of permanent taxation, fashioned a State out of the territories that had been patiently assembled by their predecessors. To do so, they had to combat various centrifugal forces, gain control over local powers, especially those of the *grands seigneurs*, and build a bureaucracy staffed by servants of the central power. Louis XIV is the classic symbol of the triumph of the monarchy in France. It was under his reign that the *intendant*, as the representative of the *bureaux* of Versailles and wielder of the sovereign's delegated authority, stamped out the traditional powers of municipalities and great families in the provinces. It was under his reign that the nobility was domesticated by the ceremonial of the Court, was confined to military activities, or enlisted in the administration of the State. The 'absolute' monarchy was built on the victory of the central power over the traditional authority of the seigneurs and the local communities.

However, that victory was a compromise. The French monarchy was not 'absolute' in the modern sense of the term, which evokes totalitarian power. In the first place, it continued to be based on the 'fundamental laws' of the realm, which no sovereign had the power to change. The rules of succession to the throne, for example, and the property of his 'subjects', were beyond his reach. But above all, the kings of France did not build their power on the ruins of traditional society. On the contrary, they built it up at the price of a series of conflicts and transactions with traditional society, which, as a result, came to be inextricably bound to the new State by a wide variety of ties. There are ideological reasons for that development, related to the fact that the French royalty never completely broke with the old patrimonial concept of power. The king of France was still first among peers, even after he had also become the head of the *bureaux* of Versailles. However, the phenomenon also had fiscal reasons: in order to afford the interminable war for hegemony that they were fighting against the Habsburgs, the Bourbon kings – and the Valois before them – had to make money out of everything, especially the privileges and 'liberties' (and the two words meant the same thing) of society. Privilege meant the imprescriptible right of any group in relation to the central power; it was the franchise of a city, the right of a corporation to co-opt its members, or the tax-exempt status of a community. Privilege had originally been granted on a variety of grounds, which were lost in the mists of time and hallowed by tradition. The king did not destroy privilege, he only renegotiated it in exchange for good money with those who were, or claimed to be, entitled to it.

Under the pressure of necessity he even created new privileges, selling a part of public power to private individuals in the form of 'offices'. The practice was not new, but the hereditary ownership of a public charge dates only from the beginning of the seventeenth century, when the first boom in the sale of offices resulted from the king's need for money during the Thirty Years War. In addition to the *intendant*, an appointed and removable official, Louis XIII and Louis XIV thus brought into being a body of servants of the State who owned their offices. That was surely a double-edged weapon, for while the massive sale of offices did indeed bring the money of the rich, both bourgeois and noble, into the royal coffers, and gave the new and powerful group of office-holders, dominated by the members of the sovereign courts, a real stake in the future of the State, the sale of offices also afforded that group the independence that comes with ownership. In the interregnum between the reign of Louis XIII and the personal reign of Louis XIV, the Fronde uprising (1648), led by the most prominent members of the *parlements*, showed the dangers inherent in such a system. Obsessed by this memory of his youth, Louis XIV was to do his utmost to cut down such opposition as long as he lived. However, as his hands were tied by financial needs and by the word of his predecessors, he was unable to suppress the potential danger, especially since he maintained the conditions that had brought it into being.

The so-called 'absolute' monarchy was thus a precarious compromise between the building of a modern State and the preservation of the principles of social organisation inherited from feudal times. A blend of patrimonial, traditional and bureaucratic ingredients, to use Max Weber's terminology, this régime was constantly contributing to a dialectic of subversion within society. In the first half of the seventeenth century, the very rapid growth of the *taille* – the direct tax from which the nobility, the clergy and many towns were more or less exempt – gave rise to many peasant revolts, secretly abetted by the traditional notables. But these unorganised revolts had no future, and only served to reunite, at least temporarily, the State and the propertied classes in common opposition to them. More serious for the 'Ancien Régime' as constituted by Louis XIV was the fact that the new power of the State, which had then reached its highest point, was never able to find a principle of legitimacy that would give a new cohesion to the ruling classes of society. It upheld, indeed 'castified' the society of orders, even while dislocating it. At the very time when it was engaged in unifying the national market, rationalising production and exchanges, breaking up the old agrarian communities based on autarky and seigneurial protection, it was more concerned than ever with upholding traditional distinctions within society. This concern led, for example, to a new rash of edicts designed to 'reform' the nobility, banishing false nobles from the order so that they could once again be taxed, yet always leaving open the possibility of negotiating their re-admission. The monarchy thereby complicated and discredited a mechanism of social advancement which, through the purchase of *seigneuries* or offices, had created a completely new French nobility since the fifteenth century. Under Louis XIV the French nobility – witness Saint-Simon – was all the more fiercely attached to its prerogatives at the same time as it lost its functions, and indeed its principle; for while 'blood' had never been more important as a badge of honour, it was also clear that one 'rose' more rapidly when backed by the State and by money than on the basis of birth alone.

The Ancien Régime, then, was too archaic for its modern aspects and too modern for its archaic aspects. This fundamental contradiction, which became obvious as soon as Louis XIV had died, was to assume ever greater scope as the eighteenth century progressed. Its two antagonistic poles, the State and society, became increasingly incompatible.

The eighteenth century was a relatively happy century, happier in any case than Soboul imagines. There were, after all, fewer wars, fewer crises and fewer famines. The population of the realm, which had been severely affected by the crises of the second half of Louis XIV's reign, first experienced a phase of recovery and then one of absolute growth, rising from 20 to 27 million inhabitants between the times of Vauban and Necker. In the absence of a decisive improvement in the productivity of labour, the increase in population probably cancelled out part of the benefit of this progress, which is another way of saying that this progress was only partly due to economic growth. At that time only England experienced a revolution in the techniques of production. France continued to be tied to the old agrarian economy, whose yields increased rather slowly through the cumulative effects of a series of minor improvements.

But there is another reason for that relative prosperity: the modernisation of the State. By the eighteenth century the French monarchy was no longer the unreliable instrument for mobilising national resources in an almost permanent war against the Habsburg monarchy; it had inherited the advances made by Louis XIV, but not the constraints he experienced, or indeed imposed. Encouraged by the spirit of the time, the monarchy was able to devote more money and attention to the great tasks of modernity, such as urban planning, public health, agricultural and commercial improvements, the unification of the market, and education. By now the *intendant* was well entrenched in the provinces, where he had precedence over the traditional authorities and was involved in everything. Deeply engaged in an immense administrative effort of fact-finding and reform, he conducted numerous economic and demographic surveys and rationalised his activities with the help of the first social statistics in French history. He stripped the clergy and the nobility of almost all their functions of local leadership, at least in secular matters. Even elementary education, that old preserve of the Church, came increasingly under his control and so received considerable impetus. Far from being reactionary or beholden to selfish interests, the monarchical State of the eighteenth century was thus one of the major agents of change and general progress – a permanent builder of 'enlightened' reform.

The problem is that, at the same time, the State continued to be bound by the social compromise elaborated in the preceding century, and that it was all the more careful to show respect for the society of orders as its involvement became increasingly destructive to that society. Society bucked under the concerted pressure of economic aspirations, the multiplication of individual initiatives and desires, and the diffusion of cultural benefits. In other words, the revolution of rising expectations took place before the means to satisfy those expectations were available; the new aspirations were thwarted by the rigid structures that allowed for social advancement in most minute doses only. Money and merit came up against 'birth'. Through ennoblement the State continued to integrate into the Second Estate of the kingdom the commoners who had served it best, and above all those who had made the most money; but, in doing so, it lost on all fronts. For the old nobility, which was often not so rich as the new, resented that practice, while the new nobility was only too anxious to close behind itself the narrow gate through which it had just passed; and in any case, the mechanism was too selective for an expanding society. All it did for the monarchy was to alienate 'its' nobility without, by the same token, creating a ruling class.

There is every indication that in the eighteenth century the French nobility experienced a crisis, though not in the sense usually understood. For the nobility was not a class or a group in decline. Never had it been more brilliant, and never was there a more aristocratic civilisation than that of the French Enlightenment. Backed by the ownership of considerable landed property, adapting the *seigneurie* to the requirements of the market economy, benefiting from the rise in landed income and frequently involved in the launching of great commercial and industrial ventures, the nobility had carved out for itself a large share in the prosperity of the period. Yet after its deliverance from the tyranny of Louis XIV it was never able to adjust its relations with the State. Having lost the essential part of its *raison d'être* along with its traditional powers, it was unable to define its political vocation. In this respect it can be said – simplifying the matter somewhat – that after the death of Louis XIV there was a stand-off among at least three nobilities, corresponding to three attitudes toward the modernisation of the State. One of these was a 'Polish style' nobility, that is, hostile to the State, nostalgically attached to its ancient local prerogatives, and ready to reconquer an idealised past. The second was a 'Prussian style' nobility that wished, on the contrary, to use the modernisation of the State for its own ends, to monopolise all public offices, and especially military grades, and to make service its new *raison d'être*. The third, finally, was an 'English style' nobility that favoured a parliamentary aristocracy in keeping with a new era.

None of those three options was viable. The first was hopeless, a backward-looking dream of lost identity. But neither did the French monarchy choose, or even encourage, one of the other two; instead, it wavered between them as clans and ministers succeeded each other. The second option would no doubt have proven too oligarchical for a rapidly expanding civil society in which the demand for public offices and titles was so great that they could not be given to men of birth alone. Nor did the kings of France ever systematically explore the means by which they might have implemented the third option, at least before 1787. And the nobility itself only belatedly accepted the price it would have to pay for it, namely the end of its fiscal privileges and the creation of a ruling class on the basis of wealth, in other words the monarchy of landowners as outlined at one point by Turgot.

That was the fundamental crisis of the eighteenth century in which one part of the Revolution has its roots. Neither the king of France nor the nobility came forward with a policy or a set of institutions that might have integrated the State and the ruling society around a minimum of consensus. In the absence of such a consensus, the action taken by the monarchy in dealing with the central problem of taxation wavered between despotism and capitulation. By the same token, the nobility had only one unifying principle, namely, hostility toward the State in the name of a social identity whose secret it had lost and whose memory it was unable to rekindle.

Louis XIV had known how to manipulate the processes of social advancement and of competition among élites within a society of orders, and indeed how to use them as the formative principle in the building of the State. Louis XV, already, was no longer able to do this, and Louis XVI even less. Perpetually torn between loyalty to the old seigneurial solidarities and the requirements of the new social and bureaucratic logic imprisoned by two contradictory modes of hierarchy and social mobility, these two kings were forever giving in to one group, and then to the other, in other words, taking sides in the multiple conflicts that were tearing the ruling élite apart. They would side first with Machault, then with Choiseul, once with Maupeou, again with Turgot. They tried every policy, yet never carried through one. Every action by the State provoked intense hostility in a large part of the ruling élites, which were never united, either in favour of enlightened despotism, for example, or in favour of liberal reform. The élites of the eighteenth century were at one and the same time in charge and in revolt. In fact they settled their internal conflicts at the expense of absolutism, which Loménie de Brienne buried once and for all in 1788. Even the crisis of 1789 did not recreate unity among the élites, except in the imaginings of the Third Estate's ideologues. The 'aristocratic revolt' that triggered the Revolution, the actions of the noble deputies to the Constituent Assembly, the subsequent work of that Assembly – none of these is intelligible unless related to the crisis of power and élites that pervaded the eighteenth century. If, in the beginning at least, the French Revolution – like all revolutions – encountered such disparate and poorly coordinated resistance, it is because the Ancien Régime died before it was struck down. Revolutions are characterised above all by the weakness and isolation of the power that is collapsing, but also by the re-invention of their history as epic: hence, the revolutionists' reconstruction of the aristocratic hydra, which allowed the redefining *a contrario* of all social values by an immense message designed to liberate, but also to create a new mystique. But one must be careful not to mistake that message for a historical analysis.

In considering the crisis of the élites, we also need to examine the rôle played by cultural differentiation, or unification, as the case may be. That, along with the entire area of historical sociology of culture, is a vast and mostly unexplored problem. At least one thing is clear, however, which is that the nobility at Versailles and in the cities was reading the same books as the educated bourgeoisie. Both were discussing Newton and Descartes, weeping over the misfortunes of Manon Lescaut, and celebrating the appearance of the *Lettres philosophiques* or the *Nouvelle Héloïse*. Thus the century's political alternative gradually took shape, not at the fringes of either of these orders, but within educated society as a whole. The demands voiced by the *parlements* and liberal thinkers prompted the inspired common sense of a Voltaire to outline the plans for a reformist monarchy, directed not so much against the authority of the king as against the structure of civil society, against inequality based on birth, the clergy and revealed religion; subsequently the physiocrats were to construct the theoretical framework for a society of landowners that would serve as the mainstay of enlightened despotism. The many cultural and political options did not coincide with the existing social cleavages; on the contrary, the highest social circles, the academies, the masonic lodges, the cafés and theatres, in short, *la Ville*, following the lead of *la Cour*, gradually fused into an Enlightened society, very largely aristocratic yet also open to non-noble talent and money. Here, once again, was a society of élites that excluded not only the lower classes but the majority of the kingdom's nobility as well. A volatile and fascinating mixture of intelligence and rank, of wit and snobbery, this society felt free to criticise everything, including and above all itself. It unwittingly presided over a profound realignment of élites and values. It was no coincidence that the ennobled ranks of the *robe* and especially of finance were playing a major rôle in this society, thereby forming a bridge between the world of their origins and the world to which they had acceded. Here is one more testimony to the strategic importance of that pivotal stratum in French society which gropingly, and with the somewhat rueful irony that comes with the two-fold feeling of strangeness and success, sought to find the way to a 'bourgeois' sociability.

To that horizontal solidarity of Enlightenment society, Albert Soboul devotes exactly eighteen lines (p. 279), which look like a twinge of remorse for long passages devoted to 'aristocratic ideology' or to bourgeois 'philosophy' – but after all, he had no choice but to classify cultural life, along with everything else, according to the principle of conflict between aristocracy and bourgeoisie! As a result, we are treated to some extra-ordinary simplifications, where ignorance of the texts and of books vies with the banality of the analysis. Montesquieu, for example, is quite simply depicted as the champion of '*parlementaire* and feudal reaction', as if the two things were the same. Soboul makes use of Althusser's book on Montesquieu[75] but strips it of the whole analysis of Montesquieu's moder-nity, just as he adduces one of Denis Richet's articles[76] but inverts its meaning. He is unable to grasp the idea that in the development of French society there was a dialectical link between privilege and freedom. Here again, the ideological categories of the period 1789–93 itself impli-citly serve as the universal yardstick of history. Encountering aristocra-tic thinking of that kind, Soboul can only invent a 'bourgeois' counter-current, which he simply calls 'enlightened philosophy and the *philosophes*'. In passing, we are also informed that 'the development of the industrial bourgeoisie was not yet sufficiently advanced to be mirrored on the literary level; that did not happen until the nineteenth century' (p. 277). On the other hand, what a raft of incomparable writers the non-industrial bourgeoisie had to speak for it! They were Voltaire, d'Alembert, Rousseau (the latter claimed, to be sure, by both the future *sans-culottes* and the bourgeoisie), and Condorcet; in short, the 'Enlightenment', which is thereby saved from aristocratic contamination and restored to its supreme

75. Louis Althusser, *Montesquieu. La politique et l'histoire* (Paris: P.U.F., 1959).
76. D. Richet, 'Élites et despotisme', *Annales E.S.C.* (January–February 1969), 1–23.

dignity as the forerunner of bourgeois and popular revolution. Such an extravagant mixture of half-truths and commonplaces defies critical commentary. Let me simply cite the final flourish (p. 381), which would have delighted Flaubert: 'The public of the Enlightenment was varied, just as the *philosophes* were diverse. But the enlightened philosophy was one and remained one.'

That is how the French Revolution, speaking belatedly but faithfully through the voice of Albert Soboul, describes the expiring or prenatal life of the great historical protagonists that it is about to enthrone: the 'feudal' aristocracy, the bourgeoisie that keeps on rising, the anti-feudal peasantry, and the future *sans-culottes*. The stage is set for the great celebration; someone should suggest to Albert Soboul that he call his second volume: 'Remembrances of a Revolutionary'.

III

Claude Mazauric takes us to a less spontaneous world. The style loses all freshness, and the preaching or the criticism takes on a militant quality. One-third of his small book[77] consists of an article already published in the *Annales historiques de la Révolution française*[78] and is devoted to the book on the French Revolution that Denis Richet and I published five years ago. But the additions to the initial article are almost exclusively of a political or ideological nature. That raises a number of problems for me.

In the first place, it is not usual for the author of a book to respond to his critics. Once a book has been written and published, it stands (or falls) on its own; it is up to the reader to decide. To publish a book is to submit to criticism. I therefore did not feel it appropriate for me to engage in a debate about Mazauric's review article; but the fact that he has written a book about our book now gives me that right. I cannot say that I am pleased to have it, for there is no pleasure either in criticising a critique or in indulging one's pride as an author concerning a book that is no longer new. That is especially true since, as far as my share in that book is concerned, I would not write it in the same way today. But if I did rewrite it I would only strengthen my prosecutor's case against me, as I have become, if I may so express myself, increasingly 'revisionist'. Thus it may be useful after all to enter into a debate, not about our book, but about some of the issues raised by Mazauric.

77. Claude Mazauric, *Sur la Révolution française.*
78. *Annales historiques de la Révolution française* (1967), 339–68.

One last preliminary remark: How does one deal with this dismal, half-scholarly and half-political prose? How, indeed why, should one respond to an author who accuses a history of the French Revolution of being anti-communist, anti-Soviet, even anti-national? If Mazauric means that in his opinion every history of the French Revolution must bear witness to the *other* revolution, and that the demonstration of that implicit goal is the touchstone of patriotism, then we are dealing precisely with the moralising teleology that may provide the historian with a good conscience but is surely not worth one minute of discussion in such rudimentary form. If he simply means that every historian of the French Revolution brings certain presuppositions of an existential and political nature to his subject – which is indeed one whose conflicts all of us have internalised to a greater or lesser extent – then he is stating something so obvious as to dispense with any need for discussion. Clearly he and I do not judge the present-day world by the same criteria, and this fact probably has some bearing on our subjective re-evaluation of the past. To be sure, history that is being written is also history. But lest we should fall prey to complete relativism, which would consist of judging different readings of the past by how they fit into the present, we must try to understand the different intellectual mediations by which an historian's experiences and assumptions make their way into his work. In other words, we must uncover the hypotheses and the presuppositions he holds before he begins to assemble his evidence. Mazauric's, it seems to me, are the same as Soboul's, which are in fact the most sterile of all, for the reasons I have exposed above. They consist of internalising, via a degenerate Marxism, the revolutionary ideology of 1789–94 according to an implicit scale of values in which the degree of popular participation in an event serves as the reference point that enables the historian to find both kindred spirits and hope for the future. My own approach is obviously just the opposite. I start with the hypothesis that the revolutionary events were, by their very nature, emotionally highly 'charged' events, and that ideology played a major rôle in masking the real processes that triggered them. Every revolution is an upheaval and a mental break; indeed it is also a tremendous summation of the past. It is the historian's first duty to dispel the underlying teleological illusion that fetters not only our understanding of the immense event, but also its agents and their heirs. One could of course endlessly debate the question whether Mazauric's presupposition is revolutionary and mine conservative. I believe that intellectually this question is meaningless. In any case, it is best to stay with such historical analysis as can be found in Mazauric's text and to confine our disagreement to precise questions.

A metaphysical personage: the 'bourgeois revolution'

Let us begin, then, with the concept 'bourgeois revolution'. It provides the historical interpretation of the events in France with an almost providential anchoring point and offers a general conceptual framework for dealing not only with the multiplicity and the sheer amount of empirical data but with all levels of reality. In other words, it is applicable, all at the same time, to economic, social and politico-ideological matters. In the economic area, the events that took place in France between 1789 and 1799 are supposed to have freed the nation's productive forces and to have induced the painful birth of capitalism; in the social sphere, they express the victory of the bourgeoisie over the traditional 'privileged' classes of the Ancien Régime; and, lastly, in political and ideological terms, they represent the advent of a bourgeois power and the triumph of the 'Enlightenment' over the values and beliefs of the preceding age. The revolution is considered to be inherent in these three historical trends, and conceived of not only as the fundamental break between 'before' and 'after', but also as the decisive result and the founding premise of these trends; and the conjunction of these three levels of interpretation is subsumed under a single concept, 'bourgeois re-volution', as if the essence of the event, its most fundamental character, were social. This theoretical shift has caused French historiography to move, insidiously and permanently, from a Marxism based on the concept of 'mode of production' to one reduced to the class struggle alone. In fact, this intellectual schema has merely given an extra twist to the self-interpretation of the French Revolution, since it harks back to the kind of historiography which, from Sieyès to Barnave, elaborated the concept of the class struggle – before Marx and in keeping with the example of the French Revolution. It is by this reduction of Marx's thought, now become a simple waystation on the road leading back to the origins, and the vehicle for a tautology and an identification, that Soboul and Mazauric find the ideology that sustains them. That ideology is not theoretical in nature, but quasi-affective for Soboul and political for Mazauric; it is the glorification of the egalitarian dialectic and of its permanent applicability, deeply embedded in our own present and henceforth endowed with living substance as a two-fold and inseparable heritage.

In reality, neither the Marxist conceptualisation by means of the mode of production, nor an interpretation based on the class struggle as borrowed from those who participated in the event, is compatible with a periodisation of the French Revolution within a short time-span, say 1789 to 1799 or, even less, from 1789 to 1794.

When one speaks of substituting a 'capitalist mode of production' for a 'feudal mode of production', it is obvious that one cannot date such a mutation by a historical event that lasted a few years. I cannot possibly review, in a single chapter, the vast literature on the nature of the Ancien Régime.[79] Suffice it to say that the discussion, whatever the meaning assigned to feudalism or 'feudal régime', stresses the idea of a transition in which were mixed social and economic factors that made themselves felt over a long period. It is therefore quite arbitrary to cut the Revolution off from what was 'upstream', and to continue to attach to the actual social process the radical break that its actors saw in it. It is true that as an idea the 'feudal mode of production' is not incompatible with the notion that eighteenth-century France had created the conditions for the demise of that mode; but one would then have to show how the hypothesis contained in the model could be proven, that is, for example, how feudal rights prevented the development of capitalism in the countryside, or how the structure of the society of orders and the existence of a nobility blocked the creation of an industrial economy based on profit and free enterprise. That is by no means easy to demonstrate, nor is it obvious, since we do know that capitalism had come to permeate seigneurial society in the countryside,[80] and very largely, so far as industry is concerned, through the efforts of the nobility itself. Moreover, the French economy, far from being 'blocked', was prospering in the eighteenth century and experienced growth-rates comparable to English ones;[81] the crisis late in the century was a slump within a generally rising trend. Finally, if one interprets the French Revolution as the shift from one mode of production to another, one is faced with the same difficulties downstream, for the unbridled capitalism whose force the Revolution is supposed to have freed took quite a while to 'take off'. In the countryside, it was checked, even more effectively than before 1789, by the growth of very small-scale ownership. Nor are there any signs that in the city the Revolution brought a rapid development of capitalism once it had, to be sure, precipitated or hastened the crisis in the last years of the century. And while it is true that, with respect to ideas and the mechanisms of social change, 1789 produced a certain number of juridical principles on

79. The size of the bibliography rules out in advance any attempt to review it in the framework of this essay. For the Marxist interpretation of this problem, I refer the reader to a discussion that has the merit of not being overly dogmatic: P. M. Sweezy, M. Dobb, H. D. Takahashi, R. Hilton and C. Hill, *The Transition from Feudalism to Capitalism. A Symposium* (London: Fore Publications, 1954).
80. Cf. above, pp. 93–5.
81. Cf. François Crouzet, 'Angleterre et France au XVIIIe siècle. Essai d'analyse comparée de deux croissances économiques', *Annales E.S.C.* (March–April 1966), 254–91.

which to base the advancement of talent and the development of a market economy, the decision to send French peasants on a vast military spree all over Europe between 1792 and 1815 hardly seems to have been dictated by a bourgeois calculation of economic rationality. Anyone who insists on interpreting history in terms of the 'mode of production' must study a far longer period than just the French Revolution; failing that, the hypothesis teaches us almost nothing about the known historical facts.[82]

That is no doubt why the Marxist approach to the problem so easily degenerates into a simplistic notion of 'bourgeois revolution', and into a socio-political analysis which postulates that, by the Revolution, the bourgeoisie succeeded the nobility in power, and bourgeois society replaced the society of orders. But here again, the Marxist framework imposes constraints. R. Robin,[83] who has the merit of taking Marxism seriously, has recently proposed the term *bourgeoisie d'Ancien Régime* to designate all the social groups that were tied to the existing structures of the Ancien Régime as 'landowners, office-holders and commoners', in order to reserve the term *bourgeoisie* for its Marxist meaning, that is, for the class that lived by the exploitation of a wage-earning labouring class. From the Marxist point of view, that is a useful classification. As far as history is concerned, however, it must be explained why, on the one hand, the Revolution was made and led in large part precisely by the *bourgeoisie d'Ancien Régime* and why, on the other, an analysis of the revolutionary process conducted in terms not of its actors, but of its objective results, shows that the constitutive elements of the bourgeoisie during the Empire were not fundamentally different from those of the pre-revolutionary period: they still were wholesale commerce, landownership, and service to the State now military more than civil.[84] Here again, the conceptual model gains in rigour what it has lost in operative value, even when applied to such a short period.

But at least R. Robin's definitions have the merit of being consistent with their own logic; by raising problems they are unable to solve, they show the impasses created by a purely structural analysis of a short-term

82. Engels wrote to Kautsky on 20 February 1889: 'You think you can get over the difficulty by bombarding us with hazy phrases and mysterious formulations about the new mode of production ... If I were you I should not talk so much about this. Every time you bring it up, it is separated by a deep gulf from the facts you discuss and thus looks like a pure abstraction which, instead of shedding light on the subject, only serves to make it obscure.' *Werke*, vol. 37, p. 155.
83. Robin, *La Société française en 1789*, p. 54.
84. L. Bergeron, G. Chaussinand-Nogaret, R. Forster, 'Les Notables du grand Empire en 1810', paper presented to the International Congress of Social and Economic History, Leningrad, 1970. Published in *Annales E.S.C.* (September–October 1971).

event like the French Revolution. With Mazauric, who clings so much to the ontology of the event that he does not define its elements, we are back to Saint Thomas: 'The Revolution is quite simply the mode of being of the crisis besetting the structures of the Ancien Régime as a whole, and the resolution of that crisis.'[85] That is why he must at all costs preserve what is both subject and object of that resolution, both its cause and meaning: the bourgeois revolution, which despite the chaotic appearance of the years 1789–94 was a single thing, its unity saved because it was an 'ascending period' marked by steadily increasing 'radicalisation' and by increasing involvement of the popular masses.[86]

Here at last we encounter the Marxist *deus ex machina*: it is more than just a social class (for 'bourgeois revolution' does not mean 'revolutionary bourgeoisie'), and more than just a 'revolution', that is, a multifarious crisis that exposes the many contradictions in civil society; it is rather a process at once subjective and objective, an actor and a script, a rôle and a message, all merged and reconciled, in and out of season, because in reality it is already the image of its own future. With Mazauric, the *deus ex machina* – which always works backwards, explaining earlier events by what came later – finds a new home. But at least he retains from Marx one basic suspicion, namely that human beings in fact experience something other than what they believe they are experiencing. Thus expelled from the individual consciousness, awareness must be rooted in collective entities, although even there doubt catches up with it: the bourgeoisie as a whole is engaged in the pursuit of goals that are not necessarily those it had in mind. Yet even that salutary suspicion stops short before the maker of 'concepts', who, in this scheme of things, is alone uncontaminated by ideology. By what sign can he (our historian) recognise himself as the trustee of a meaning that is at last genuine? By the fact that in light of later historical configurations he has been able to 'elaborate' the concept of bourgeois revolution. The reader has to be satisfied with that as guarantee.

The reader, it is true, cannot sink to quibbling over the providential character of that all-purpose concept. Just as Descartes's God, whose attributes include existence, must for that reason exist, so Mazauric's bourgeoisie is similarly endowed with a splendid essence. Just about everything is contained 'potentially' in it. Popular support and the alliance with the peasantry are always latently there, so that, in accepting them, the bourgeoisie merely developed its 'nature' and was never truer to

85. Mazauric, *Sur la Révolution française*, p. 52.
86. *Ibid.* p. 55.

itself. But the price of this shamefaced Spinozism is a totally immobile history, paralysed by an overdose of logic. It is easy to see its advantages for a demonstration that is unsure of itself, for it enables the historian to disregard the many facets of the crisis, the fortuitous events, and the unending series of improvisations that are part of it. Contained and absorbed from the outset within the total essence of the concept – just as, by the way, the counter-revolution is contained in the revolution and the war in the counter-revolution – such contingencies are at most the patterns overlying a single design; they bear witness, for all eternity, to its irrefragable unity. The 'bourgeois revolution' is a metaphysical monster that keeps unfolding a succession of coils with which to strangle historical reality in order to turn it, *sub specie aeternitatis*, into a birthplace and an annunciation.

The French Revolutions

In fact, the concept is useful to the historian – and I do believe that it is useful – only if it is applied in a controlled and limited manner. To analyse the 'bourgeois revolution' is first, and on the simplest level, to study not only the participation of the different bourgeois groups in the Revolution, their projects and their activities, but also their reactions to the pervasive upheaval of society. It seems probable, as the late Alfred Cobban used to emphasise, that the bourgeois groups that were most committed to revolution generally had few ties to the capitalist mode of production; but it also seems probable that there were, as early as 1789, several revolutions within the Revolution,[87] and especially that there was from the very beginning, even when the *Cahiers* were being drafted, a peasant revolution that was largely autonomous in relation to the bourgeois undertaking. It is in my opinion the very great merit of Georges Lefebvre, and probably one of his most outstanding contributions to the history of the French Revolution, to have been the first to show that.[88] Since his day, a number of very important studies, like those of Paul Bois[89] and Charles Tilly,[90] have expanded the demonstration by pursuing

87. Mazauric seems at first to accept this idea (p. 26), only to reject it later (p. 55), although I fail to understand how he reconciles these two analyses.
88. See his 'La Révolution et les paysans' (1932), in *Études sur la Révolution française*, in which Lefebvre very clearly shows both the plurality of revolutions within the Revolution and the autonomy of peasant action.
89. Bois, *Paysans de l'Ouest*.
90. Charles Tilly, *The Vendée* (Cambridge, Mass.: Harvard Univ. Press, 1964; French trans., Paris: Fayard, 1970).

different questions involving the relations between town and country. Even though these studies come to different and on certain points opposite conclusions, both of them do stress the great political autonomy of the peasant world, which was essentially grounded in distrust for all urban people, whether seigneurs old or new, or bourgeois old or new. In Bois's book, as we have seen,[91] the anti-seigneurial grievance of 1789 coincides with, and to some extent presages, the anti-bourgeois distrust of 1790–1, as well as the anti-republican *chouannerie* [counter-revolutionary movement] of those years. Bois shows, for example, that the peasantry of the Haut-Maine did not *become* hostile to the bourgeois revolution because of any disappointment with what had been achieved, as Mazauric, locked into his schema, imagines;[92] this peasantry simply was, if not hostile, at least indifferent and distrustful toward the town as early as 1789. Moreover, it was exactly the same frustration that was expressed in their hostility toward seigneurial rights and toward rural capitalism, whose symbol was the bourgeois, the city-dweller. If the bourgeois revolution attempted to establish social relations of the capitalist type, the peasant revolution was working to attain its own and different ends; and the shared 'anti-feudal' attitude of the two movements conceals two very different images of change, both in people's consciousness and in reality.

For it is a false though very common notion to believe that revolutions invariably arise from the desire of certain classes or social groups to speed up a change that in their opinion is too slow. Revolution can also be, for certain sectors of society directly affected by the upheaval of the traditional order of things, the wish to resist a change that is considered too rapid. The revolutionary line of battle is not drawn, like a pitched battle depicted in an old manual of warfare, in keeping with a linear scheme of history, where all the classes on the march desire and foreshadow an identical future. The single image of the past developed quickly by all those who resist that movement should not mislead on this point. On the contrary, the revolutionary line of battle is always fluctuating and dependent on a rapidly changing political situation; above all, the battle-ranks are heterogeneous, since the objectives of their different components may well be different and even contradictory.

When the French Revolution broke out, the kingdom of France was not characterised by a lack of change; quite the opposite is true. For more than fifty years, it had undergone extremely rapid social and economic changes, to which the State had difficulty adapting. Nothing is more

91. See above, p. 93–6.
92. Mazauric, *Sur la Révolution française*, p. 235.

difficult – or more dangerous – for an absolutist system than to alter its essential ways of functioning and, above all, to liberalise itself. But the same holds true for social classes; and not only for the nobility, but also for the popular classes, which are particularly vulnerable to disruption of the traditional equilibrium and are politically less aware of the stakes and the objectives of the competition for power. The situation, then, was far more complex than Mazauric imagines,[93] for example, when he describes those whom the popularly-supported bourgeois left behind, on either side of the road they marched on toward revolution. Two groups were unfit for the great adventure and excluded from national unity: the Parisian *sections* on the left, and the peasants of the Vendée on the right. The fact is that between 1789 and 1794 the revolutionary tide, though dammed up and channelled by the groups that successively came to power – having first fallen in line with it – was never really controlled by anyone, because it was made up of too many opposing aims and interests. That no doubt explains the fundamental importance, as compensation, assumed by a highly integrative ideology such as Jacobinism. But does that mean that the historian should take what it says at face value?

To be sure, much remains to be done to round out the internal analysis of the political ingredients of the revolutionary movement. We have learned a great deal, thanks to Daniel Guérin, Albert Soboul, Georges Rudé, and Richard Cobb, about the demands of the 'little people' of the towns and their political rôle in 1793–4. But we know little about the impact on the towns of the abolition of the guilds and about the ensuing rivalries between and within various occupational groups.[94] We know even less about the rôle played by the massive migration to the towns that marked the eighteenth century, and about the impact of an urban population recently uprooted from its native soil, a population that, once arrived in Paris, as the example of Nicolas de Restif suggests, felt dispossessed and cut off from its own identity. It is quite possible that to some extent the puzzling political behaviour of the *sections* is related to such phenomena, rather than to older and more usual sociological differentiations. Similarly, we still do not know enough about the behaviour of the peasants, about their motivations, and about the relations

93. *Ibid.* pp. 235–6.
94. Some interesting intuitions concerning this aspect of the urban revolution can be found in one of Engels's letters (21 May 1895) to Kautsky on the French Revolution, where Engels stresses the rôle played in the Terror by what he calls the '*déclassés*', the social left-overs of the old corporate and 'feudal' structures. (*Werke*, vol. 39, pp. 482–3.)

   Cf. also, in the same vein, Louis Bergeron's article in 'Les sans-culottes et la Révolution française', *Annales E.S.C.* (1963, no. 6).

between town and country during the Revolution; but we do know that the urban domination of the rural world was only very partially restored after the summer of 1789: large numbers of peasant-proprietors refused to 'repurchase' seigneurial rights, that is, to compensate their owners, as stipulated by the decrees of 4–11 August 1789;[95] the 'Montagnard' decrees of August 1792 and July 1793, which freed the peasants from paying such compensations, were but the juridical sanction of an accomplished fact. When the urban revolutionary bourgeoisie sacrificed its bourgeois property rights (for that is what the seigneurial rights had become when they were made redeemable), they yielded to the peasantry. Georges Lefebvre aptly summed up the matter when he said that, even outside the specific cases and zones of armed conflict (Vendée, *chouannerie*) where it had to fight, the bourgeoisie had always to 'come to terms' with the peasantry, that is, negotiate with it at every crucial stage of the Revolution: on 4 August 1789, during the Constituent Assembly's great task of 'reconstruction', after 10 August 1792 and after 2 June 1793.

War, terror and ideology

One also wonders how to explain the war without taking into account that extraordinary fragility and fragmentation of the revolutionary front, a fragility that characterised both the new ruling class – whose various factions vied to fill the power-vacuum by means of ever-escalating rhetoric – and the social coalition, which was subjected to the conflicting pull of divergent, sometimes irreconcilable, interests obscured by utopian visions and nostalgic yearnings. I am well aware that Mazauric considers that a subordinate question. In fact, he states that the war was a '*natural* component'[96] of the Revolution. Marvellous! For by this pompous return to a simplistic providential notion of Nature, not unworthy of the good old *abbé* Pluche, the 'bourgeois revolution' is transferred without effort to its second-stage rocket, which was providentially encased in the first and bound for the same target all along. To be serious about it, however, the outbreak of the war between the French Revolution and the rest of

95. This problem is still largely unexplored. I am generalising here, by way of a plausible hypothesis, the indications furnished for south-west France by the following studies: Ferradon, *Le Rachat des droits féodaux dans la Gironde, 1790–1793* (Paris, 1928), pp. 200–311; Daniel Ligou, *Montauban à la fin de l'Ancien Régime et aux débuts de la Révolution* (Paris: M. Rivière, 1958), pp. 384–5. The same general interpretation is found in Ernest Labrousse's contribution to Roland Mousnier, Ernest Labrousse and Marc Bouloiseau, *Le XVIIIe siècle*, vol. 5 of *Histoire générale des civilisations*, 5th edn (Paris: P.U.F., 1967), p. 383.
96. Mazauric, *Sur la Révolution française*, p. 57. The word is italicised by Mazauric.

Europe is probably one of the most important and telling problems in the history of the Revolution. The war, for reasons I shall not go into here, was accepted rather than desired by the European monarchies, despite pressure from the *émigrés* and the French royal family. By contrast, it was desired in France by the court and the social forces that hankered after the Ancien Régime; but in the winter of 1791–2 those forces were far too weak to trigger the conflict they wished for. In reality, it was the Revolution that, over Robespierre's objections, wanted to go to war against the kings. The Revolution, yes. But here again, which one?

I realise that there are reasons for regarding the great adventure that was about to begin as a typical conflict in which a 'bourgeois revolution' would become involved, namely, the old mercantile competition between France and England and the special pressure from the Girondin group. Yet, as far as the first point is concerned, I believe that I am in agreement with most historians of the French Revolution[97] in stating that the economic rivalry between France and England played a relatively minor rôle in the outbreak of the war. Considerations of French domestic politics clearly took precedence, both subjectively and objectively, over the conflicting interests of the two countries in international trade. As for Brissot and those who came to be called the Girondins, it must be said that, although they were eloquent advocates of the war, they were not responsible alone for its outbreak. In the Assembly the future Montagnards kept silent: the great opinion-makers, Danton, Desmoulins, and Marat, abandoned Robespierre as early as December. Moreover, since they were as interested as the Girondins in radicalising the Revolution, their strategy in this instance was better than Robespierre's, for the war would indeed become the focus of unity and of an ever-escalating revolutionary rhetoric.

The fact is that the international conflict was not only, nor even mainly, a bourgeois war. The king wanted it as a last chance to reassert himself; the people seized upon it to give wider scope to their liberating mission. They turned it into a war of liberation, whose impressive battalions would be formed by an urban and especially peasant[98] democracy under arms. It was a conflict of values rather than of interests. Nationalist feeling was no longer limited to the new France; it became an ideological model, the banner of a crusade. In making this extraordinarily

97. At least with Georges Lefebvre, but not with Daniel Guérin, who considers the economic ambitions of the 'Girondin bourgeoisie' to be the main reason for the outbreak of the war (*La Lutte de classes*, vol. 2, p. 501).
98. Cf. J.-P. Bertaud, *Valmy* (Paris: Julliard, 'Archives' series, 1970).

early synthesis between the messianic calling of an ideology and nationalist fervour – a synthesis that was destined to have a great future –
the French people did not exactly discover a miraculously exemplary form
of human community; but surely they were the first to integrate the
masses into the State and to form a modern democratic nation.

The price of that historical experience was open-ended war. The
conflict of values that was touched off in the spring of 1792 could not, by
its very nature, have any defined or definable goals, and so it could only
end in total victory or total defeat. All the 'bourgeois' leaders of the
Revolution would try to stop it at one time or another; Danton tried, then
Robespierre, then Carnot. But the revolutionary ideology had already so
assimilated the war that in ideological terms, and even when the
Revolution was going well, war meant revolution and peace meant
counter-revolution. On the French side the war was a reckless venture by
the revolutionary coalition, a way to exorcise its precariousness by fusing
bourgeois, popular and peasant attitudes into a single ideology, which
merged the military heritage of the old society with Enlightenment values,
now expressed in a democratic form by the cult of the new State and of
the 'grande nation', henceforth entrusted with the mission of universal
liberation. The concept 'bourgeois revolution' is simply not suited to
account for this internal revolutionary dynamic, for the political and
cultural tidal wave unleashed by Jacobinism and the revolutionary war.
Henceforth, the war conducted the Revolution far more than the
Revolution conducted the war.

Knowing my classics, I realise that at this point Mazauric is ready for
me with a quote from Marx,[99] to the effect that Jacobinism and the
Terror were simply a 'plebeian way' of carrying through the bourgeois
revolution and of eliminating the enemies of the bourgeoisie. Both propositions are wrong. The bourgeois revolution was accomplished as early
as 1789–91 and achieved without compromise of any kind with the old
society. By 1790, all of the essential features of the new bourgeois order
underlying our contemporary world were finally in place: the abolition of
social orders and of 'feudalism', the opening of careers to talents, the
substitution of the social contract for divine-right monarchy, the birth of
homo democraticus and of the representative system, free labour and free
enterprise. The counter-revolutionary elements of the nobility had fled
without a fight, the Ancien-Régime king was no longer but a prisoner,
and, as we have seen, compensation for feudal rights largely remained a

99. K. Marx, 'La Bourgeoisie et la contre-révolution', article of 12 December 1848 (*Werke*,
    vol. 6, pp. 107–8).

dead letter. Moreover, the popular classes, and above all the enormous pressure exerted by the peasantry in the summer of 1789, had already played a crucial rôle in that decisive break with the past.

Those who take at face value the ideology of the time and the reasons by which the Jacobins of 1793–4 justified their conduct will no doubt claim that the progressive radicalisation of the bourgeois revolution was brought about by counter-revolutionary resistance. But to do so they must explain why this radicalisation existed as early as the summer of 1789, after 14 July, at a time when the counter-revolution was objectively quite weak; and why it was sustained not so much by the force of resistance to it as by its symbolic value and by its very ineptitude, as the crucial episode of Varennes shows so well. In fact, the true danger of a counter-revolution came with the war, with the invasion in the late summer of 1792, and in the summer of 1793. But the war had been desired by the Revolution, precisely because it 'needed great acts of treason'.[100] Whether those acts of treason actually took place or not – and they did take place, of course, though by no means as often as the militant revolutionary imagined – the Revolution invented them because it considered them necessary for its own progress. For, in the main, Jacobin and terrorist ideology functioned autonomously, unrelated to political and military circumstance, expressed in hyperbole all the more inclusive as politics was subsumed under morality and the sense of reality faded. Indeed we know that while the first two waves of terror, in August 1792 and the summer of 1793, were clearly related to the national emergency, the 'Great Terror' did not coincide with the greatest distress of those terrible years: it arose instead in the spring of 1794, just as the military situation was improving, as an administrative machine designed to implant an egalitarian and moralising metaphysical system. It was the fantasy to compensate for the political impasse that had been reached, the product not of real struggle, but of the Manichaean ideology that would separate the good from the wicked, and of a pervasive social panic. On 4 September 1870, when he feared that the French workers might overthrow the Provisional Government, Engels analysed the Terror in the following terms in a letter to Marx:[101]

100. The expression, it will be recalled, was Brissot's.
101. Marx–Engels Correspondence, 4 September 1870, *Werke*, vol. 33, p. 53. This text, among others, reveals that Marx and Engels varied greatly in their judgment on this phase of the Revolution, indeed on the Revolution as a whole, depending on their involvement in specific events of their own time as well as on their predominant intellectual preoccupations at different periods of their lives. It can be said, to put it briefly, that Marx and Engels were relatively pro-Jacobin in 1848–9, at the time of the German revolution, and very anti-Jacobin between 1865 and 1870, when they were fighting 'the French', as they said, in the First International. Will Mazauric, here again, appeal to the older Marx for help against the young Marx?

Thanks to these perpetual little terrors mounted by the French, one has a much better idea of the Reign of Terror. We imagine it as the reign of those who spread terror, but, quite to the contrary, it was the reign of those who were themselves terrorised. To a large extent the terror was nothing more than useless cruelty, perpetrated by frightened people who were trying to reassure themselves by it. I am convinced that the Reign of Terror *anno* 1793 must be imputed almost exclusively to overwrought bourgeois playing the rôle of patriots, to philistine petits-bourgeois who were messing their pants with fright, and to the dregs of the people, who made the Terror their business.

In an earlier analysis, in *The Holy Family*,[102] Marx had given a less psychologically-oriented critique of the Jacobin illusion. He had shown that the core of the illusion was the idea of a 'virtuous' State, patterned on a school-book model of Antiquity that disregarded and went far beyond the objective facts of a civil society that, in his opinion, was already 'modern bourgeois society'; the Terror was precisely the State conceiving of itself as its own end because it had no roots in society; it was the State alienated from society by ideology and escaping from the control of what Marx calls the 'liberal bourgeoisie'. The history of the Revolution, he maintained, shows us the two high points of that alienation, first the Robespierrist dictatorship, then Napoleon:

Napoleon was the last stand of *revolutionary terror* against *bourgeois society* – which the Revolution had also proclaimed – and against its policy ... *Napoleon* still regarded *the State* as *its own end*, and bourgeois society as a provider of funds, a *subordinate* forbidden any *will of its own. He carried the Terror to its conclusion* by *replacing the permanent revolution with permanent war.*[103]

The young Marx's brilliant analysis of the rôle of Jacobin ideology in the mechanisms of Terror and war, and the interchangeable nature of Terror and war, might have served as epigraph to the history of the Revolution I wrote with Denis Richet. It is implicit throughout in the analysis we propose,[104] especially in what we have called the Revolution's 'skidding out of control'. Not that I would insist on this automobile metaphor if anyone were to find a better one. But I do insist on the idea that the revolutionary process, in the course it took over the relatively short tun, cannot be reduced to the concept of a 'bourgeois revolution',

102. *La Sainte Famille* [The Holy Family], pp. 144–50.
103. The italics are Marx's.
104. For example, we treat the Constituent Assembly period (1789–91) and the Directory as periods of relative identification between bourgeois civil society and the revolutionary process. By contrast, we view the Jacobin and terrorist phase as the period of greatest discrepancy between civil society and the historical process and point out that this discrepancy was due to ideology.

even if that bourgeoisie is qualified as 'with-popular-support', 'rising', or whatever else today's Leninist jargon-mongers might write; for its permanent tendency to skid out of control and to contradict its own social nature marks the revolutionary process as an autonomous political and ideological movement that must be interpreted and analysed as such. Hence, it is not the concept of bourgeois revolution, but that of situation or revolutionary crisis that must be developed in greater depth.[105] It seems to me that such matters as the pre-1789 power vacuum and abandonment of the State, the crisis within the ruling classes, the autonomous but parallel mobilisation of the popular masses, and the elaboration in society of an ideology that was both Manichaean and highly integrative are indispensable for understanding the extraordinary dialectic of the French revolutionary phenomenon. The Revolution was more than the 'leap' from one society to another; it was also the conjunction of all the ways in which a civil society, once it had suddenly been 'opened up' by a power crisis, let loose all the words and languages it contained. This enormous cultural emancipation, whose meaning society was hard put to 'keep within bounds', henceforth fuelled the competition for power conducted through an ever-escalating egalitarian rhetoric. Internalised by the popular masses – or at least by certain sections of them – and all the more ruthless as the people was the only reference mark, indeed the new source of legitimacy, revolutionary ideology had become the arena *par excellence* of the struggle for power among groups. Through this ideology passed the dialectic of successive schisms within the leadership during the years 1789–99, as well as the language assuring continuity of the new élites. It was in the name of equality that Robespierre sent Barnave and Brissot to the guillotine; yet equality was also the principle to which Sieyès remained faithful, despite his many apparent breaches of faith, from the spring of 1789 to 18 Brumaire 1799. The revolution was the process by which the collective imaginings of a society became the very fabric of its own history.

What, then, can possibly be gained by trying to turn it, willy nilly, into the absolutely inevitable result produced by a single metaphysical essence

105. This subject has generated an abundant literature, especially in America. Cf. for example Chalmers A. Johnson, *Revolution and the Social System* (Stanford: Hoover Institution, Stanford Univ., 1964); Lawrence Stone, 'Theories of Revolution', *World Politics*, vol. 18, no. 2 (January 1966), 159 (a review of Johnson's book). On the French side, some recent studies have brought a fresh approach to the phenomenon of revolution: A. Découflé, *Sociologie des révolutions* (Paris: P.U.F., 'Que sais-je?' series, 1968); by the same author, 'La Révolution et son double', in *Sociologie des mutations* (Paris: Anthropos, 1970); J. Baechler, *Les Phénomènes révolutionnaires* (Paris: P.U.F., 1970).

that unveils one by one, like a set of Russian dolls, the various episodes supposedly contained within it from the very outset? Why try to construct at any cost that fanciful chronology in which an ascending 'bourgeois' phase is followed by a period of triumph for the popular classes, to be superseded by a comeback of the bourgeoisie, albeit a 'descending' one, since Bonaparte is waiting in the wings? Why this poverty-stricken schema, this resurrection of scholasticism, this dearth of ideas, this passionate obstinacy disguised as Marxism? The vulgate according to Mazauric and Soboul is not grounded in an original approach to the problem, such as might arise from newly acquired knowledge or from a new doctrine; it is but the feeble afterglow of the great shining flame that illuminated the entire history of the Revolution in the days of Michelet or Jaurès. The product of a confused encounter between Jacobinism and Leninism, this mixed discourse is unsuited for discovery; it amounts to nothing more than a residual shamanic function destined to comfort any imaginary survivors of Babeuf's utopia. That is why it is both contradictory and convincing, incoherent and irrefutable, moribund and here to stay. One hundred years have passed since Karl Marx, in speaking of the French left-wing republican and workers' movement that had founded the Third Republic, denounced its nostalgic Jacobinism as the vestige of a certain French provincialism, hoping that 'events' would 'put an end, once and for all, to this reactionary cult of the past'.[106]

106. Letter to César de Paepe, 14 September 1870 (*Werke*, vol. 33, p. 147).

2. De Tocqueville and the problem of the French Revolution*

Tocqueville's attachment to history did not spring from a love of the past but from his sensitivity to the present. He was not of that breed of historians who wander in the past, seeking the poetry of bygone ages or the diversions afforded by scholarship; he was totally committed to a different kind of historical curiosity, in which an examination of the present leads to the search for filiations. Unlike his contemporary Michelet, he was free of the obsessive passion for the past, the lugubrious and sublime fanaticism of a haunter of graveyards. The object of the lifelong search that gave his intellectual work its penetrating insight and its coherence was to find the meaning of his own time. He began his quest not in time, but in space, using geography as a kind of comparative history. To test his inspired reversal of the traditional hypothesis, he went to study the United States, not in order to recapture the childhood of Europe, but to gain a sense of its future. The history of Europe was but a second voyage for him, closely related to the first and subjected to the set of hypotheses that had resulted from sounding out the present.

Moreover, these two voyages – in space and in time – are linked not only by the intellectual meaning Tocqueville gave them, but also because he wrote about them very early in his career, between 1830 and 1840. The first two parts of *Democracy in America* appeared in 1835, the last two in 1840. In between, in 1836, Tocqueville published a short essay entitled 'Political and Social Condition of France' in the *London and Westminster Review*.[1] Tocqueville's first major creative period, which preceded his actual political career, thus shows the link between his two major intellectual concerns.

*Originally published as a contribution to *Science et Conscience de la société* (Mélanges en l'honneur de Raymond Aron), 2 vols. (Paris: Calmann–Lévy, 1971).

1. *London and Westminster Review* (January–April 1836), 137–69. The essay, which appeared anonymously, had been translated by John Stuart Mill. Cf. the original French text, 'État social et politique de la France avant et depuis 1789', in *L'Ancien Régime*, vol. 1, pp. 33–66.

After retiring from politics, Tocqueville returned only to the historical part of his project, which he had simply outlined and shelved, as it were, in 1836; this time he locked himself up in the archives, read the primary sources, took copious notes and for several years practised the hard discipline demanded by the historian's craft. Yet the ultimate purpose of his research remained unchanged: he still wanted to understand, and thus foresee, where France's contemporary history was headed. History, for him, was not a resurrection of the past, even less a description or a narrative, it was a set of materials to be organised and interpreted. The similarity between Tocqueville's 1836 and 1856 writings is therefore not so much in his sources – which were infinitely better and more complete in *L'Ancien Régime* – as in his system of interpretation. In the spirit of the Tocquevillean method itself, this may well be the best approach to a history which openly acknowledges that it is inseparable from an explanatory theory.

I

Tocqueville's general interpretation of the French Revolution can thus already be found in a short essay published in England in 1836, after his visit to America. The full title of the original text was 'État social et politique de la France avant et depuis 1789', a surprising anticipation of the title that Tocqueville was to give to his last book twenty years later. Strictly speaking, Tocqueville's essay corresponds only to the first part of the title, as it just deals with pre-revolutionary France. The sequel, referred to in a ten-line transition that gives this text a curious conclusion, never seems to have been written; it is not fully clear why Tocqueville interrupted his work on the subject at that date. In 1836, as he was to do twenty years later, Tocqueville concentrates on the Ancien Régime more than on the Revolution, on pre-1789 more than on post-1789 France. The article can be summarised as follows:

The introduction states the central idea of the essay: the Revolution was merely a local and particularly violent explosion of universally held ideas. The first part is mainly a description of French civil society at the end of the old monarchy. For Tocqueville, the Church had become a political institution cut off from the population, and the nobility a caste rather than an aristocracy (that is, an English-style ruling class). While the Church is dealt with rather summarily, the nobility is analysed in great detail. Politically, the nobility was cut off from power by the monarchy; deprived of its local administrative authority without having been compensated with a share in government power, it was powerless to oppose the king on behalf of the people or to exert any real influence on the king against the people. Hence the anachronistic character of noble privileges (the nobles were no longer loved or feared), notably economic and honorific ones.

Economic redistribution benefited the Third Estate, which controlled the country's non-landed wealth. Hence the fragmentation and changing ownership of noble estates, the breaking up of the nobility into a mass of moderately well-to-do individuals and the phenomenon that might be called the 'democratisation of the nobility'.

Finally, the author discusses the rise of the Third Estate, which took place independently of the nobility (here Tocqueville almost echoes Sieyès), for it 'created a new people', with its own aristocracy. That rise accounts for the division within the ruling class and for the revolutionary spirit of the Third Estate. 'The division among the various aristocratic elements had pitted the aristocracy against itself in a kind of civil war from which democracy alone was to profit in the end. Rebutted by the nobility, the leading members of the Third Estate could fight back only by adopting principles that served their purposes at the time, but were dangerous precisely because they were so effective. As one section of the aristocracy in revolt against the other, the Third Estate was therefore compelled to endorse the idea of equality for everyone in order to combat the specific idea of inequality that thwarted it' (p. 46).

Tocqueville emphasises the fact that the aristocratic principle rapidly lost ground, partly as a result of the influence of the intelligentsia on society and a kind of 'egalitarian' fusion between the nobility and the intellectuals. This 'imaginary democracy' in spirit was matched by a real democracy of wealth, brought about by the fragmentation of landed property; the consequent rise in the number of small-scale fortunes created favourable conditions for political democracy. Eighteenth-century France was thus marked by a discrepancy between its institutions (based on inequality) and its way of life, which already made it 'the most truly democratic nation in Europe'.

Tocqueville then proceeds to describe the *political* consequences of these social conditions: just as aristocratic societies tend toward local government, so democratic societies tend toward centralised government. Democratic society begins by wresting local government from the aristocracy, but since it is too weak and too fragmented to exercise power on its own, it entrusts it to the king – the only force that can hold it together despite its interests and its weaknesses – through the mediation of its natural leaders, the jurists.

In France the effects of these 'general causes' were compounded by 'accidental and secondary' factors: the dominant rôle of Paris, the need to maintain national unity among very diverse provinces, and the personal rather than parliamentary nature of power.

Yet governmental and administrative centralisation had by no means extinguished the spirit of liberty, which Tocqueville considers to be one of the characteristic traits of French national temperament. That is why, in the eighteenth century, the aristocratic notion of liberty (the protection of privilege at every level) was superseded by a democratic one, based on common law instead of privilege.

So the Revolution did not create a new people, nor a new France: 'It regulated, coordinated, and put into law the effects of a great cause but it was not itself that cause.' It was the end result of long-term trends in Ancien-Régime society, far more than a radical transformation of France and the French. These trends toward democracy, which Tocqueville analyses according to their impact on civil society, on attitudes, on government and on ideology, formed a kind of common rootstock for both the old and the new régime, and the Revolution simply appears as one stage in the development of their effects – a stage to which Tocqueville does not attribute a specific character. In his view, the continuity of French history has wiped out the traces of its discontinuities.

The main conceptual elements of this interpretation of the French Revolution in a long-term historical setting, an interpretation that stresses the weight of the past and reduces the significance of the change for which the Revolution wanted to take the credit, did not originate with Tocqueville. But since he was always so discreet about his readings[2] – there are very few explicit references to other authors in his books, and relatively few in his correspondence – it is hard to identify his sources. One of them, however, is clear: he had obviously read Guizot, with whom he was engaged in a continuous intellectual and political exchange marked by a mixture of complicity and hostility,[3] which is a most telling example of the ambiguities of French liberalism in the first half of the nineteenth century. His senior by eighteen years, Guizot had already written his most important works when Tocqueville was writing his 1836

2. He was as discreet about his readings as he was eloquent in discussing his manuscript sources, as in *L'Ancien Régime*: the double snobbery, perhaps, of an aristocrat and intellectual.
3. Cf. an interesting paper by Stanley Mellon, 'Guizot and Tocqueville', read at the annual meeting of the Society for French Historical Studies, Chicago, 1969.

essay. Although Guizot was more fundamentally a historian than Tocqueville, they shared the same basic political creed, liberalism, the same view of history as interpretation, and the same central frame of reference within which to structure a very long past, that is, the concept of the French Revolution as both the culmination of a universal (i.e. European) history and the mystery specific to French history. Given this common approach, it is interesting to find out to what extent Tocqueville followed, or learned from, Guizot and to analyse the differences between their interpretations.

Having gone back to teaching history after his fall from political power in 1820, Guizot published the essential parts of his explanatory system in his first major historical works, notably in his *Essais sur l'histoire de France* (1823). Charles Pouthas[4] points out that in his 1828 lectures, later published as *Histoire de la civilisation en Europe et en France*,[5] Guizot modified some of his judgments and above all corrected some factual errors, notably concerning early French history and the barbarian invasions. Yet these are minor changes so far as the question discussed here is concerned, for between the 1823 *Essais* and the 1828 lectures, the main lines of Guizot's interpretation of French history remained the same. All of the great protagonists are already present in the *Essais:* the seigneurs, the Church, the king, the *communes* (free towns); and so are the societies and types of government – aristocratic, theocratic, monarchical, democratic – that are or should be embodied by those protagonists, along with the conflicts or periods of equilibrium with which they fill the history of France. In 1828 as in 1823, this history was merely the empirical confirmation of an intellectual schema that remained essentially unchanged.

Guizot sought to define the history of France as a march toward a 'society', that is, toward an organised social whole all of whose strata are linked by a unifying principle. Feudalism, which emerged from chaos or non-society around the tenth century, under the Capetians, was the first form of organised society in French history. It was hard on the people, but its internal dialectic pointed to 'a better future',[6] for it rested both on the oppression of the people, 'the nation as personal property', and on egalitarian relations within the dominant class, 'the sovereign nation' of fiefholders: 'Here I come upon a different sight; I see liberties, rights, and guarantees which not only bestowed honour and protection on those who

---

4. Charles Pouthas, *Guizot pendant la Restauration* (Paris: Plon–Nourrit, 1923), chapter 10, 'L'enseignement de Guizot', especially pp. 329ff.
5. Six vols. (Paris, 1838).
6. The quotes used here are taken from the fifth '*Essai*' on the history of France.

enjoyed them, but by their nature and intent opened to the subservient population a door to a better future.' The complex hierarchy of fiefholders established a network of reciprocal relationships of relative equality among the seigneurs, from the least among them all the way up to the king; yet the fief consolidated its holder's individualism and his independence from the authorities. 'Such a situation looked like war rather than a society; yet it preserved the energy and dignity of the individual; a society could arise from it.'

Guizot was referring to the type of society that he saw as a culmination of history, and was founded on a redefinition of 'individuals' and 'public institutions', of the liberty and order that had been sacrificed to feudalism. As soon as feudalism had been established, it was attacked at both ends: from below in the name of liberty, and from above in the name of public order. 'Such efforts were not made amidst the clash of diverse and ill-defined systems reducing each other to impotence and anarchy [as in the first five centuries of French history, according to Guizot]; they arose within a single system and were directed against it alone.' And Guizot concludes his analysis with these admirable lines: 'This monarchical system, which Charlemagne, despite his genius, had been unable to found, was gradually made to prevail by much lesser kings. The rights and guarantees that the Germanic warriors had been unable to preserve were recovered one by one by the *communes*. Only feudalism could be born of barbarism; but feudalism had hardly reached maturity when the monarchy and liberty began to take shape and grow within it.'

In a detailed examination of those two processes, Guizot shows that both the monarchy and liberty were given a chance to develop by the political weakness of the feudal aristocracy. Isolated in its respective fiefs, disunited for lack of a collective organisation comparable to that of the Roman patriciate, the Venetian Senate, or the English barons (for the inequality of the feudal hierarchy precluded any such organisation), the aristocracy was not only worn down locally by the opposition of the population, but also held down by the most powerful overlord, the king.

It soon became clear that feudalism was useful only for guiding society's first steps out of barbarism, and was incompatible with the progress of civilisation; *it did not contain the seeds of any durable public institution*;[7] it was lacking not only the principle of aristocratic government, but any other principle as well; and, once it had perished, it would leave behind it a nobility around the throne, aristocrats above the people, *but no aristocracy to govern the State*.[8]

The opposite development took place, according to Guizot, in

7. Italics mine.
8. Italics mine.

medieval England, where kingship and feudalism were born together at
the time of William the Conqueror: 'England had two social forces, two
public powers, neither of which existed in France at the time: an
aristocracy and a king. These forces were too barbaric, too dominated by
passion and personal interest to permit the development of either despotism or free government; yet they also needed each other and were
often obliged to work together.' Out of the struggle between the English
barons *forming an aristocracy* and the king *embodying a monarchy* came the
charters ('a beginning of public law'), followed by institutions, that is, 'a
free and national government'.

For Guizot, the historical development of France was thus characterised by feudalism's failure to create an aristocracy, and by the *communes'*
failure to create democracy. Hence the absence of free institutions, hence
also the absolute monarchy, the end-result of a double impotence. It was
the Revolution – the culmination of a centuries-long class struggle
between feudalism and the *communes* – that finally created democracy, that
is, both a society and free egalitarian institutions; it was the Revolution
which rallied society round a single unifying principle.

The major features of Guizot's and Tocqueville's general interpretations have a number of points in common. First, both authors try to fit
so-called 'events' into a wide time-span and conceptual framework. Both
feel that the Revolution was but the culmination of a very long historical
process that had its roots in the formative stages of French society. In that
sense, their history of France, though it implicitly contains the future it is
supposed to explain, and is obsessed, as it were, by the French Revolution,
was nonetheless bound to be not so much a history of the Revolution as a
description of its origins.

For the fundamental dialectic that produced the revolutionary conflict
and accounts for the course of history is the same in both authors; it is the
dialectical relationship between civil society and institutions, between the
state of society and government. Within this general approach to the
problem, the two authors' conceptual framework for their historical
analysis is also very similar. Both feel that, from the outset, French civil
society was essentially composed of two rival groups, the nobility and the
Third Estate, both of them existing since the Frankish conquest, and both
potential bearers of a system of socio-political values, respectively aristocracy and democracy. Their relations with the central authority, the king,
are the underlying pattern of French history – yet they also account for its
special nature in comparison with the English model.

But Guizot, unlike Tocqueville, did not think that there had ever been a true aristocratic political society in French history. For him, as for Mably, the Middle Ages and feudalism were nothing more than a state of anarchy, unbearable for the people and incapable of building any genuine political institutions. And since the French – unlike their English contemporaries – were too weak to develop such institutions, the growth of royal power was an indispensable period of transition toward democracy and liberty.

Tocqueville, by contrast, felt that there had indeed been an aristocratic society, accompanied by a paternalist local government that protected individual liberty against encroachment from the central power. It was the gradual erosion of that aristocratic society under the impact of the royal administration and more general trends that opened the way, not to liberty, but to equality.

Both Tocqueville and Guizot, therefore, saw the fundamental dialectic of French history in socio-political terms, as centred on the growth of royal power supported from below by the mass of the democratic 'people'. Guizot, however, spoke of liberty where Tocqueville spoke of democracy or equality, because Guizot felt that aristocracy was an obstacle to liberty, while Tocqueville saw it as the foundation and bulwark of liberty. The fundamental disagreement in their interpretations concerns the rôle played in French history by the king and the aristocracy, and the political and moral values they embodied.

It is therefore tempting to compare the underlying political commitments of these two men – and to contrast Guizot's pride as a commoner ('I am of those who were raised by the tide of 1789 and who will never consent to step down') with Tocqueville's nostalgia ('Everywhere in the world, the societies that will always have the greatest difficulties in holding out against absolute government will be precisely those where aristocracy has been lost once and for all.'). The contrast in their experiences and existential attitudes shows up even more clearly the similarities in the major conceptual elements of their historical analysis. The originality of Tocqueville's 1836 essay in relation to Guizot's work was due no doubt more to the insights accidentally afforded by his family background than to his intellectual imagination.

Twenty years later, on the other hand, *L'Ancien Régime* arrived at an infinitely more complex synthesis of Tocqueville's aristocratic inheritance. Tocqueville had brought to it not only many more years of thought and research, but also his experience as a politician.

II

L'Ancien Régime et la Révolution is written in an extremely brilliant and compact style. Tocqueville's notes and drafts, now published in full in the second volume of the Gallimard edition, testify to his great concern with form, and to the painstaking work he devoted to polishing and repolishing his expressions. Yet this apparently limpid prose is in fact infinitely less clear than the 1836 text, for neither the historical conceptualisation nor the steps in the demonstration are easy to identify.

Yet that must be done; for even in the later work Tocqueville deliberately refused to write in the classical style of contemporary 'histories of the Revolution' and altogether shunned narrative. Moreover, he did not cite Thiers, Lamartine, or Michelet, all of whom he had probably read[9] or at least skimmed; and if he broke with the historians' time-honoured tradition – which is still alive – of criticising or copying his predecessors, it was not so much from disdain as from a desire to place his work at a different level than that of narrative history. His history, which in this sense is extraordinarily modern, is an examination of selected problems for the purpose of constructing a general explanation and interpretation of the Revolution. Hence his exclusive reliance on manuscript or printed primary sources; hence also the general design of the book, which sacrifices chronology for the sake of logical coherence.

The book is divided into three major parts. The first defines the historical significance of the Revolution and its essential content, which was not religious (since religion was, in the medium term, actually 'revived' by the Revolution) nor exclusively social or political, but indissolubly socio-political: the substitution of egalitarian institutions for the old 'feudal' ones – and Tocqueville used the word 'institutions' to refer to both the social and the political order, that is, to both equality of conditions and the modern administrative State. Hence the universal character of the Revolution, expressed in the almost religious form that democratic ideology gave it in France. Tocqueville thereby makes it clear from the outset that he was more interested in analysing the deeper significance and origins of events than the visible forms they took. He was convinced that by finding out how the dialectic between the State and civil society had evolved in France, how it was experienced, interpreted and retrospectively imagined in the last centuries, and especially the last

---

9. We know that he had read Thiers, whose historical works he comments on in his *Correspondence*.

decades, of the Ancien Régime, he would unlock the secret of the French Revolution and account for its chronological precedence and its intellectual impact on European history. Tocqueville thus went from comparative sociology to the sociological statement of a problem in French history.

The rest of the book is arranged according to two types of causal explanations: long-standing and general causes (Book 2) and specific and recent causes (Book 3). Tocqueville thus establishes a hierarchy of causes according to their time-scale. General causes are those that have been at work for a long time, deeply embedded in several centuries of history; their effects have arisen out of the remote past; unbeknownst to anyone, indeed beyond the reach of human memory, they were preparing new social and political conditions. Specific causes made themselves felt only in the eighteenth century, sometimes just in the last decades; they do not explain why change had become inevitable – those reasons are inherent in the long-term evolution – but why it took place at a specific date and in a specific manner.

Let us begin with the long-term causes, which are analysed in the twelve chapters of Book 2. For the most part, their treatment follows the theoretical premises outlined in Book 1, since Tocqueville first reviews the historical features of administrative centralisation (chapter 2–7) and then of civil society (chapters 8–12). Yet the first chapter, devoted to feudal rights and the peasantry, seems oddly out of place. Why did Tocqueville use it to introduce his description of the imbalances of the Ancien Régime, and why did he return to the study of the rural world in the last chapter of Book 2 (chapter 12), as if to say that this problem is important enough to frame the general analysis as a whole? I am unable to answer that question. Admittedly, the two chapters look at the peasant world from two different angles, since the first is devoted to the relation between peasant and seigneur, while the last deals with the relations between peasant and State. Nonetheless one would expect those two topics to have been created together at the end of Book 2, after the study of administrative centralisation and its effect on all levels of civil society.

Tocqueville, of course, may have wanted to begin his general analysis of the Ancien Régime with an examination of what the revolutionaries considered its most outrageous aspect, in order to present, at the very outset, by means of this special example, one of his fundamental ideas: the continuity between the Ancien Régime and the Revolution. Tocqueville was convinced that feudal rights had become hateful to the French not because they were particularly burdensome (they were more onerous in the rest of Europe) but because the French peasant was already, in many respects, a nineteenth-century peasant, that is, an independent owner in relation to his seigneur. Because feudal rights were no longer accompanied by an exchange of services, they had ceased to be institutions and had become survivals. Tocqueville thereby also accounts for an apparent paradox: given that, on the one hand, the Revolution was more than three-fourths accomplished before it even began and that, on the other hand, such vestiges of feudalism as did subsist in the countryside were particularly resented precisely for that reason, it becomes understandable why the Revolution attached such exaggerated importance to the liberation of the peasants.

By examining objectively the real content of the revolutionary break, Tocqueville shows the rôle played by ideological distortion. That was an exceptionally fruitful idea, considering how many of yesterday's and today's historians tend to take revolutionary discourse at face value, whereas probably no consciousness is more 'ideological' (in the Marxist sense of the term) than that of the revolutionaries.

Having used the theme of feudal rights to characterise the dialectic between continuity and break (one might almost say: continuity in fact, yet perceived as a break) that marked the Revolution, Tocqueville turns to the crucial development that provided the historical continuity between the Ancien Régime and the Revolution: the growth of public power and administrative centralisation. It should be noted – and we shall return to this point later – that here Tocqueville reverses the logical or chronological order of his 1836 text and begins where he had left off twenty years earlier. Highly original as well – in comparison not only with his own 1836 article but also with his contemporaries – is his treatment of the classic theme of the growth of royal power, for he places the emphasis not on the purely political victories of the monarchy but on its increasingly firm administrative hold over society. For him, the administrative conquests of the king of France were the dominant feature of French history since the end of the Middle Ages, and the central power exerted its influence on civil society through the administration of the country's everyday affairs. The picture he presents is too well known to be summarised here; yet it involves a number of problems that deserve to be reviewed.

The first is that of its historical accuracy. Tocqueville was remarkably knowledgeable about administrative archival sources for the eighteenth century; moreover, he had the intelligence to look at them at both ends of the hierarchical ladder. On the one hand, he went through the documents in series F (central administration) of the Archives Nationales, and many of the complementary manuscripts preserved at the Bibliothèque Nationale. On the other hand, at the local level, he systematically explored the papers of the *intendant*'s office at Tours and carefully studied Turgot's account of his experiences as *intendant* of the Limousin. He wanted to know how power really worked, how it reached down from the central bureaucracy to the smallest village community, through the all-important mediation of the royal *intendants*. In doing so, he came face to face with the contradiction familiar to every historian of the Ancien Régime: from above, extraordinarily minute regulations for everything were handed down; below, disobedience was chronic, a situation reflected in the fact that the same edicts or *arrêts* were promulgated every few years. Tocqueville's description takes that double reality into account. He begins by analysing the inroads of the royal administration in town and country (chapters 2–5), only to show, from chapter 6 on, the limits of its reach: 'rigid rules, lax practices; such is its character [i.e. of the Ancien Régime]' (ch. 6, p. 134). To this he adds a lucid and unwittingly self-critical remark, considering that in the preceding chapters he has in a sense done what he now criticises: 'Whoever would set out to judge the government of that time by its law codes would end up with the most preposterous errors.' This statement is echoed in an even clearer sentence found in the appendix: 'The administration of the Ancien Régime was so diverse and so heterogeneous that it would survive only so long as it *took very little action*' (italics mine).[10] Thus, it was not so much the administration's real power in the Ancien Régime that struck Tocqueville, as its disintegrating effect on the body politic, its annihilation of all intermediary power of recourse, whether seigneur, priest, communal syndic, or alderman. The State-as-Providence was not yet a reality, but it already existed in people's minds. By obliterating everything but arbitrary central power and the isolated individual, the Ancien Régime invented the *mould* which the Revolution used to shape its institutions. It presented all the political inconveniences of State control, without as yet providing any of its practical advantages.

Yet Tocqueville's dialectic between administrative and government

10. Yet in other passages, for example, Book 2, chapter 6, p. 133, Tocqueville notes the 'prodigious activity' of government in the Ancien Régime. The solution to this apparent contradiction lies in the distinction – to be found throughout Tocqueville's work – between government and administration, even though the distinction, which is perfectly clear in certain passages of *Democracy in America*, becomes blurred in the chapters of *L'Ancien Régime* analysed here. At what level, for example, did the *intendant* operate? It is the contrast between the government's increased activity and its impotence in practice that accounts for the progressive loss of faith in the law.

power entails a number of difficulties. Some are related to his interpretation of the facts. For instance, despite his close attention to certain
obstacles to the exercise of power under the Ancien Régime – resulting
from the extraordinary diversity in customs and procedures, and in the
legal status of persons and communities – Tocqueville tended on the
whole to overestimate the extent of administrative centralisation in the
Ancien Régime. His opinion is summarised in one of his preliminary
notes, where he attempts to define that system of authority in a single
phrase: 'A very centralised and very preponderant royal power, deciding
all important matters, and endowed with imprecisely defined but vast
prerogatives which in fact *it exercises*' (italics mine, vol. 2, p. 375). This
fundamental belief, which ultimately contradicts other statements about
the limits within which royal power had to operate, makes for some
strange silences or unwarranted simplifications in Tocqueville's treatment
of the real historical forces of centralisation. At this stage of his analysis,
for example, he says nothing about the sale of public offices, a key factor
in the formation of a monarchical bureaucracy, but ambiguous as far as
his thesis is concerned, since the sale of public offices was both a means
employed by the central power and an obstacle to its autonomy. But
when Tocqueville does try to define the bureaucracy of the Ancien
Régime, he writes (chapter 6): 'The administrative officials, almost all of
whom were commoners, already formed a class with its own particular
attitudes, its own virtues, honour and pride. It was the aristocracy of the
new society, which, already well-formed and alive, was only waiting for
the Revolution to make room for it.' For Tocqueville this type of analysis
had the advantage of creating, above and, as it were, outside of society, a
homogeneous social group, defined by its function, sharing a common set
of values, and actively involved in centralisation. Unfortunately, this
analysis is based throughout on mistaken assumptions. In the first place,
the administrative officials of the eighteenth century – one has only to
think of the *intendants* – were by no means 'almost all ... commoners'.
Secondly, they were deeply divided, not only by their personal ambitions
and their networks of patronage, but also by their political and ideological choices – witness the sharp division between physiocrats and anti-
physiocrats. Moreover, the most 'functional' administrators, i.e. those
directly connected with the central power – the bureaucracy of Versailles,
the *intendants* and their deputies (*subdélégués*) – would not survive the
Revolution, not even its first phase, while those who owned their offices
would, on the contrary, form one of its leading groups. Tocqueville's
probably exaggerated view of governmental and administrative central-

isation led him to deduce its presumable agents from the process he had described.

Tocqueville was on even shakier ground when it came to chronology and causes; indeed he proceeded by allusions and by a succession of unconnected remarks, without ever advancing a general theory of political change. Here, no doubt, he was not in his field. Having come to history fairly late in life, and not being familiar with pre-eighteenth-century sources, he was visibly indebted to his predecessors, whose materials he rearranged according to his own intuitions and presuppositions. The broad historical picture in chapter 4 of Book 1 is faithful to the classic periodisation of French history: medieval political institutions broke down in the fourteenth and fifteenth century under the advancing administrative monarchy, which impinged upon the power of the nobles. Tocqueville is faithful not only to that traditional chronology but also – without having made a special study of the field – to his own 1836 interpretation: he retrospectively places great emphasis on the nobles' traditional power, which he views as a sort of local self-government based on an exchange of services or as an idyllic relationship of trust between the seigneur and the peasant community. But none of that is truly analysed in historical terms. Tocqueville seems to believe that between the fifteenth and eighteenth centuries centralisation developed in a regular manner, although he never discusses its causes or its phases: Louis XIV is not even mentioned. Nor are the wars of the monarchy, a crucial factor in the growth of the State, ever evoked. Concerning the eighteenth century, he writes (Book 2, chapter 5) these sibylline words: 'The rapid progress of society constantly created new needs, each of which was a new source of power for it [the government], for it alone was in a position to satisfy them. While the administrative sphere of the law courts remained fixed, that of the government was moving, and constantly expanded at the same pace as civilisation itself.' The progress of centralisation is thus simply and vaguely related to that of 'civilisation'. Tocqueville's way of sharing his contemporaries' belief in progress consists of using one of the most obscure words of historical vocabulary to express his deep and abiding feeling of inevitability. That is as much as we shall ever know.

Having described in the first seven chapters of Book 2 (with the exception of chapter 1) the functioning – or rather what would now be called the dysfunctions – of the eighteenth-century administrative monarchy, Tocqueville, from chapter 8 on, turns to the analysis of civil society. As was pointed out earlier, this arrangement reflects a reversal of his usual approach, by comparison not only with the 1836 essay but also with *Democracy in America*. In the latter, the broad picture of 'the social state of the Anglo-American' (part 1, chapter 3) precedes the analysis of political institutions, and Tocqueville expressly notes at the end of the chapter: 'The political consequences of such a state of society are easily deduced. One could not possibly expect that equality would fail to penetrate the political world as it had penetrated all others.' Tocqueville emphasises the predominance of social factors (in the widest sense, including mental attitudes, mores, and the 'public spirit') over political factors, but at the same time he implicitly formulates a global typological theory of society *à la* Montesquieu or Max Weber, which is clearly present in the 1836 article as well. It postulates that 'aristocratic' societies tend toward local government, while 'democratic' societies tend toward centralised government. In fact, in the earlier period, Tocqueville does not seem to have been hostile to civil equality (which is the essential feature of his definition of 'democracy') or to governmental centralisation (so long as it went hand in hand with administrative decentralisation). That is the underlying meaning of his study of America.

Yet, twenty years later, the organisation of *L'Ancien Régime* very probably reflects a change in his judgment and his thinking. It has been pointed out,[11] incidentally, that the word 'democracy' is used much less frequently in *L'Ancien Régime* than in the 1836 text, as if Tocqueville had gradually abandoned that key concept of his earlier analysis without, however, completely striking it from his vocabulary. What had happened? Tocqueville had just experienced as a politician, not simply as an intellectual, the upheavals of the years 1848–51. In 1848, the popular and socialist explosion, a new French version of the 'trend' towards democracy, clearly showed the outer limits of social democratisation, which Tocqueville had described as accomplished; moreover, the 1848 risings were a sight that filled him with horror. The well-reasoned optimism that had underlain his analysis of American society gave way to fear. The reformer of the days before the Revolution had become a conservative intent upon preserving the order restored at such great cost. Hence he was faced with a two-fold problem, the theoretical one of defining his terms and the existential one of making a value judgement. In 1851, the government of notables, which Tocqueville had supported and in which he had even participated, believing it to be the best of all French régimes since 1789 (as he put it in his *Souvenirs*), had come to an inglorious end on

11. Seymour Drescher, *Dilemmas of Democracy: Tocqueville and Modernization* (Pittsburgh: Univ. of Pittsburgh Press, 1968), p. 242.

2 December 1851, to be succeeded by the worst centralising despotism since 1789. It had now become difficult to explain a set of political institutions as diverse as the July Monarchy, the Second Republic or the despotic rule of the second Napoleon in terms of a single state of society, a concept whose extreme flexibility was being demonstrated before Tocqueville's very eyes.[12] The reversal in his approach and his new emphasis on the autonomy and the primacy of purely political factors – more specifically of political-administrative structures – are probably related to his experiences during those years.

Actually, one can find traces of this reversal in the notes for *L'Ancien Régime*, in which Toqueville worked out his concepts more freely than in the final text. Here, for example, is a note about the meaning of the word 'democracy' (vol. 2, p. 198):

The greatest intellectual confusion arises from the use of the words *democracy, democratic institutions, democratic government*. So long as we are unable to define these words clearly and to agree on their definition, we shall live with an inextricable confusion of ideas, to the great advantage of demagogues and despots.

It will be possible to say that a country governed by an absolute prince is a *democracy*, because he governs by law or in the presence of institutions favourable to the welfare of the people. His government will be called a *democratic government*. He will be said to form a *democratic monarchy*.

Now the words *democracy, democratic monarchy* or *democratic* government can mean only one thing when used in their true sense: a government in which the people participate in government to a greater or lesser extent. Its meaning is intimately related to the idea of political liberty. To call 'democratic' a government in which political liberty is absent is to utter an obvious absurdity, if one considers the natural meaning of those words.

This note is rather perplexing, since Tocqueville here condemns precisely the meaning he had hitherto given to the word 'democracy'. In fact, his correction consists in transferring the concept from the social sphere (equality) to the political sphere (sharing in power, and liberty), as if the former were now conditioned by the latter.

Another telling indication of this shift can be found in an appendix to chapter 5 of Book 2, on centralisation. Here Tocqueville makes a remarkable comparison between French colonial rule in Canada and English colonial rule in America, noting that in the colonies the underlying character of the two administrations is magnified to the point of caricature. In Canada, there is no nobility, no 'feudal tradition', no pre-

12. Marx faced the same problem in his *18 Brumaire*, even though his system of explanation rested on different premises. In reading him one never understands why the divergent interests of the ruling classes (landowners versus capitalists) made a common government first possible then impossible, and why they should have led to such a catastrophic recurrence of blind obstinacy.

dominant church power, no set of old judicial institutions firmly rooted in the mores of the population, in short, nothing carried over from civil society in old Europe, nothing to oppose absolute government. 'It already looks just like modern centralised administration, like Algeria.' By contrast, in neighbouring English America, where social conditions were comparable, 'the republican element, which is the basis, as it were, of the English constitution and way of life, expresses itself freely and flourishes. The administration proper did very little in England, and private citizens did a great deal; in America the administration practically did not take care of anything, and individuals, working together, did everything. Whereas the presence of upper classes made the inhabitant of Canada under French rule even more subservient to government than the inhabitant of France at the same period, the absence of upper classes in the English provinces made their inhabitants increasingly independent of authority. Both colonies eventually established an entirely democratic society; but in Canada, at least so long as it belonged to France, equality went hand in hand with absolute government, while in America it went hand in hand with liberty.'

It seems to me that two striking ideas are expressed in this note, written at the same time as *L'Ancien Régime*:

1. Political liberty is not necessarily related to the presence of upper classes, an 'aristocracy' in Tocqueville's sense. The contention that in English America 'the absence of upper classes' made individuals 'increasingly independent of governmental power' marks a clear break with the conceptual schema of 1836, in which aristocracy, local government and political liberty are equated.

2. The decisive factor in the development of these two societies is not, therefore, their social state – which in both cases is 'democratic' – but their tradition and political-administrative practices.

And that is indeed the conclusion to be drawn from the analysis of the essential features of *L'Ancien Régime*. It is not, of course, that Tocqueville is carred away by any single-cause explanation, which is totally alien to his way of thinking. On the contrary, he continues to pay close attention to the tangled web of reasons and consequences that is empirically revealed to him by his sources. Nonetheless, in his last book, civil society is less a cause than a result of the political and moral environment. That is perhaps the most fundamental intellectual originality of *L'Ancien Régime*, both in comparison with Tocqueville's earlier work and in relation to nineteenth-century political sociology as a whole.

Thus the central phenomenon and essential aspect of historical change in France is the growth of royal power and of government centralisation, both of which in turn are related to the development of direct taxation (the *taille*). This process both dislocated and unified civil society ('the division into classes was the crime of the old monarchy', Book 2, chapter 10, p. 166), which was split up into increasingly rival groups composed of increasingly similar individuals. The upper classes' inability to preserve their traditional political power, or to unite in order to gain a new kind of power, gave free rein to administrative despotism, which in turn compounded the consequences of government centralisation.

In analysing French civil society in the second part of his book, Tocqueville, faithful to the legacy of Restoration historiography, speaks of 'classes': 'One can, of course, cite individual examples to the contrary, [but] I am speaking of classes, which alone have a place in history' (Book 2, chapter 12, p. 179). Yet his use of this fundamental concept is ambiguous throughout. At times he defines classes as the orders of the Ancien Régime, at other times he defines them by a combination of Ancien-Régime legal criteria and an extremely vague criterion of wealth and social status, which includes the well-to-do bourgeoisie in the upper classes. The real reason for this ambiguity and for the constant shift from one meaning to another is the central question that Tocqueville was trying to answer about eighteenth-century French society: why was it unable to move, without a revolution, from the rigid hierarchy of the society of orders to the modern dichotomy between the notables and the people, the upper classes and the lower classes? But if that is really, as I believe it is, the crucial question for him, then it also shows how far he had come since *Democracy in America*. Tocqueville's approach was no longer centred on social equality and political democracy, but on the rôle of the upper classes and the élites. It is true that, as he himself had intimated in *Democracy in America* (vol. 1, end of chapter 9), he was no longer dealing with a society formed *ex nihilo* by republican immigrants who believed in equality, but on the contrary with a world firmly rooted in aristocratic tradition; and it is also true that he could not subject the two societies to the same kind of analysis. Yet the fact remains that there is a marked difference in tone between the two books, and that the prose of *L'Ancien Régime* is suffused with an atmosphere of sadness: what had been a hope for the future in the 1830s has become a nostalgic longing for the past.[13] Tocqueville is always looking back to the nobility, evoking the mythical image of its glorious past, when the rural communities were

---

13. Additional evidence for this change in tone, the shift from optimism to nostalgia between *Democracy in America* and *L'Ancien Régime*, is provided by two texts in which Tocqueville seeks to define the kind of person who thrives in democratic societies, and where he implicitly gives his opinion on the matter. (*To continue next page.*)

united under its wings, when civil society was relatively close-knit and held together by fraternal bonds and in any case free: such was the society that the monarchy had destroyed.

Yet this 'existential' change in Tocqueville's attitude, however evident and indeed understandable for a man so attuned to his time – not many speculative thinkers have been so teleological and so clearly motivated by practical needs – naturally fitted into a conceptualisation of the history of the nobility which, on the whole, remained faithful to his 1836 arguments, even if it changed their effective connotation. *L'Ancien Régime*, being less schematic, makes it easier to understand Tocqueville's approach, with all its unresolved contradictions.

Parodying Bainville's dictum, one might summarise Tocqueville's dialectic as follows: eighteenth-century society had become too democratic for the residue of noble domination it preserved, and too noble-dominated for its democratic aspects. The 'too democratic' aspect is treated in chapters 7–10 of Book 2 – which describe the move toward intellectual unification and the gradual isolation of upper-class groups from one

Democracy in America (Henry Reeves translation [New York, 1953]) vol. 1, ch. 14 (end of chapter): 'We must first understand what is wanted of society and its government. Do you wish to give a certain elevation to the human mind and teach it to regard the things of this world with generous feelings, to inspire men with a scorn of mere temporal advantages, to form and nourish strong convictions and keep alive the spirit of honorable devotedness? Is it your object to refine ... habits, embellish ... manners, and cultivate the arts, to promote the love of poetry, beauty, and glory? Would you constitute a people fitted to act powerfully upon all other nations, and prepared for those high enterprises which, whatever be their results, will leave a name forever famous in history? If you believe such to be the principle object of society, avoid the government of democracy, for it would not lead you with certainty to the goal.

But if you hold it expedient to divert the moral and intellectual activity of man to the production of comfort and the promotion of general well-being; if a clear understanding be more profitable to man than genius; if your object is not to stimulate the virtues of heroism but the habits of peace; if you had rather witness vices than crimes, and are content to meet with fewer noble deeds, provided offenses be diminished in the same proportion; if, instead of living in the midst of a brilliant society, you are contented to have prosperity around you; if, in short, you are of the opinion that the greatest object of a government is not to confer the greatest possible power and glory upon the body of the nation, but to ensure the greatest enjoyment and to avoid the most misery to each of the individuals who compose it – if such be your desire, then equalize the conditions of men and establish democratic institutions.'

L'Ancien Régime, Book 2, chapter 11, p. 175: 'The men of the eighteenth century hardly knew that passionate attachment to well-being which is like the mother of servitude, a temperate yet tenacious and unchangeable passion, which often goes along and indeed becomes intertwined with a number of private virtues, such as love of family, unimpeachable mores, respect for religious beliefs, and even a lukewarm and assiduous practice of the established religion. This passion permits honourable conduct and prohibits heroism, and is an excellent means of producing steady people and unspirited citizens. Our forebears were better and worse.

In those days the French loved life and adored pleasure. Perhaps their manners were more dissolute, their passions and their ideas more reckless than they are today, but they were free of that tempered and well-mannered sensualism we see around us.'

another – as well as in chapter 12, where Tocqueville treats the peasant problem separately, as he had done at the beginning of Book 1. The 'too noble-dominated' aspect it treated in the curious chapter 11, where Tocqueville analyses, in order to celebrate it as the opposite of 'democratic' mediocrity, the independent spirit and the sense of liberty with which the aristocratic traditions had imbued French society under the Ancien Régime; yet he emphasises that this spirit, being tied to the idea of privilege, was not suited to survive the advent of democratic institutions, much less to give rise to them.

Just where, then, are we to look for this contradictory development, which bore the seeds of the revolutionary explosion? Since the answer is never very clearly stated, it is important to elucidate this point. Tocqueville deals with economics, society and something one might call, for lack of a better term, ideology.

His economic analysis is always superficial and vague, but at least one can understand why certain factors are not mentioned. Economics was a dimension of human life that had interested him only for its interaction with social or intellectual life, but never in itself or as a basic mechanism of change. That is why he did not make a systematic study of the specifically economic documents of the Ancien Régime, even though he was thoroughly familiar with the sources for the social, administrative, political and intellectual history of the period. He noted the growth in industrial activity in Paris (Book 2, chapter 7, p. 141) only in order to indicate that 'industrial affairs' were attracted to the capital by the centralisation of 'administrative affairs'. Concerning the changing patterns in the distribution of wealth among classes (which is only partly a matter of economics), his approach is strangely simplistic: he speaks of the impoverishment of the nobility and the enrichment of the 'bourgeois' (Book 2, chapter 8, p. 145) without relating the alleged process to economic causes. Noting the kingdom's urbanisation through the massive migration of the 'middle class' to the towns, he simply returns to his 'administrative' explanation: 'Two causes had been most important in producing this effect: the privileges of the *gentilshommes* and the *taille* [direct taxation]' (Book 2, chapter 9, p. 153). Finally, his explanation for

14. This statement contradicts what Tocqueville says earlier about the impoverishment of the nobility. We now know that the notion of an impoverishment of 'the' nobility as a social unit does not hold for the eighteenth century, since economic circumstances in fact favoured a steep rise in landed income of every kind (feudal dues, rents, and direct management). Tocqueville's second statement thus seems more accurate than the first; but it is also less characteristic of Tocqueville's thinking, which requires him to *deduce* the nobility's economic decline from its political decline.

peasant misery remains extremely vague: 'The progress of society, which made for the wealth of all other classes,[14] brought despair to the peasant; civilisation turned against him alone' (Book 2, chapter 12, p. 185). Moreover, his picture of peasant life as a whole is marked by a complete ignorance of the technical aspects of rural economy.

The economic development of French society is thus either simply deduced from another development (that of the political-administrative sphere) or reduced to vague abstractions ('progress of society', 'civilisation'); in other words, it is ignored as a factor in its own right. Moreover, matters of economic doctrine are also similarly approached. Tocqueville has read the physiocrats, for example, but he never mentions their specifically economic analysis (which probably did not interest him), not even the crucial anti-mercantilist implications of the 'laissez-faire, laissez-passer' doctrine; the one part of physiocratic thought he does mention, only to criticise it, is the theory of 'legal despotism' (Book 3, chapter 3), which in fact is but the corollary of the definition of economic rationality (and moreover not even accepted by 'marginal' physiocrats who, like Turgot, were rather Gournay's disciples). Tocqueville referred to the only aspect of physiocratic thought that squared with his analysis of the eighteenth century; but in restricting one's vision in this manner one is condemned to miss the extraordinary vogue of economic liberalism that pervaded the upper strata of society. And indeed Tocqueville does not breathe a word about it.

In his sociological description – in the narrow sense – Tocqueville is once again on familiar territory. Not that, as we have seen, the tools of his investigation were novel or even precise. But in this area it was easier for him to go back not only to his own history, which virtually obsessed him, but also to his fundamental discourse, for he was once again in an area that responds more directly to the effects of politics and administration. Society offers a vast field in which to document the consequences of legislation and government action. Yet how often does Tocqueville beg the question! Take the statement that the nobility became impoverished. Here is the explanation: 'Yet the laws that protected the nobles' property were still the same; seemingly their economic condition remained the same. Nonetheless, they were becoming poorer everywhere in exact proportion to the rate at which they were losing power.' And further on: 'The French nobles were gradually becoming poorer as they came to lack the practice and the spirit of government' (Book 2, chapter 8, p. 144). The fragmentation of noble property was thus itself only a sign and a consequence of that fundamental fact.

This type of analysis compounds its logical obscurity with disregard for established facts. The correlation between power and wealth, for each social group, is as as dubious in Tocqueville as it is in Marx (where wealth comes *before* power). Moreover, Tocqueville establishes this correlation merely to give us a biological comparison that does nothing to satisfy the reader: political power, we seem to be told, is 'that central and invisible force which is the very principle of life', the very heart of human society. Besides, it is all the more difficult to follow Tocqueville's analysis as he never reckons with the redistribution of wealth within society by the State, a study that might well have led him, for the eighteenth century, to opposite conclusions.[15] Finally, as has already been pointed out, the eighteenth-century French nobility – at least a part of it, but Tocqueville never makes any distinctions within the group – was by no means excluded from power. Of the eighteenth-century nobility that occupied, conquered, and crowded all the avenues to power in France, one might say that it had lost the 'spirit of government', but certainly not its 'practice'.

Tocqueville, however, may be assuming more or less explicitly – more, if at all – that the recent nobility, ennobled and made wealthy by the king for its services to the State – men like Colbert or Louvois – were not part of the ideal model of the nobility and its traditional political values. This implicit exclusion would at least fit in with the idea that in the eighteenth century the machinery of the State was run exclusively by 'bourgeois'. But that merely moves the contradiction one step back, for Tocqueville criticises the French nobility for having become a 'caste' defined by birth alone, and for having ceased to be an aristocracy, i.e. a *corps* that, although limited in numbers, is relatively open to citizens who wield political power. In fact, the French nobility never was that 'aristocracy' of which Tocqueville dreams, in the sense in which sixteenth-century Venice, for example, governed by its Senate, was an aristocratic State. Yet the French nobility had been open throughout the Ancien Régime[16] to the advancement of commoners, for by its end the old families who traced their lineage back to the Middle Ages had become a distinct minority within the order. It was as a result of the sale of offices[17] and

15. For this essential mechanism of absolutism as it functioned in the eighteenth century, one must read Herbert Lüthy's perceptive description in his *La Banque protestante en France*, vol. 2, pp. 696ff, which presents Calonne's management of the public finances as the ultimate field-day for the nobility.

16. Indeed, in the very chapter where he defines the French nobility as a 'caste' (ch. 9) Tocqueville writes: 'At no period of our history was nobility acquired as easily as in [17]89', only to add that this fact did nothing to change the *consciousness* of separation between the orders.

17. *L'Ancien Régime* is strangely contradictory with respect to the sale of offices. Chapter 10 of Book 2 condemns the institution as a source of servitude, while the following chapter praises the independence of the French magistracy in the eighteenth century – an independence very obviously sustained by the sale of offices.

ennoblement by the king, in other words, *as a result of absolutism and consubstantially with it*, that the nobility ceased to be a closed *corps* of hereditary landowning seigneurs and incorporated into its ranks, in the name of service to the State, the sons of the wealthiest merchants and the most deserving of the king's servants. When Tocqueville writes, 'The more the nobility ceased to be an aristocracy, the more it seemed to become a caste' (Book 2, chapter 9, p. 151), one could reverse his statement and say that the more the nobility ceased to be a caste, the more it became an aristocracy.

Here we may well have reached the core of Tocqueville's system of interpretation and its ambiguities. For the entire sociological analysis of *L'Ancien Régime* is based on an opposition between aristocracy and nobility, a dialectic in which aristocracy is posited as the 'should-be' of the nobility, as its very essence. But then Tocqueville, whose historical learning, except for the eighteenth century, was quite superficial, had a rather banal, indeed legend-like, notion of the history of the French nobility (and aristocracy). As for its origins, he never went beyond the classic argument that identified the nobles with the Frankish conquerors,[18] making them an aristocracy created by the conquest. They soon lost this character ('during the Middle Ages', writes Tocqueville at the beginning of chapter 9 of Book 2, although this statement seems to contradict his description of medieval institutions in chapter 4 of Book 1) as a result of royal usurpations of power and became a 'caste'. A 'caste', in the very unusual meaning Tocqueville attributes to the term, was not so much a group closed to all who were born outside it as a group deprived of all political power and therefore all the more fiercely determined to preserve its compensatory privileges. It thus becomes clear that this history provides the nobility with origins and at the same time sets its goals for the future. It implies that the nobility was ruining itself not because its real past and the historical mechanism by which it had renewed itself inextricably tied it to the absolute monarchy, but because it was unfaithful to its origins and to its aristocratic principle. This historical account also shows that the political aspect was always paramount in Tocqueville's interpretation. Tocqueville was ultimately no more interested in society *per se* than in economics *per se*. Despite his close

18. Cf. in particular the last chapter of volume 1 of *Democracy in America* ('The Present and Probable Future Condition of the Three Races that Inhabit the Territory of the United States') or the beginning of chapter 9 of Book 2 of *L'Ancien Régime*. In the passage of *Democracy in America* Tocqueville curiously asserts that ever since human society began to exist, all aristocracies and the inequalities they imposed were the products of military conquest. One wonders how Tocqueville would fit into this schema, for example, Renaissance Italian republics or eighteenth-century England.

attention to fiscal sources, census data, and seigneurial rent rolls (*terriers*), which is obvious from his notes, and despite some marvellous comments on specific points, he was quite indifferent to the history of that society. The actual process by which the French eighteenth-century nobility, with its groups and sub-groups, had come into being did not interest him. For him, classes, above all his own, the nobility, were the trustees of traditions and values they could betray or embody; and he felt very strongly that nobility was inseparable from the political principle of aristocracy and that the notion of a nobility consisting of the king's servants was a contradiction in terms, since a nobility defined by function was not a nobility at all. Tocqueville was therefore bound to see the king as Saint-Simon had seen Louis XIV, surrounded by bourgeois who were busily engaged in ousting the nobility from all its traditional positions. Here is the last and belated echo of a specific political conflict, as well as the reaffirmation of a principle.

Tocqueville's historical description in *L'Ancien Régime* is thus essentially not concerned with economics, nor even with the structures of society and the history of its classes. Rather, it is concerned with the frame of mind of the French, with what one might call their national temperament or character. To him this was the arena *par excellence* of the clash between democratic and aristocratic tendencies, between consent and opposition to centralisation. One would have to apologise for speaking in such vague terms if it were possible to define Tocqueville's thinking more clearly. In volume 2 of *Democracy in America*, where he studies the effects of 'democracy' on the American mentality, Tocqueville successively defines the 'intellectual movement', the 'feelings' [of the Americans] and finally their 'actual mores'. It is not always easy to make a clear distinction between the levels of his study – notably between what he calls 'sentiments' and 'mores' – but at least a guiding thread is provided. *L'Ancien Régime* is totally different: Tocqueville not only modifies, as we have seen, the ranking of causes by shifting the emphasis to governmental and administrative centralisation, but he also fails to distinguish between types of effects. Actually, the notion of traditions (intellectual or emotional) or of mores fits in fairly well with the picture of French society in Book 2, for Tocqueville contends that centralisation had brought about the development of 'democratic mores', which clashed with the aristocratic tradition, and that the two trends reinforced and exacerbated each other by dint of their very incompatibility. Eighteenth-century Frenchmen were becoming ever more similar yet ever more distinct, ever more subservient yet ever more independent-minded. The closing years of the Ancien Régime were marked by the judicial combat between two principles and their conflicting influence on public opinion. In *L'Ancien Régime* democracy is not so much a state of society as a state of mind.

This modification permits Tocqueville to bring into his analysis a revolutionary dialectic that is clearly indispensable for dealing with his subject. For 'democracy', as he had studied it in the United States, was not only a state of society, but a founding principle, brought over and built-up *ex nihilo* by democratically-minded men who never had to struggle against an opposing principle, an opposing history and opposing traditions. In such conditions, he argues, society as a whole develops in harmony, for its democratic principle, embodied in actual facts, pervades every area of life, notably mentalities and manners. France at the end of the Ancien Régime presented Tocqueville with a completely different problem, for it involved a *history*, a *change*, and a *revolution*. Democracy (equality of conditions) cannot characterise the state of society before the Revolution, since it defines the state of society after the Revolution. Hence his recourse to a different conceptualisation: what was common to 'before' and 'after' was centralisation, as the vehicle for change and for the spread of democratic attitudes in a society that clung to its aristocratic forms, emptied though they were of their content. Defined in historical terms, the contradiction that brought this society to revolution was thus not essentially of a social, but of an intellectual and moral order;[19] it coincided only secondarily – and quite belatedly, i.e. in 1788 – with an awareness of of an internal conflict within civil society between the nobility and the Third Estate. It was thus the expression of a conflict of values deeply embedded in society as a whole, and notably in the mind of every 'enlightened' individual: democratic individualism and the nobility's caste spirit, both equally degenerate forms of their respective models, but for that very reason all the more incompatible and hostile to each other. The only principle that ultimately brought them together was despotism.

III

This interpretation accounts for the content of Book 3 of *L'Ancien Régime*, which, unlike the earlier books, is not devoted to the long-term causes of the Revolution but to the 'specific and more recent facts that finally determined its place in history, its birth and its character' (Book 3,

19. Cf. Sasha R. Weitman, 'The Sociological Thesis of Tocqueville's "The Old Regime and the Revolution"', *Social Research* 33, 3 (1966).

chapter 1) – in other words, to the examination of what we would call its short-term causes.

Tocqueville feels that toward the middle of the eighteenth century, specifically in the 1750s, the phenomena he had studied and the contradictions they produced were rapidly gathering speed. The first change, understandably, involved mentalities and ideas. It is as if the long process of administrative centralisation and social disintegration that he had analysed in the preceding books culminated in a cultural revolution during these years: France, at least its élites, that is, the groups whose political impact was decisive, was massively won over by an abstract philosophy of the political and social order that was all the more incompatible with existing society as it arose precisely from the very lack of political experience that characterised the individual in that society, whether nobleman or bourgeois. Deprived of true liberty, Frenchmen turned to natural law; incapable of collective experience, unable to test the resistances of a political process, they unwittingly set their course toward a revolutionary utopia; without an aristocracy, without organised leadership, without the possibility of calling upon professional politicians, they turned toward men of letters. Literature took on the rôle of politics. This phenomenon was subsequently fostered and intensified by an internal dialectic, for the intellectuals were by nature, and not just by the force of circumstance alone, the social group most lacking in political experience. In destroying the aristocracy, the monarchy had turned writers into make-believe substitutes for a ruling class. France then went from a debate about how to run the country to the discussion of ultimate values, from politics to revolution.

It is not so much the ideas of the period that were completely new. In fact, Tocqueville stresses that they were old. What was new was their impact throughout society, their resonance, their reception and their rôle. Nor were these ideas specifically French: they were shared by the entire European Enlightenment, yet all of Europe did not move toward the same revolutionary future. By this outline of a sociology of the production and the consumption of ideas in France in the second half of the eighteenth century, Tocqueville suggests that the Revolution was above all a transformation in values and patterns of thought, and that this transformation encountered particularly favourable conditions and was already well under way in France during the 1750s, owing to the long process of monarchical centralisation. The cultural (or, if one prefers, intellectual and moral) revolution, which had been a minor factor in the long term, became the essential element in the revolutionary process in the short term, for it channelled religious sentiments toward the imaginary cult of the State-as-model, thereby neutralising from the outset any liberalising tendencies that might be stimulated by this new awareness. For Tocqueville the chief goal of the revolution was 'democratic despotism', as prefigured and already developed in the physiocratic doctrine, rather than parliamentary liberalism; it was the 'preparation' of 1793 much more than a working toward 1789.

Tocqueville sees this sudden change of pace in French history, which he had first analysed in the intellectual sphere, in the economy and in society as well: he points out that – notwithstanding the beliefs of the actors in the great drama, who were obsessed with the idea of 'regeneration' – the Revolution did not strike a country in decline, but a prosperous one, which had experienced a great period of growth since 1750. Indeed the regions that were struck hardest were those that had responded most readily to the century's economic and social development, such as the Île-de-France. That is the famous thesis of chapter 4, which, in a general sense, though not in every detail,[20] has been largely confirmed by modern studies in eighteenth-century economic history. Unlike today's Marxist or Marxist-oriented historians, however, Tocqueville does not see that situation as a factor in the struggle between social classes with opposing interests, but diagnoses it instead as one more element that upset traditional attitudes and beliefs: the régime was too old to accommodate innovation, and the people were too liberated to tolerate the vestiges of their servitude, or rather their feeling of servitude. Reforms, which were incapable of overcoming the awareness that the situation was intolerable, only served to accelerate the disintegration of society: it was in 1787, not 1789, that Loménie de Brienne destroyed the Ancien Régime with his administrative reform, which replaced the *intendants* with elected assemblies. That, Tocqueville points out, was a more important revolution than all those France was to undergo after 1789, for the later ones affected only political institutions and not the 'administrative constitution'. The year 1787 marked the complete upheaval of the traditional relationship between the French people and the State, and of the very texture of social life. In short, the Ancien Régime was already dead in 1789, and the Revolution could kill it only in spirit, since that was the only place where it was still alive. Hence the extraordinary ease with which events followed their course. Was 1789, then, merely a hoax?

But if the actual content of the Revolution, thus defined, was indeed

20. I did not feel it necessary, in the context of a study on Tocqueville, to review the immense bibliography concerning the causes of the French Revolution.

already secured before the outbreak of the Revolution, then the revolutionary phenomenon, in the narrow sense of the term, was circumscribed from the outset. It did not bring a political and social transformation – for that transformation either had already been accomplished or, to the extent that it was incomplete, would be accomplished as a matter of course. The revolutionary process merely expressed two modes of historical action, namely, the use of violence and the use of ideology (or intellectual illusion); and in reality these two modes are one. For violence and political radicalism are inherent in the eschatological ideology of a 'before' and an 'after', of the old and the new, that characterised the revolutionary endeavour. The formation of the centralised democratic State, which for Tocqueville is the very meaning of the French Revolution, was also the meaning of the Ancien Régime. The Revolution only gave a new name to that process; but it was the Revolution *because it believed* that it had invented it. Here Tocqueville shows an admirable intuitive understanding of the discrepancy between the rôle objectively played by revolutions in historical change and the perception of that rôle by contemporaries or its intellectual fascination for succeeding generations. Unlike the many historians who, for almost 200 years now, don the costumes of the period when they recount the Revolution by means of a commentary on the Revolution's interpretation of itself, Tocqueville suggests that revolutionary times are precisely the most difficult to understand, since they are often periods when the veil of ideology hides most completely the real meaning of the events from the protagonists. That, no doubt, is the fundamental contribution of *L'Ancien Régime* to a theory of revolution.

Yet the central intuition of the book is never stated that explicitly. Tocqueville could only have done so had he written the history of the revolutionary events from the two-fold perspective he had announced in *L'Ancien Régime*; that is, if he had treated the events in themselves and then, above all, the ideology, or successive ideologies, that served to justify them.[21] But in 1856 he never did write the second volume of his book, thereby repeating – unintentionally this time – his silence in 1836. His death, eighteen months after the first volume appeared, may well not be the only explanation. Tocqueville, in his systematic approach, having finally succeeded in constructing a historical interpretation of the Ancien

21. Cf. his letter to Lewis of 6 October 1856: 'Since my purpose is far more to depict the evolution of the sentiments and ideas that successively produced the events of the Revolution than to recount the events themselves ...' Quoted by André Jardin in *L'Ancien Régime*, vol. 2, p. 21.

Régime, had yet to master the problems he saw in formulating a commensurate historical theory of the French Revolution.

The very history of the book, and the posthumous fragments that have come down to us, attest to that.[22] We know[23] that Tocqueville began the research that eventually led him to write *L'Ancien Régime* by studying the Consulate; in mid-1852 he wrote two chapters devoted to the public spirit at the end of the Directory,[24] which he intended to use as the preamble to that study. Then, toward the end of 1852, he gave up the project in order to return to the analysis of the Ancien Régime. He spent the summer of 1853 studying the archives of the *intendance* of Tours, and so deliberately abandoned his initial line of research. These two successive projects clearly indicate his major preoccupation, which was to study administrative institutions and their continuity, beyond the Revolution, from the Ancien Régime to the Consulate settlement. He himself indirectly admitted as much when, in April 1853, he made the following comment on the Paris municipal archives: 'These boxes contain few documents dating before 1787; from then on, the old administrative constitution was profoundly modified, and one comes to a rather uninteresting period of transition that separates the administration of the Ancien Régime from the administrative system created by the Consulate, which is the system that still governs us today.'[25]

In point of fact, that 'rather uninteresting period of transition' – a truly astounding phrase for a man who wanted to write a history of the Revolution – has left few traces in his posthumous fragments. Most of his reading notes are devoted to the Ancien Régime and the years just before the Revolution, specifically to the administration of the Ancien Régime and to pre-revolutionary ideology. They contain very little about the Constituent Assembly, nothing at all about the Legislative Assembly or the Committee of Public Safety, and practically nothing about the Convention: just a few rather banal pages about the Terror. Yet one cannot explain this impressive silence only by the reason Tocqueville had given in 1853. For we have seen that although he had begun by examining administrative centralisation, the underlying theme of his study of the Ancien Régime, Tocqueville had become increasingly interested in the ideological aspect of the Revolution. Why, then, did he so carefully read the pre-revolutionary pamphlets, but not the speeches of

22. *L'Ancien Régime et la Révolution*, vol. 2, 'Fragments and unpublished notes about the Revolution.'
23. Cf. A. Jardin's *Note critique* at the beginning of vol. 2.
24. Published as Book 3 of vol. 2, pp. 267–93.
25. Jardin, *Note critique*, p. 15.

the *conventionnels*? Why Mounier and not Brissot? Why Sïeyès and not Robespierre?

That is all the more puzzling as some of these fragmentary notes indicate that Tocqueville did perceive the dynamic character of revolutionary ideology. At one point, for instance, he comments on a page of Burke as follows:

It is quite true that, almost on the eve of the Revolution, France was very far from the state of mind that was to be exhibited by the Revolution. It is only too true that the spirit of liberty was not yet present among the masses (and it never was found there). These people still lived by the ideas of a different order and of a different century (vol. 2, p. 342).

He also repeatedly (vol. 2, Book 5, chapter 2) noted the rôle of the 'uncivilised' lower classes in the revolutionary process. Moreover, it is well known that in *L'Ancien Régime* he expressed his admiration for the men of 1789 and his loathing for those of 1793. The trouble is that those scattered remarks are difficult to reconcile with Tocqueville's detailed analyses of the emergence of the 'true spirit of the Revolution' (vol. 2, Book 1, chapter 5) based on the pamphlets of 1788–9 and the *Cahiers de doléances*, for those analyses convey the impression that revolutionary ideology, fully developed at this early stage, was already speaking 'the final word of the Revolution' (vol. 2, p. 196). Even more extraordinary are some of Tocqueville's omissions: he says almost nothing, except for the sentence quoted above, about intellectual and ideological differences within the French population. One simply finds Enlightenment culture above, and a kind of cultural nothingness, a non-civilisation, below. There is not a word, finally, about the messianic mission of Jacobinism and ideological warfare as both an outgrowth and a tremendous intensification of revolutionary patriotism after 1792, despite its being, in terms of Tocqueville's own analysis, the most general ideological expression of the attachment of the masses to the new democratic State and their participation in it. Even in the only two completed chapters of volume 2, where he analyses the state of mind of the French at the end of the Directory, Tocqueville manages to avoid a discussion of the problem of war and peace, which, at that time, was probably the overriding issue in domestic politics and also precluded, for emotional and practical reasons, a liberal solution to the political crisis.

But if so great a thinker could remain blind to such overwhelming evidence, he must have suffered from a kind of conceptual block, which may well have been the price he paid for his penetrating insight. Tocqueville, basically, never ceased to waver between two major lines of research, two basic hypotheses about French history. One is the hypothesis of administrative centralisation. It almost naturally led him to write on the Ancien Régime, and it might have led him to write a similar account of the Consulate or the Empire, for it provided him with a guiding thread for the long-term continuity of French history. But while this hypothesis gave a content to the Revolution, it also deprived it of its special character as historical process or mode, that is, of its specificity. Moreover, if the Revolution crowned and completed the work of the Ancien Régime by producing the administrative 'constitution' of the Consulate, then why 1830, why 1848, why all the additional revolutions that Tocqueville never ceased to study with passionate interest? Henceforth, the administrative constitution was established once and for all, and yet the political constitution was subject to sudden change every fifteen or twenty years.

It is probably this realisation that led Tocqueville to adopt his second major line of research, in which he defined revolution as a rapid transformation of the customs and mentalities of a society and as a radical ideological venture. This vast cultural split, which individuals desired all the more fervently as it was favoured, not thwarted, by the evolution of society, is analysed first as a consequence of centralisation and of the dislocation of traditional social groups. Tocqueville then endows it with a kind of autonomous force in 1788, which is meant to explain the outbreak of the Revolution; yet, imprisoned by his first hypothesis, he never carries the second one to its logical conclusion. The reason is, partly, that in this area he never clearly states just what he means by 'mores', 'frame of mind', 'habits', 'feelings', and 'ideas'. But, above all, once he had analysed the factors that touched off the Revolution as a cultural process, he seems to have failed to put together the elements needed for the history of that cultural dynamic.

Perhaps it can be said that Tocqueville has given us not so much the history of 'The Ancien Régime and the Revolution' he had meant to write as an interpretative description of the Ancien Régime and some fragments of a projected history of the Revolution. The first text constitutes Books 1 and 2 of L'Ancien Régime; the second was never written, and the preparatory notes for it are all that has come down to us. In between, Book 3 of L'Ancien Régime acts as a very subtle yet necessary transition, for the two texts do not follow the same internal guide-lines. The first, despite its hidden contradictions, is based throughout on a relatively static analysis of administrative centralisation and its effects on society. In the second, that is, starting with Book 3, history suddenly comes into play at the beginning of the 1750s; it is precisely the history of which Tocqueville had thorough and first-hand knowledge only from that date onward. In the second approach, therefore, cultural phenomena in the widest sense tend to become largely independent of the growth of administrative structures and are treated as determining factors of the revolutionary explosion. The Revolution is no longer defined as the building of the democratic State, since that was already accomplished by 1788, but rather as the application of an eschatological ideology: hence Tocqueville's detailed analysis of the 1788–9 pamphlets and the *Cahiers*.

Nonetheless, most of Tocqueville's notes on the revolutionary years show him to be locked into his first approach to the problem. That is not surprising, since they were taken at the time he was writing his book. There is no indication, then, that before his death Tocqueville ever clearly resolved the problem that had stymied him in 1836: how to work out a theory of the revolutionary dynamic. Yet in the last years of his life, unlike in 1836, he was able to chart the direction for further research. That is the real legacy of this great unfinished work.[26]

26. By way of a postcript: after I had written this essay, a new text (new at least to me) came to my attention. It is a letter from Tocqueville to Louis de Kergolay (16 May 1858), which seems to confirm the cogency of my analysis.

   Less than a year before his death, at the time when he was in the midst of his work on the second volume, that is, on the Revolution itself, Tocqueville spoke about his problems and the state of his research to his friend Kergolay. He complained about the enormous number of contemporary works to be read and then came to the interpretation itself: 'There is moreover in this disease of the French Revolution something very strange that I can sense, though I cannot describe it properly or analyse its causes. It is a *virus* of a new and unknown kind. There have been violent Revolutions in the world before; but the immoderate, violent, radical, desperate, bold, almost crazed and yet powerful and effective character of these Revolutionaries has no precedents, it seems to me, in the great social agitations of past centuries. Where did this new race come from? What produced it? What made it so effective? What perpetuates it? [F]or the same men are still with us, even though the circumstances are different now; and they have a progeny everywhere in the civilised world. I am exhausting my mind trying to conceive a clear notion of this object and seeking a way to depict it properly. Independently of all that can be explained about the French Revolution, there is something unexplained in its spirit and in its acts. I can sense the presence of this unknown object, but despite all my efforts I cannot lift the veil that covers it. I can palpate it as through a foreign body that prevents me from grasping it or even seeing it.' Tocqueville, *Oeuvres complètes*, XIII, *Correspondance Tocqueville–Louis de Kergolay*, ed. André Jardin and Jean-Alain Lesourd, vol. 2 (Paris: Gallimard, 1977), pp. 337–8.

3. *Augustin Cochin: the theory of Jacobinism*

Augustin Cochin is probably the most neglected historian of the French Revolution, yet he devoted his entire life to the subject.* Born in 1876 into the great family of conservative notables that lent such distinction to Social Catholicism in the nineteenth century, especially in the person of a grandfather whose first name he bore, Cochin graduated from the École des Chartes and then began, in 1903, to specialise in the French Revolution. Freed from professional obligations by his family fortune – in fact, he lived very frugally – he devoted his short life to two fundamentally important investigations. The first of these concerned the electoral campaign of 1789 for the Estates General, first in Burgundy and then in Brittany. The second, focusing on the period of the Terror, led him to assemble a collection of sources, the *Actes du gouvernement révolutionnaire (23 août 1793 – 27 juillet 1794)*, whose first volume, though completed in 1914, was published only in 1920. Meanwhile, in 1909, he had also intervened in Aulard's constant attacks on Taine's memory by publishing a brilliant historiographical essay entitled *La Crise de l'histoire révolutionnaire: Taine et M. Aulard.*

Augustin Cochin was drafted in 1914 and killed at the front in 1916. In 1925 his collaborator, Charles Charpentier, brought out the only book Cochin had completed, *L es Sociétés de Pensée et la Révolution en Bretagne.* In addition, his mother arranged for the publication of two volumes of essays, *L es Sociétés de Pensée et la Démocratie moderne* (1921) and *L a Révolution et la libre pensée* (1924). Some of these essays, such as the commentary on Aulard's attack on Taine, had been published before the war; others, such as the introduction to the *Actes du gouvernement révolutionnaire* (signed, in fact, by both Cochin and Charpentier), had appeared shortly after the

* I should like to express my gratitude here to Baron Denys Cochin, Augustin Cochin's nephew and trustee of the family archives, for the extreme kindness with which he gave me access to the papers left by his uncle and shared with me his precious personal recollections.

164

war. Most, however, were unpublished. Some are based on Cochin's research on the 1789 elections, notably an article on the electoral campaign in Burgundy; others are theoretical analyses of the phenomenon of revolution and what Cochin considered to be its principal manifestation, Jacobinism. This second category of texts was intended by Cochin to set out his conceptual interpretation of the Revolution with a minimum of specific historical references. Except for a few lectures, they were working papers designed to guide his empirical research.

For Cochin had one quality that is rarely found among modern historians in any circumstances, and altogether improbable in a historian of a traditionalist bent and moreover trained at the École des Chartes at the height of positivism: he had a philosophical cast of mind. To be more precise, he had learned the rules of scholarship without losing his taste for general ideas; indeed he continued to cultivate this taste, as is shown by his interest in Durkheim, surely his opposite in every sense, given Cochin's family background, his Catholic traditionalism and his hostility toward the republican régime. Yet Cochin always tried to blend history with sociology, since he recognised that sociology attempts to discover the general laws that govern individual patterns of behaviour. Cochin had conducted archival research in two areas, the electoral campaign of 1789 and the revolutionary government of 1793, but only the former topic was given a final synthetic form, in the book on Brittany and the article on Burgundy. As for the second topic, we have only, on the one hand, the edition of source materials and, on the other, the series of posthumous theoretical texts, which the author regarded simply as preliminary steps toward a history of Jacobinism. Although Cochin was both sociologist and historian, he temporarily had to separate the concepts and hypotheses of the two disciplines in order to carry out his empirical research; owing to the author's premature death they have remained separate in these writings.[1]

1. The following is a list in chronological order of Augustin Cochin's works:
   With Charles Charpentier: *La Campagne électorale 1789 en Bourgogne* (Paris: H. Champion, 1904) (reprinted in *Les Sociétés de Pensée et la Démocratie*, pp. 233–82).
   La Crise de l'histoire révolutionnaire: Taine et M. Aulard (Paris: H. Champion, 1909) (reprinted in *Les Sociétés de Pensée et la Démocratie*, pp. 43–140).
   'Comment furent élus les députés aux états généraux', *Société d'histoire contemporaine*, 22ᵉ Assemblée générale (1912), pp. 24–39 (reprinted in *Les Sociétés de Pensée et la Démocratie*, pp. 209–31).
   With Claude Cochin: *Le Grand Dessein du nonce Bargellini et de l'abbé Desisles contre les Réformés (1668)*, in *Annuaire-Bulletin de la Société d'histoire de France*, 1913 (Paris, 1913).
   'Quelques lettres de guerre', *Pages actuelles*, no. 105 (Paris: Bloud & Gay, 1917).
   Actes du gouvernement révolutionnaire (23 août 1793–27 juillet 1794). Recueil de documents publiés par la Société d'histoire contemporaine par MM. Augustin Cochin et Charles
   (*To continue next page.*)

That is one of the reasons for the rather chilly reception of Cochin's posthumous works on the part of professional historians. The *Revue historique* of January–April 1926, in which G. Pariset devoted a 'Bulletin historique' to the historiography of the Revolution, summarised *La Révolution et la libre pensée* in twenty-five lines and concluded: 'The thesis is presented in an abstract and somewhat disconcerting form. Had the author lived, he would undoubtedly have recast, condensed and clarified many pages before publishing them. At least one would like to think so, if only out of respect for his memory.'[2] In Aulard's journal, *La Revolution française* (January-December 1923), the high priest of the academic field, equally disconcerted by the book's obscurity, summarised it with the help of the editor's preface, from which he gathered that Cochin had revived *abbé* Barruel's old thesis that the Revolution came out of the Masonic Lodges. The fact that Louis XVI and his two brothers were freemasons makes one wonder about the cogency of this thesis. But the author's reasoning is not concerned with facts and never, or almost never, cites facts at all.[3] Nor did Aulard find the much more 'historical' work on the philosophical societies (*sociétés de pensée*) and the Revolution in Brittany any clearer when he wrote two years later, in 1925: 'It is a rather confused jumble of learned comments encased in a kind of system under abstract and strange headings. . . It makes such difficult reading that I have been unable to finish it; nor do I really understand what the author meant to do.'[4]

In the shop across the street, in the offices of the *Annales révolutionnaires*, later to become the *Annales historiques de la Révolution française*, the head of

---

(Foonote 1 contd.)

Charpentier. *Tome I* (23 août–3 décembre 1793) (Paris: Picard, 1920). (Foreword reprinted in *Les Sociétés de Pensée et la Démocratie*, pp. 141–208).

Les Sociétés de Pensée et la Démocratie. Études d'histoire révolutionnaire (Paris: Plon-Nourrit, 1921; reprint by Éditions Copernic, 1978, under original title; also reprinted, but with the omission of the essay 'Le Catholicisme de Rousseau', as *L'Esprit du jacobinisme: une interprétation sociologique de la Révolution française*, preface by Jean Baechler, P.U.F., 1979. References here are to the first edition.).

La Révolution et la libre pensée: la socialisation de la pensée (1750–1789); la socialisation de la personne (1789–1792): la socialisation des biens (1793–1794) (Paris: Plon-Nourrit, 1924; reprint by Éditions Copernic, 1979. References here are to the first edition.).

Les Sociétés de Pensée et la Révolution en Bretagne (1788–1789), vol. I, *Histoire analytique*, vol. II, *Synthèse et justification* (Paris: H. Champion, 1925).

Sur la politique économique du gouvernement révolutionnaire (Blois: J. de Grandpré, 1933).

Abstractions révolutionnaires et réalisme catholique (Bruges, Paris: Desclée de Brouwer, 1935); introduction by M. de Boüard.

With M. de Boüard: *Précis des principales opérations du gouvernement révolutionnaire* (Paris: H. Champion. 1936).

2. 'Bulletin historique. Révolution', *Revue historique* 151 (January–April 1926), 199–200.
3. *La Révolution française* 76 (January–December, 1923), 362–5.
4. *La Révolution française* 78 (January–December 1925), 283–4.

the Robespierrist school was no more indulgent toward *La Révolution et la libre pensée* than his old Dantonist rival, with whom at least he shared a positivist conception of history. A few years earlier, Mathiez had called attention to the useful publication of the *Actes du gouvernement révolutionnaire*,[5] but his reaction to the volume of theoretical essays was as severe and uncomprehending as Aulard's (even though, as we shall see, his short critique was somewhat less peremptory):

M. Cochin's book . . . lies outside history that moves in time and space. It is, one assumes, part of the new science that claims to absorb all others and calls itself Sociology. This sociology floats upon the clouds. Owing no doubt to insufficient training, I have never been able to see the value of these so-called 'explanations', which usually amount to no more than commonplaces of a disconcerting banality. I leave it to the initiates of this new science to appraise the value of this politico-philosophical chemistry.[6]

Strangely enough, the reviews in right-wing historical journals such as the *Revue d'histoire de l'Église de France*, or even the *Revue des questions historiques*, showed greater tolerance for Cochin's 'sociological' methods.[7] Their political sympathy with the author's opinions made them put up with his eccentricity. But of course the tone was given by Aulard and Mathiez, whose criticism expelled Cochin from the academic historiography of the French Revolution for a long time to come. In fact, their criticism was repeated as a matter of course by their successors, who are still administering the same cultural patrimony. The fact that the two great academic patrons of the Sorbonne were in agreement about Cochin is far more important than their theatrical duel over Danton and Robespierre. Their agreement is more than the expression of Jacobin opinions shocked by Cochin's counter-revolutionary position. It showed quite clearly that the tremendous resistance to conceptualisation of the sociological type had become an integral part of a field of historical study such as the French Revolution. Because it is overlaid with a set of political notions shared by its actors and its historians, this period continues to derive its meaning from the conflict of values in which its actors were involved. Revolutionary history in its conventional form, whether right-wing or left-wing, has only one task, and that is to bring back to life the

5. *Annales révolutionnaires*, journal of the *Société d'études robespierristes* 13 (1921), 514–16.
6. *Annales historiques de la Révolution française* (nouvelle série) 2 (1925), 179–80.
7. R. Lambelin, 'La Révolution et la libre pensée par Augustin Cochin', *Revue des questions historiques* (3ᵉ série) 6 (1925), 435–96; E. Lavaqueray, 'Augustin Cochin: la Révolution et la libre pensée', *Revue d'histoire de l'Église de France*, 12 (1926), 226–7; J. de La Monneraye, 'Les Sociétés de Pensée et la Révolution en Bretagne (1788–1789)', *Revue des questions historiques* (3ᵉ série) 11 (1927), 123–8; E. Lavaqueray, 'Augustin Cochin: les Sociétés de Pensée et la Révolution en Bretagne', *Revue d'histoire de l'Église de France*, 13 (1927): 228–31.

terms of the conflict, the men who embodied it, and the actions it produced. History may arrive at different and even opposite judgments about values, men and actions – and in this particular case Aulard and Mathiez, though both 'Jacobins', agreed about the values but disagreed about the men – but in practice it is based on the shared conviction that the narrative itself provides the evidence; such history does not admit of, and indeed detests, any distance between the conscious experience of human behaviour and its interpretation. What hampered Aulard's and Mathiez's understanding of Cochin's work was not his counter-revolutionary stance, with which in fact they had a long-standing familiarity; nor was it his historical scholarship, which they were competent to judge. It was the distance inherent in the conceptual approach, which went against their own belief in history as narrative.

The most egregious misconception of Cochin's work was advanced by Aulard, who saw it as a new version of the thesis that the Revolution was an outgrowth of the masonic plot. Since this misconception is still widely shared and is *a contrario* a means of understanding Cochin's basic hypothesis, it can serve as a starting point. The 'masonic plot' theory is part of right-wing historiographical tradition and dates back to the end of the eighteenth century. *Abbé* Barruel[8] had explained the Revolution by the joint conspiracy of the intellectuals (he said: the 'sophists') and the freemasons. Cochin, however, explicitly and repeatedly took exception to that part of the counter-revolutionary legacy. A historical interpretation in terms of plot, that is, in terms of conscious human endeavour, seemed altogether too superficial and commonplace to him, for he felt that the political psychology of the revolutionaries was totally inadequate to explain their language, their behaviour or even their rivalries:

Is it conceivable that the revolutionary party amounted to no more than a vast conspiracy in which each participant thought only of himself when he played the rôle of the virtuous and acted only for himself when he accepted an iron discipline? Personal interest does not have such perseverance or self-denial; and yet that is the explanation given by authors who hold extreme opinions, such as Father Barruel on the one hand and several historians of freemasonry on the other. Schemers and egoists have always existed; revolutionaries have been in existence only for the last one hundred and fifty years.[9]

It was in his 1909 essay on Aulard's attack on Taine that Cochin most clearly stated his rejection of all 'psychological' history based on the actors' conscious intentions. For while this essay was written to defend Taine against Aulard's criticisms (notably with respect to his scholarship

8. *Mémoires pour servir à l'histoire du jacobinisme*, 4 vols. (London, 1797–8).
9. *La Révolution et la libre pensée*, p. xxv.

and his knowledge of the sources), Cochin nonetheless did not go along with Taine's interpretation, which he saw as marked by a 'psychologism' that did not explain anything. If, as Taine claimed, the Jacobins were simply alloys of abstract virtue and unscrupulous practical ambition, then it is impossible to understand the power of their collective fanaticism, unless one attributes to them a 'Jacobin spirit', which is rather like attributing a 'soporific quality' to opium. Just as one cannot explain freemasonry by looking at the individual freemason, so one cannot account for the nature of Jacobinism, let alone for its birth, by looking at the individual Jacobin's psychology.

Yet this very problem was at the core of Cochin's investigation: he wanted to account for the origin and the development of Jacobinism. Like Taine, but also like Aulard and the republicans, Cochin approached the Revolution *as a single phenomenon.*

Indeed it is clear to anyone who bases his judgment on the texts rather than on sentiment that we are dealing with a single historical phenomenon between 1788 and 1795. One finds throughout the same principles, the same language, the same expedients. It will not do to see the 'patriotism' of 1789 as the voice of the people and that of 1793 as the great lie of scheming individuals. 'Quatre-vingt-neuvisme' [the cult of 1789] may be a wise position to take in politics, but it is indefensible in history, as M. Aulard, in agreement on this point with Taine, has very well understood.[10]

But if Taine had at least the merit of perceiving the strangeness of the Jacobin phenomenon – an indispensable first step in any scientific enquiry – Aulard actually participated in its celebration. Taine raised a problem he failed to resolve, or resolved inadequately; Aulard commemorated a myth, the Defence of the Republic. Aulard shared Taine's shortcoming, the psychological method and the explanation by the actors' intentions; but Aulard used the method for apologetic purposes, while for Taine it had a critical function. In the form of a posthumous plea, Aulard adopted the discourse of the protagonists of the event in his commentary on their own interpretation. This historiography, as old as the Revolution itself, subsumes the supposed psychology of its protagonists under that of an entity endowed, despite its abstract nature, with a subjective will. This entity, of course, is the people, struggling to overcome its enemies, who, though equally abstract, are nonetheless endowed with evil intentions and assumed to be capable of criminal activities: the aristocrats.

Cochin, who criticised Taine for reducing Jacobinism to a collection of individual psychological traits, felt that Aulard's republican historiography was a mere caricature of this naive explanation, packaged for

10. 'La crise de l'histoire révolutionnaire', in *Les Sociétés de Pensée et la Démocratie*, p. 131.

political consumption. He felt that the theory of the 'conspiracy', whether masonic, Jacobin or aristocratic, was but a primitive form of the interpretation by the actors' intentions and moreover borrowed from the contemporaries of the events. He considered the 'circumstances' theory to be of the same nature, though beneficial only to the republican brand of history, since it sees the Revolution, and notably the Terror, as an organised response to the plot and the aggression of the reactionary forces. Cochin realised that this dialectic between antagonistic intentions conformed to the way the revolutionary era had actually been experienced, as a period in which the universe had been so subjectivised that every event was identified as the outcome of wilful intentions, and that the global conflict was perceived as a battle between the good and the wicked, with the use of these terms depending on the political persuasion of the protagonists or their historians. The overlay of this psychological dimension on political events is an integral part of the revolutionary phenomenon as it appeared for the first time in France. It provides republican historians with rationalisations by which the 'situation' or the 'circumstances' (which in reality refer to the aggressiveness of the Revolution's adversaries) become not just external factors in the radicalisation of revolutionary behaviour, but also, at the very least, a set of attenuating circumstances for the Terror, if not its full and complete justification.

Cochin, on the contrary, felt that a true understanding of the Revolution had to start by a break with the type of explanation furnished by the protagonists of the events themselves.

Though unacquainted with Marx's work – I do not find a single reference to it in his books – Cochin at least shared Marx's conviction that men who make history do not know the history they are making and simply rationalise their rôle through mental representations that the historian must, precisely, subject to critical evaluation. In short, Cochin distinguished between actual experience and critical analysis of it, an all the more fundamental distinction as the revolutionary experience is characterised by a much more abundant output of representations and ideologies than are 'normal' periods of history. In fact, that distinction divides the historiography of the Revolution into two separate camps, not between the Right and the Left, as lazy thinkers on both sides are wont to assume, but between a critical history that relies on conceptual analysis rather than on subjective experience and is exemplified by Tocqueville, and a descriptive history that is based on the protagonists' mental representations and may therefore be right-wing or left-wing, aristocratic or Jacobin, liberal or leftist. The most brilliant of the second kind of practitioner of history is still Michelet, who, as Cochin said, had 'a sense of the Jacobin spirit that comes close to divination.'[11]

Descriptive history may, for example, insist on the importance of one of the ideological obsessions of the period: the plot (royalist or republican), the idea of the advent of a totally new era, the casting of the political conflict in moral terms (the conspiracy of the wicked), or the appeal to the notion of public safety. In each instance the illusion consists of using those notions as explanatory factors, whereas they are precisely *what must be explained*. For instance, with respect to the notion of public safety, of which Aulard made such great use, Cochin advanced the following critical theory: '"Public safety" is the requisite fiction for a democracy, just as "divine right" is in an authoritarian régime.'[12] He did not regard it as an objective situation or even strictly speaking a policy, but as a system of legitimation for democratic power, and so the instrument and central feature of the new consensus.

What makes Cochin's work extraordinary, if not unique, is the harmony between the topic of his research on the Revolution and the theoretical nature of his thinking. Cochin was not interested in the problem raised by Tocqueville, that of the long-term *consequences* of the Revolution; nor did he approach the Revolution as part of the institutional, social and administrative continuity between the old régime and the new. On the contrary, what he wanted to understand was the explosive character of the event, the rending of the historical fabric, and all the factors which, for six or seven years, came together like an irresistible current to carry the revolutionary movement forward: in short, its internal dynamic, or what the eighteenth century would have called the 'mainspring' of the Revolution. It is therefore no coincidence that he spent his life as an archivist selecting and publishing, just like Aulard, documents relating to the Committee of Public Safety and Jacobinism. For he was interested in the same problem as Aulard or Mathiez; he too felt that Jacobinism was the central phenomenon of the Revolution; but, unlike them, he tried to conceptualise the nature of the phenomenon instead of seeing it simply as the matrix of the 'defence of the Republic'.

He detested Jacobinism yet tried to comprehend it. I do not believe that there is a clear connection between these two premises, for neither a distant nor a sympathetic attitude toward a historical event or phenomenon is in itself a sufficiently powerful incentive for working out an explanation. Hatred of or admiration for Jacobinism can lead no further

11. *Ibid.* p. 91.
12. *Ibid.* p. 70.

than to condemnation or unqualified praise of the Jacobins or their leaders. Cochin tried to find out what made them possible. In doing so, he carried his analysis to the very core of the Revolution's most mysterious feature, its political and cultural dynamic. In order to understand it, Cochin, unlike Tocqueville, had no need to deny it as an event and to bracket it, as it were, between its origins and its outcome. His undertaking was unique because it combined the historian's fieldwork, indeed the archivist's knowledge of Revolutionary sources, with an attempt to conceptualise the most fundamental yet most elusive aspect of the Revolution: its impetuousness.

Augustin Cochin's family patrimony also included sociology. His grandfather had collaborated in Le Play's famous surveys.[13] Like Le Play, the intellectual and Catholic upper bourgeoisie so brilliantly exemplified in the nineteenth century by the Cochin family was obsessed with the 'social problem', a term that designated both pauperism and the decline of traditional – notably Christian – values in the working-class. This bourgeoisie opposed socialist solutions by working for a counter-evangelisation designed to restore the virtues of bygone communities. It shared with Le Play not only the ambition to restore moral values, but also the concept of a social milieu responsible for certain outwardly individual characteristics.

Cochin himself had read and reflected on Durkheim. He naturally rejected Durkheim's prophetic vision of science as the solution to all problems, since he remained faithful to the Catholic tradition. Nonetheless, one of his highest scientific ambitions was to wrest the social dimension from the realm of psychology in order to establish it, at last, as a field of knowledge in its own right. Durkheim was ultimately concerned with the same problem that Cochin had raised in connection with Taine: the relation between the individual and society. Durkheim's hypothesis, indeed his conviction, was that a society is not defined by the sum of the individuals who compose it and that society, because it is of an altogether different nature, cannot be reduced to the sum of its parts. He was convinced that it was this different nature, the subject matter of sociology, that determines individual behaviour. The fact that Durkheim had re-established the primacy of social factors over psychological motivation provided Cochin with his starting point:

M. Durkheim mentions neither Taine nor Jacobinism. Yet his critique seems made to order for them, for Taine as a historian is the outstanding practitioner of

13. He even wrote two précis on the subject: *Les Ouvriers européens, résumé de la méthode et des observations de M. F. Le Play* (Paris, 1856); *La Réforme sociale en France, résumé critique de l'ouvrage de M. Le Play* (Paris, 1865).

the psychological method, while the Jacobin problem is the very model of a social problem. The tool is not suited to the task at hand – that is the reason for the book's inadequacies ... The psychological school, M. Durkheim tells us, attaches too much importance to *intentions*, and not enough to situations, when it seeks to explain social facts. It only sees the calm behaviour of human beings whereas a more powerful cause is at work in the slow and deep-reaching evolution of institutions and human relations.[14]

Thus Cochin did not see Jacobinism as a plot, nor as the political response to a contingency, nor even as an ideology. For him it was a particular *type of society*, whose constraints and rules the historian must discover in order to understand it without relying on the intentions and the discourses of its protagonists. In the historiography of his time, indeed in the historiography of the French Revolution as a whole, his approach to the problem of Jacobinism is so original that it has been either not understood or buried, or both. For in the nineteenth century, and until fairly recently, history ceased to be what to some extent it still was in the eighteenth century, namely, the interpretation of a given society in its different 'states'. Precisely since the French Revolution, history had been totally preoccupied with drawing up inventories of the proprietary claims each society could make on its own history, in other words, with exploring the fabric of national consensus. It thus addressed only the question: what is the nation? without ever turning to the equally important question: what is a society? Yet Augustin Cochin did ask the second question, and deserves all the more credit for doing so as the period and the political structure about which he asked the question were so overwhelmingly concerned with defining 'the nation'. It could be objected that the conservative tradition of his milieu and his own counter-revolutionary bent may have made the conceptual shift easier for him; but then he had precisely to forget his background in order to read Durkheim. In his time the right-wing historiography of the Revolution was, like the left-wing one, a historiography of the nation.[15] So far as I can see, Cochin was the only author to tackle the problem from the other end.

His main argument, therefore, was this: Jacobinism was the fully developed form of a type of political and social organisation that had become widespread in France in the second half of the eighteenth century and that he called the 'philosophical society'. Literary circles and societies, masonic lodges, academies, and patriotic and cultural clubs were different manifestations of this phenomenon. Just what was a philosophical

---

14. *La Crise de l'histoire révolutionnaire*, p. 58. A. Cochin had obviously thought at length about Durkheim's *Les Règles de la méthode sociologique*, published in 1895.
15. Witness, for example, A. Sorel's or A. Vandal's work on the one hand, and Aulard's or Mathiez's on the other.

society? It was a form of social life based on the principle that its members, in order to participate in it, must divest themselves of all concrete distinctions and of their real social existence. It was the opposite of what the Ancien Régime called a corporate entity (*corps*), defined by a community of occupational and social interests. Membership in a philosophical society was strictly a matter of ideas, and in that sense these societies were a prefiguration of the functioning of democracy. For democracy too makes for equality among individuals, since they are all members of society by virtue of one abstract right, their citizenship, which by definition endows each individual with his share of popular sovereignty. Cochin therefore does not view democracy, as Tocqueville had done, as a movement toward true economic and social equality, but rather as a political system based on abstract equality among individuals. Jacobinism was the French variant of this system, as it traced its origins and its political model not to a political entity proper, such as the English Parliament, but to literary and philosophical societies.

For the purpose of the philosophical society was not to act, to delegate or to 'represent': it was to deliberate and to cull from its members and from discussion a common opinion, a *consensus* to be subsequently expressed, propounded and championed. A philosophical society had no authority to delegate nor any representatives to elect on the basis of shared ideas or as a voting block; it served as a tool designed to produce unanimous opinion, regardless of the content of that unanimity – whether it be that of the Compagnie du Saint Sacrement in the seventeenth century or that of the Grand Orient a hundred years later. The novel feature in the second half of the eighteenth century was that the consensus of the philosophical societies, commonly referred to as 'enlightened philosophy', tended to permeate the fabric of society as a whole.

Cochin never dealt with the causes of the shift, which he considered to be under way by 1750. Taking it as a kind of self-evident truth, he sought to remove it from the pure history of ideas in order to reconstruct its institutional and social itinerary. In fact, the working of the mechanism he analysed presupposes the breaking up of society into individuals, the end of what Louis Dumont has called 'holistic society',[16] and the decline of corporate solidarity and traditional authority. The search for, and the production of, a democratic consensus by the philosophical societies filled a need whose origins Cochin never discusses, although it is essential for understanding political society in eighteenth-century France.

16. Louis Dumont, *Homo hierarchicus, essai sur le système des castes* (Paris: Gallimard, 1967); cf. also his *Homo aequalis* (Paris: Gallimard, 1976).

But at least he showed in all his writings that in the eighteenth century the philosophical society of the 'enlightened' type was the matrix of a new network of political relations that was to be the main characteristic and the outstanding innovation of the French Revolution. In the consensus of the lodges, the circles and the 'musées' [cultural associations], one can already see the outlines of Rousseau's general will, the imprescriptible part of the citizen that cannot be reduced to his particular interests, 'the pure act of understanding that, undisturbed by passions, reasons about what man can demand from his fellow man and about what his fellow man has a right to expect from him.'[17] The philosophical society was thus the first example of collective constraint, and arose from the encounter between a sociological mechanism and a philosophy of the individual. The sum total of individual wills produced the tyranny of society, which was to become the religion of the French Revolution and of the nineteenth century.

The centre-piece of Cochin's analysis was the opposition between two notions of society and of its political action. The first can be called, for lack of a better term, the 'corporative' or Ancien-Régime notion, which entitles power to call upon a nation composed of '*corps*' to express its opinion. The second is the 'democratic' notion, which Cochin sometimes also calls the 'English' notion, and which entitles power to seek advice from a people of voters consisting of the entire society atomised into equal individuals. In the first type, society preserves its actual state, its hierarchies, its long-standing decisions and rights, its network of leadership and the diversity of its values; it does not modify its structures in order to become a political entity or an interlocutor of power, but keeps the form it has acquired through its interests, its values and its history. It therefore has no need to create a professional 'political' personnel, since politics is merely an extension of its activity as a society. Moreover it has its natural leaders, whose mandates are binding.

In the second type, society must revamp itself to accede to politics; it must become an abstract society made up of equal individuals, in other words, a people of voters. In such a society, power addresses itself to each individual, regardless of his milieu, his activities and his values, since only by his vote does this abstract individual become a real, individual. Hence the need to invent a field for this new reality, politics, with its specialists, the politicians, who will act as mediators. For once the people has been reduced to its democratic definition as the sum of equal individuals, it is

17. This famous phrase from the *Social Contract* is quoted by Cochin in his article 'Le Catholicisme de Rousseau', in *Les Sociétés de Pensée et la Démocratie*, pp. 25–42.

no longer capable of autonomous activity. On the one hand, it has been stripped of its real ties to the social world, and so it no longer has either particular interests or the competence to debate the issues; on the other hand, the act that constitutes it, the vote, is prepared and determined elsewhere, so that the people is only asked to express consent. 'Professional politicians must propose catch-phrases and leaders to the people.'[18] Politics is thus presented as a corollary of democracy and as a special characteristic of consensus at the stage when it has been mythically freed from social constraints. It therefore demands substitutes for the 'natural' conduct of public affairs by organised bodies, a rôle that will be played by politicians, parties and ideologies.

But democratic politics does not necessarily have to rely on terrorism. Popular sovereignty, in its parliamentary version, will be periodically delegated according to rules laid down by the constitution; it will be mediated by independent men, so allowing for genuine debate. The philosophical societies, however, set up a model for pure, not representative, democracy, in which the collective will always lays down the law. The same principle is applied in the expanded Jacobin version of the model, which extends not just to the original Republic of intellectuals, but to the entire nation: since self-government by the people, the only means to achieve the great revolutionary ambition of a total identification [*transparence*][19] between society and power, is technically impossible, a substitute is provided in the form of permanent debating societies, supposed microcosms and mandatory spokesmen of society as a whole. The philosophical society naturally offered itself as a precedent and a model.

The philosophical society thus involved not just any kind of democratic practice; it was 'pure' democracy, almost the outer limit of democracy. It was the infallible self-expression of the community, achieved through each of its members' exclusive concern with ideas, that is, through the social production of truth (as opposed to the apprehension of truth by individual thought). The philosophical society, being the locus of the general will, was thereby the enunciator of truth. For Cochin, the victory of the *philosophes* – or of what he also calls 'free thinking' – is not exclusively in the province of the so-called history of ideas, which is merely the genealogical chart of authors and works; it belongs on the contrary to the sociological study of the development and spread of ideologies. That victory was the result of the collective endeavour of the

18. *Les Sociétés de Pensée et la Démocratie*, p. 213.
19. M. Richir, 'Révolution et transparence sociale', preface to J. G. Fichte, *Considérations destinées à rectifier les jugements du public sur la Révolution française* (Paris: Payot, 1974).

philosophical societies. Individualism, characterised by each person's 'free' relationship to ideas, amounted to an abstract equality that negated the conditions of real society; by putting together in a new shape the scattered fragments of society, individualism produced a new consensus founded on the constant reaffirmation of Society as the highest good: its ultimate form was pure democracy, with no leaders and no delegates.

The cult of Society is indeed the natural product of democracy, a substitute value for the transcendency of the divine. To this substitutive divinity, Cochin applies, probably without knowing it, a variant of Feuerbach's critique of religion when he claims that the real individual becomes alienated in and through democracy, just as Feuerbach had claimed that the individual is alienated in and through religion. Democracy, Cochin feels, imprisons modern man in the ideological illusion that Society is everything, an illusion that also motivates his political commitment. A philosophical and theoretical critique thus leads Cochin to perceive one aspect of the fiction of democracy.

His theoretical critique is inseparable from a practical critique of the procedures of democratic action. For if democracy, defined in the abstract as political endeavour, is indeed characterised by an egalitarian relation of all members of society to ideas, then the concrete action it has to take and the concomitant obligation to establish power or a set of powers are incompatible with the system's ideal egalitarianism. Even when the result is a representative system, duly elected after a public contest that has offered choices to the citizenry, the preliminary organisation of the contest is nevertheless handled by professional politicians who specialise in manipulating 'opinion'. Here Cochin's argument falls in line with a current of thought exemplified by such contemporaries as Michels or Ostrogorski.[20] But Cochin's interest went beyond the problem of representative democracy, since he was studying 'pure' democracy, which does not delegate authority and power and is subject at all times to direct citizen control. He believed that this system was the very essence of Jacobinism. In this type of régime, which mythically depends on the daily approval of the community, symbolically represented by the Jacobin society, the rule of equality can be broken only in the most covert manner, and the transgression will be all the more reprehensible for being clandestine.

The key to the secret of Jacobinism is the 'machine' hidden in the shadow of the 'People'. Cochin therefore studied the laws and mechanisms

---

20. R. Michels, *Les Partis politiques. Essai sur les tendances oligarchiques des démocraties*, trans. from the German (Paris, Flammarion, 1971); M. J. Ostrogorski, *La Démocratie et l'organisation des partis politiques*, 2 vols. (Paris, 1903).

by which the societies of equals developed a fictitious image of historical reality and then proceeded to 'activate' it, so to speak, by means of small militant groups who were professionally qualified to deal with this surrealist entity. For the price exacted by the fiction of pure democracy, the reverse side of ideology, was the existence of an all-powerful machine, the 'inner circle' of a society or an organisation that prefabricated consensus and had exclusive control over it. It was an anonymous oligarchy, a company of obscure, mediocre, expendable and interchangeable men. Brissot, Danton and Robespierre were not so much the leaders as the products of Jacobinism.

They were merely the temporary instruments of the different historical phases through which the machine ensured its ascendancy, and they had no freedom to influence the direction it would take. The successive purges, a characteristic feature of this period, must therefore not be interpreted as the classic episodes of a power struggle; they are instead an objective mechanism, a law regulating the machine and allowing it to produce the spokesmen it needed as it extended its influence and assumed more radical control over all society. The 'string pullers' were only clogs in the machinery: the manipulators were manipulated and imprisoned in the logic of the system.

This logic, moreover, was all the more compelling as the philosophical society, by definition, did not think: it spoke. The 'socialised truth' that emerged from the peculiar chemistry of the assemblies was not thought but consensus, a set of notions crystallised into a few simple verbal figures designed to unify and mobilise individual minds and wills. In short, it was what we would call ideology. That is in fact why dominance in a 'society' or in the 1793 committees called for a type of talent that was neither put to use nor recognised in society at large: Robespierre was not a minister; his function was one of 'surveillance'. He watched over the consensus, sniffing out the slightest deviance. But then ideology is not a matter of thinking, at least not in the sense that thinking might make it susceptible to criticism; it spoke, or rather expressed itself, through its spokesmen and above all through the machine. So the Revolution was not so much an action as a language, and it was in relation to this language, the locus of the consensus, that the ideological machine established differences among men. Ideology spoke through the Jacobin leaders much more than they spoke through it. In a subtle way, Cochin showed a very modern understanding of the constraints of language, and of how political discourse turns the political speaker into a mere mouthpiece for the ideology he is conveying. But far from seeing this situation as a natural propensity of the human mind, he attributed it to a pathological state of cognition in which ideology takes precedence over thought and 'socialised truth' over the genuine search for truth.

If the theory of manipulation by the 'machine' (we would now call it the 'apparatus') is the one aspect of Cochin's analyses that has been retained by hasty or superficial readers, it is because they can reinterpret it, albeit mistakenly, in the voluntarist terms of 'plot'. In fact, it is just the second conceptual element of what Cochin called the 'sociology of the democratic phenomenon', which must lead to the core of the French Revolution. The first element, without which the second cannot be understood, is the theory that the consensus was produced by a discussion among equals that did not concern real situations but was exclusively devoted to the relationship of individuals with a set of stated goals. Once obtained, the consensus became a 'socialised' truth that derived its legitimacy from its democratic character. Its mission was to permeate all of society and to act as the unifying principle replacing the traditional division into '*corps*', i.e. interest groups. The consensus could then take over the spheres of power, and so the State. At this culminating point of its development, the philosophical society became a political party that claimed to embody both society and the State, which were now identical. Yet concrete action – first the transfer of the consensus from the philosophical societies to society as a whole and then the takeover of the State by that consensus – was needed to make the two-fold mythological 'leap' through which the régime of 'pure democracy' could be established. Such action could be taken only by militant minorities in whom the new legitimacy was vested.

In short, pure democracy achieved the breakthrough from intellectual power to political power through the mediation of the philosophical societies and their unofficial representatives (since formal delegation of power was contradictory to the nature of the system). That breakthrough, for Cochin, constituted the French Revolution.

The process began around 1750, when democracy as a social and political phenomenon (characterised by the disintegration of the old society under the pressure of individualism and the rise of a new legitimacy based on equality, which was making inroads on established authority) first took shape in the philosophical societies. France was then experiencing for the first time the conflict between two types of political society. The first was traditional society, broken up into interest groups and founded on inequality (both as a social reality and as a collective mental representation); the second was the new and ideally egalitarian society of what Cochin calls 'social opinion', founded on the fictitious consensus of the philosophical societies, the laboratories where new values were being produced: 'Which of these two opinions, the social or the real one, would be recognised as sovereign, declared to be the People and the Nation? This question, which was raised as early as 1789, was decisively settled in the autumn of 1793.'[21]

Once it was officially proclaimed in the autumn of 1793, the dictatorship of public safety became the truth of the Revolution. It marked, to use Cochin's vocabulary, the triumph of 'social opinion', henceforth the sole representative of society, which was rechristened the 'People'. The triumph was achieved by the dictatorship of the societies, which formed the core of Jacobinism. Although their unconditional victory made revolutionary government possible, it came up against the reality of power and of the State: revolutionary government was not a matter of reigning in the Republic of Letters or even in society, but of ruling *over* society. Here pure democracy came face to face with its own impracticability, arising from the fact that society and the State cannot be treated as one and the same thing. As Marx realised, 9 Thermidor marked the comeback of society.[22]

Cochin's revolutionary chronology thus includes a first period of gestation from 1750 to 1788, during which 'social opinion' was developed and propagated among the intellectuals and within the societies and the lodges, without yet exercising power over persons and things. Then, from 1788, the Revolution was the period in which the consensus of the intellectuals encountered the reality of power through the mediation of the revolutionary societies, which reproduced and expanded the mechanisms of the philosophical societies. In 1793, for a few months, that process reached its culmination when Jacobinism, under the fictitious guise of the 'People', took the place of both civil society and the State. Through the general will, the people-as-king achieved a mythical identity with power; this belief is the matrix of totalitarianism.

Cochin is restating here, in new terms, a classical conservative theory concerning the origins of the Revolution (a theory he also applies to the revolutionary process itself), namely, that the intellectuals of the eighteenth century prepared and provoked the Revolution. He does not simply say that the ideas of the *philosophes*, once they had penetrated the nation as a whole, led to 1789 or 1793; for he realised that the problem was precisely how to explain that penetration and the seizure of social

21. *Les Sociétés de Pensée et la Démocratie*, pp. 148–9.
22. Marx, *La Sainte Famille* [The Holy Family], pp. 148–9.

power. Nor did he adopt Tocqueville's infinitely more subtle thesis (which, curiously, he never discussed),[23] according to which the rôle played by the intellectuals in eighteenth century society devolved upon them *by default*, since in Tocqueville's view society, in its futile search for trustees, followed the lead of the intellectuals only because it lacked independent and qualified representatives. Cochin differed from Tocqueville because he believed the old society still had its natural trustees in the established *corps* – from guilds (*corporations*) to social orders – and because he overestimated the prestige of these traditional spokesmen, whereas Tocqueville stressed their decline. But his most original contribution in comparison with Tocqueville is his analysis of the way in which the philosophical societies produced the new political legitimacy; the *philosophes* did not invent it 'by default' but in conformity with their social practices. They were not substitutes for politicians; they were the essence of democratic politics itself, in its pure abstract form.

The difference between Tocqueville and Cochin is that Tocqueville, despite his natural distaste for democracy (which may also be related to his family background, but the result would be the same), accepted it as an inevitable development that had to be made compatible with liberty, while Cochin, more traditionalist and, so to speak, more 'reactionary', viewed it as the artificial creation of a milieu that gradually established, through the interplay of the internal laws that governed it, a political machine and tradition. Both authors related the concept of democracy to individualism as well as to equality. But Tocqueville was mainly interested in democracy as a state of society produced by a long historical evolution dominated by the development of the absolute State and of administrative centralisation. As the climax of this process, the Revolution in turn accelerated it by destroying the nobility and creating the modern administrative State.

Cochin, on the other hand, never dealt with the causes or rather the origins of the explosion of egalitarian ideas he observed in mid eighteenth-century France. He was not interested in pinpointing the rôle of the French Revolution in the long-term evolution of French society, but in understanding its tremendous political dynamic between 1788 and 1794. He wanted to explain the break rather than the continuity, the event rather than its outcome. That is why he concentrated his attention on the areas in which the break in national continuity was most clearly visible: politics and ideology. The Revolution, for him, was the transition from a

23. In all of Cochin's writings there is only one allusion to Tocqueville, and it concerns a minor point: see *La Révolution et la libre pensée*, p. 131.

'traditional' royalty (in a nearly Weberian sense) to the dictatorship of the Jacobin committees. Cochin wanted to elucidate the mechanism of the break, the rise and proliferation of this new political entity within the space of a few decades, indeed of a couple of years, as democracy became the new system that gave power its legitimacy. Cochin's entire work is ultimately related to two objectives that seem strangely modern for a man so deeply attached to tradition: a sociology of the production and rôle of democratic ideology, and a sociology of political manipulation and machines.

It is therefore not surprising that his strictly historical work – the part of it that he was able to finish, as opposed to what he intended to do – focused on 1789 and 1793: in 1789, the great political battle fought by the philosophical societies over the calling of the Estates General; in 1793, Jacobin dictatorship, the final avatar of pure democracy. Cochin's historical contribution proper is particularly important for the period 1788–9, since his two thorough studies of the elections of 1789 in Brittany and Burgundy were completed before the First World War, whereas his great work on the *Actes du gouvernement révolutionnaire* was interrupted by his death.

The 1789 elections provided the theatre for a confrontation, not between two camps but between two principles and sets of choices: Liberties in the French sense or liberty in the English sense? The traditional consultation of the 'estates' or the democratic vote of the electors? The corporate bodies of the old society or the new party discipline? Dominance of the notables or dominance of the politicians?

Necker, however, did not choose between the two principles. The key text of 24 January 1789, which states the rules of the electoral procedure and was inspired if not actually written by him, mixes the principles without perceiving their contradictory logic, and so institutionalises incoherence. On the one hand, it calls for an electoral body of the English type, based on the principle of one man/one vote, that would cast votes and select delegates in a virtually uniform manner and thus become emancipated from its habitual social leadership. In short, it called for a democratic consultation by vote, whose procedures were also applied to the nobility, even though that order, along with the clergy, was isolated from the rest of the nation. That contradiction was fraught with murderous consequences, yet it was minor in comparison with the other contradiction, which spelled the complete breakdown of the regulation. For Necker treated the newly formed community of voters as if he were dealing with the corporate bodies and traditional notables of the old society, for centuries the interlocutors of royal power. It never occurred to him that the new sovereignty delegated by millions of voters might be governed by different rules than the traditional and limited consultation of the corporate bodies. Consequently, no arrangements were made to organise the conflict between men and ideas that was bound to ensue from universal suffrage: there was to be no political pluralism, no campaigning and no competition among candidates and programmes. These novel assemblies, ostensibly meeting to ascertain the collective will under majority rule, were supposed to function as if they had been called upon to express the unanimous wishes of the old communities or craft guilds. They were to vote, which means that they were expected to express different opinions; yet they were also expected to draw up *Cahiers*, and so express a single opinion. They were to choose deputies, but there were no candidates. They were already electorates, yet they were assumed to vote with a single voice.

The text of 24 January is marked throughout by that ambiguity. The procedures for convening the assemblies and the voting rules so disrupted corporative society that such vestiges of it as were maintained became preposterous and therefore intolerable. But it was not that aspect – one might call it the 'Tocqueville effect' – that interested Augustin Cochin. What struck him most in the incoherence of the royal regulation was the fact that it opened the door to the manipulation of the assemblies by anonymous groups. Since there were no fixed rules for the competition among men and ideas, and since that competition was both implied and denied, the regulation 'did not set the voters free but placed them in a void'.[24] Yet the void was filled, the *Cahiers* were drawn up and the deputies were elected without major difficulties, all within a month. 'The reason is that alongside the real people, which was unable to respond, there was another, which spoke and acted in its name: the membership of the philosophical societies, which, though small in numbers, was united in a common purpose and present everywhere.'[25]

Cochin then points out that since new electoral alignments broke the traditional networks within communities, and since there was no public debate and controversy to circulate information, only the philosophical societies were in a position to provide the voters with ideas and with the kind of leadership that would hold them together. The two offerings were closely related, for ideology was the only principle on which to base the selection of the 'pure', that is, the members of a philosophical society or a

24. *Les Sociétés de Pensée et la Démocratie*, p. 217.
25. *Ibid.*

manipulating group. It thus functioned as a substitute for collective experience and for non-existent public competition, causing the assemblies to coalesce around a set of values that integrated only by means of exclusion. In order to ensure the election of the 'good' it was necessary to detect the 'wicked' in the light of accepted principles; and that is why from the very beginning of the Revolution the struggles for power were characterised by ideological exclusion. The nobility was the first victim of this exclusion, as early as September 1788; excluded also were all those members of the Third Estate who were in any way connected with it: ennobled commoners (*anoblis*), seigneurial dues collectors (*fermiers*) and all the agents of what was now becoming the Ancien Régime. For exclusion, by virtue of its very principle, proceeds by anonymous and abstract classes of individuals.

Thus, since the 'nation' did not speak, someone had to speak for it. The old corporate bodies and communities had had their day; moreover they were unable to wield the new language and to adjust to the new image of Society. The patriotic party, by contrast, was well adjusted to both; not so much the party as a whole as the small urban groups that formed its backbone and, through a mechanism of exclusion and purges inseparable from 'pure democracy', soon appropriated the function of representing society. Their aim was to reconstruct the old kingdom along the lines of their own party: as one mythical entity, united under the ideological and political guidance of the committees. The year 1793 was already contained in 1789.

In Burgundy, for example, in the autumn of 1788, political activity was exclusively engineered by a small group of men in Dijon, who drafted the patriotic platform calling for the doubling of the Third Estate, voting by head and the exclusion of *anoblis* and seigneurial agents from the assemblies of the Third Estate. The next stage was the systematic takeover of the corporate bodies: first the *avocats*' corporation, where the group's cronies were most numerous, then all the lower echelons of the magistrature (*robe*), the physicians, the trade-guilds and finally the town hall, won over thanks to one of the aldermen and under pressure from a group of 'zealous citizens'. In the end, the party platform appeared as the freely expressed will of the Third Estate of Dijon. Promoted by the usurped authority of the Dijon town council, it then reached the other towns of the province, where the same scenario was acted out as the aldermen yielded to the pressure of *avocats* and *robe* magistrates. *Intendant* Amelot, a protegé of Necker and foe of the *Parlement*, watched complacently as events unfolded.

Opposition arose in early December, not from the nobility as a whole or from the existing representative authorities (even though the Estates of Burgundy did have a standing committee), but from a group of nineteen noblemen, which later grew to fifty. Setting out to combat the first group, these nobles refused the doubling of the Third Estate and advocated voting by order, yet they patterned their procedures on those of the rival group. The reason is that the second group, recruited primarily among *robe* magistrates (and supported by the *Parlement*) constituted the noble faction of the philosophical and *parlement* party. These men were therefore well aware and capable of practising the manipulatory techniques of the *avocats*, having long been on their side. But since they could not go along with the party's ever-escalating egalitarianism, they soon – by mid-December – became the issue in a first split within the philosophical party, a split that benefited the *avocats* and the Third Estate.[26]

Cochin's analysis is significant in two respects. First, it reveals how, by the end of the eighteenth century, established institutions in France had been dispossessed by the new networks of power that civil society had set up beyond the reach of the State. This dispossession preceded the regulation of 24 January 1789, which ratified rather than provoked it (although the process was thereby certainly accelerated). It indicates that there had been a revolution before the Revolution, a transfer in the networks and the means of power toward the forces of social initiative and in the name of new principles. But these networks, means and principles were established by the entire society for its own purposes; they were not yet a way to ensure the advancement of the bourgeoisie, the aristocracy or any other social class. Democratic legitimacy and democratic ideology first developed within the framework of a dialectic between society and the State, in which there was room for the cultivated and dominant society as a whole. The philosophical party had its nobles, its aristocrats and its bourgeois. The break that occurred in the autumn of 1788 was not a parting of the ways between supporters of the old régime and adherents to the new one, but a split between two equally non-representative groups (in terms of the old legitimacy), both of them engaged in the hidden manipulation of the traditional corporate bodies and both submitting in advance to arbitration by democratic legitimacy, which was the common principle of their existence. It was the first of the revolutionary purges, carried out, like those that were to follow, in the name of equality and directed against the nobility as the incarnation of inequality. The egali-

26. This account summarises Cochin and Charpentier's study *La Campagne électorale de 1789 en Bourgogne*.

tarian democracy of the philosophical societies had become a policy principle.

Cochin presents an even more detailed though not always clearer analysis of the pre-revolution in Brittany, from the revolt of the 'Bastion' [the noble Establishment] to the ensuing insurgency of the students and the *avocats* of the Third Estate. Here again, the decisive turn occurred in September–October 1788, somewhat earlier than in Burgundy: the revolutionary movement took a step forward by purging itself, thereby providing the first illustration of a mechanism that was to operate until 1794 and successively liquidated every leadership group of the Revolution, from the *monarchiens* to the 'Triumvirate' (Barnave, Duport and Lameth), the Feuillants, the Girondins, the Dantonists and the Hébertistes. In the summer of 1788 the group to be liquidated was the party of the nobility and the *Parlement*, which, although it had given the signal of revolt against the established power, was excluded by the patriots in the course of the debate about voting by order or by head.

In the case-study of Brittany, Cochin once again analyses the mechanism of the purge, which was consubstantial with 'pure democracy'.[27] In Brittany the process began with the rise of the 'societies' in the 1760s: the Society of Agriculture was given letters patent by the king after it had been established upon deliberation by the Estates (1757–62); above all, Brittany had a patriotic society, whose founding, though not so clearly documented, was related to the *parlements'* battle against 'ministerial despotism'. In Cochin's view, these organisations were characterised by two features. First, they were held together by the tenets of 'enlightened philosophy', and their adherence to a certain number of ideas that had no relation to their real social practices, so that they became microcosms of a different society, based not on special interests but on an ideological sense of community. Secondly, they propagated their ideas throughout the province through their affiliated chapters, thus producing, by means of opinion, an influence and a manipulating force that progressively came to take the place of established power and of the administration itself. Infused with new vigour by a collective movement of opinion (which Cochin simply records), the old academic form of the learned society gave birth to embryonic forms of democratic power in response to a civil society's search for autonomous expression.

What was the nature of that power or, until 1788, that counter-power? In Cochin's eyes, 'philosophical' opinion was characterised by the fact that it created, in the name of values and principles that were bound to

27. *Les Sociétés de Pensée et la Révolution en Bretagne (1788–1789).*

destroy the old society, an organisation and a form of pressure. Like all power, this pressure could not be completely public, even at this early stage, particularly since it did not acknowledge its rôle in society. That is why it had its hidden strength, its inner circles and, above all, its secret associations, such as freemasonry. The typical and inevitable expression of a power that refuses to abide by its constraints, freemasonry served to weave networks of solidarity and hierarchical discipline by recruiting its members on the basis of opinion alone. Freemasonry was a very important part of Augustin Cochin's historical and conceptual world; not, as Barruel believed, because it was the tool of a conspiracy against the Ancien Régime, but because it was an exemplary embodiment of the chemistry of the new power, which transformed a social phenomenon into politics and opinion into action. In this sense, it embodied the origin of Jacobinism.

Originating in freemasonry, an attitude that Cochin calls '*esprit de société*' came to replace the *esprit de corps* in the old kingdom. The new spirit invaded the nobility, the *parlements*, the masters' guilds, the corporations and all of the representative institutions of society, disseminating its abstract principles and the ideology of the people's will, which supplanted the self-interests that had been safeguarded by the *esprit de corps*. The same circles also espoused the religion of consensus, the cult of a Society unencumbered by its usual constraints, and the belief that power and society are one.

The kingdom's traditional administration, thus undermined, ended up as a mere façade. It definitively collapsed in 1788, with the general social uprising against the reform of the *parlements*: the '*esprit de société*' now encountered the realities of power. Throughout the summer of 1788, the 'Bastion', united with the Third Estate of Brittany, led the battle against the king's *intendant*. Yet they marched under the banner of the societies: the rights of the People, the will of the Nation. The cast of characters also came from the societies, for the great official *corps*, forming a rather mediocre troop, was backed by a network of patriotic activists. By autumn, however, their 'democratic' unanimity broke down in the first encounter between ideology and history, occasioned by the debate on the holding of the Estates General: the nobility was excluded from the sovereign People and the 'string pullers' of the societies isolated and liquidated the 'Bastion'.

The reason is that ideology, in order to move from the fictitious society of abstract individuals – as embodied in the philosophical society – to real society, had to compose a new society by excisions and exclusions. It had to designate and personalise the powers of evil. For if there was a discrepancy between values and facts, if society, which should be as good as the individuals that compose it, was bad, it could only be because institutions and social forces artificially stood in the way of natural good. It was therefore necessary to define, combat and exclude them. That is what happened in the autumn of 1788 to the nobility, which, as the very symbol of inequality, was guilty, as a body, of contradicting the new principles. *Individual* nobles might well be revolutionaries, but *the* nobility became by definition the opposite of the Revolution.

Even after the camps had been labelled and the principles and their social opposites had been defined, individuals still had to be placed into categories. This was a practical task for which principles were no help at all, since the facts often did not square with them. After all, there were nobles who were patriots and artisans who were not; and in any case it was impossible to replace, in one fell swoop, the entire leadership of the kingdom. Hence the selection of men, which was bound to deviate from the social criteria laid down by ideology, was carried out in secret, through the 'machine' controlled by the members of the societies.

Cochin's analysis of the events of 1788–9 thus contains a theory of ideology and a theory of politics. Ideology is born when an optimistic philosophy sees the abstract individual as corrupted or impeded by society and feels called upon to take concrete action in order to lead that individual to the enjoyment of his rights. Ideology endows all aspects of society and all institutions, powers and classes with either favourable or nefarious significance, using them as reference points for the militant action that must combat and exclude the wicked in order to recreate in real society the philosophical society's consensus. Yet when militant action is faced with interests and passions instead of ideas, it cannot follow the guide-lines of ideology, for it is subject to mechanical laws inherent in revolutionary politics, and so must resort to manipulation, secrecy and small groups of activists. When ideology turns into politics, the philosophical society turns to its inner circle. In every democratic power, all the more so in every 'pure' (i.e. undelegated) democratic power, there is a hidden oligarchy that is contrary to its principle yet indispensable to its functioning.

The story of Brittany in 1788 is that of a very old civil society that disowned its traditional means of expression and reorganised itself entirely on the pattern of the philosophical societies, which by then had also begun to take concrete action. The nobility, which was the first to appear on the local revolutionary stage by protesting against the Lamoignon reforms, paid for its defence of *parlement* rights with its own disintegration; though it believed it was fighting against power in defence of traditional values, it had in fact become a coalition for the dissemination of propaganda and opinion, composed for the most part of *anoblis*, adolescents and rural *gentilshommes*. In playing this rôle, the 'Bastion' had dug its own grave, for the logic underlying the philosophical society was that of the abstract individual, and hence that of egalitarian ideology. Once it had won the summer battle against the king, the nobility therefore had to face the consequences of its own victory. It became apparent that it had cleared the way not for the restoration of the *parlements* but for the rising tide of democracy. On this battleground it was defeated in advance.

Indeed, once the debate was transferred to the philosophical societies, the 'machine' of the Third Estate soon proved its absolute mastery of the game; moreover, the king's *intendant* at Rennes, smarting from the revolt of the nobility, did nothing to stop it. The issue of voting by head provided an ideal terrain for egalitarian propaganda and for the exclusion of the nobility. In the ensuing debate, the societies, manipulated by the activists of the Third Estate – jurists or students at Rennes – became the 'Nation'. In short, the same dynamic that would account for 1792 and 1793 was already at work in 1788: an egalitarian ideology implicitly accepted as the common point of reference in the political struggle and manipulated at every turn by unrepresentative groups pushing for a more radical policy. This dynamic was at work as early as the autumn of 1788 not only against the nobility, its first and, as it were, natural victim, but *within the Third Estate* as well:

The progress of the Enlightenment pursued its inexorable course, even more rapidly than anyone had hoped. Indeed, it had skipped over one of its stages, the ascendancy of the *avocats* and the wealthier wholesale merchants, who were left behind by December. A number of these men, to be sure, stayed in politics and would reappear in April in the wake of the official elections, which, by calling for the votes of all inhabitants rather than those of the patriots only, were to put worthier candidates in the running. But for the moment patriotism reigned supreme, through its own means, according to its own principles, over a people of its own making, unimpeded by the royal or provincial authorities, and helped rather than hindered by the complementary work of the 'Bastion'; in its earliest stages it had reached a degree of 'purity' that was not to be seen again until the great purge following 10 August 1792. Already its membership was recruited from the same milieu – small shopkeepers, petty clerks of the courts [*basoche inferieure*], merchants, attorneys of the crown in the presidial courts and country lawyers – that composed the six or seven official and unofficial patriotic *corps* of Rennes, in other words, the *Commune*.[28]

28. *Ibid.* vol. 1, ch. 12, p. 293.

The battle between the nobility, by now a philosophical society, and the Third Estate, by now a political party, was joined in late December – early January in the provincial Estates over the issue of voting by head. The 'Bastion' was swept away by the January riots, which sealed the triumph of patriotism and established the control of the political machine of the urban Third Estate over town and country. Yet to come was the election to the Estates General, which, under the terms of the regulation of 24 January, gave the 'machine' the practical means to exercise the 'sovereignty' attributed in the abstract to the people of the *bailliages*. The control by the machine is evident, in fact, not so much in the content of the *Cahiers*, which remained relatively varied, as in the selection of the deputies, for the *Commune* of Rennes received the lion's share (five of the nine elected deputies), while the three towns of the *bailliage* obtained eight of the nine deputies with only 38 electors out of a total of 880.

In Cochin's view, the revolutionary explosion was thus not brought about by economic or social contradictions. It had its roots in a political dynamic, the manipulation of society and the conquest of power by anonymous groups, trustees of the new sovereignty in the name of equality and the 'people'. Yet their trusteeship was a perversion, not because they had seized it by force or intrigue, through concerted action or conspiracy, but because the new legitimacy – direct democracy – was bound by its very nature to produce a cascade of usurpations whose cumulative effect constituted revolutionary power. It was an anonymous and unstable power, condemned by its ideological nature to periodic acts of exclusion and to reckless escalation.

All of Cochin's archival work was devoted to publishing the texts relating to that power at its apogee, when it had destroyed all opposition to its reign, in other words, during the Terror. Once he had analysed the dynamic of revolutionary power, its internal mechanism as it were, by studying the period 1787–8, he set out to examine it at the other end of its short history and to show it in its full maturity between 23 August 1793, the date of the *levée en masse* (mass conscription) decree, and the fall of Robespierre. During this period the consensus of the philosophical society had become the mandatory political model for the entire country. By the 23 August 1793 decree the revolutionary government 'implemented the social fiction by which a single collective will was substituted not just in law but in actual fact for each individual will'.[29]

Cochin's archival work proper therefore consisted of assembling all the administrative documents in which the directives of the Comité de Salut

29. *Actes du gouvernement révolutionnaire*, p. 1.

Public were laid down, explaining and set in motion. It affords the historian an inside view of the processes by which those texts were implemented and of the problems posed at the local level by the generalised regulations handed down from Paris. This collection of documents, published in three posthumous volumes, seems to have been completed in 1914. It is thought that Cochin intended to introduce it with a lengthy *Discours préliminaire*, which would have contained his historical interpretation of Jacobinism; but in the end he substituted a brief foreword written during the war and in which he summarised the substance of his argument. This text was published in 1920 with the first volume of documents. The *Discours préliminaire*, postponed until better days, was to become the afterword of the publication. Cochin did not have time to give it its definitive form, but he probably worked on it even before 1914 and also intermittently during the war.[30] Various drafts for this *Discours préliminaire* were published in 1924 under a title that was antiquated even for that period and in any case somewhat misleading: *La Révolution et la libre pensée*. In fact, they attempt to systematise the conceptual intuition Cochin had already outlined in his 1907 essay. It was this intuition that gave his archival work its purpose: 'The answer to the enigma of the Revolution will not be the psychology of the Jacobin; *it will be the sociology of the democratic phenomenon.*'[31]

This statement is striking because Cochin's vocabulary is rarely so modern, so 'Durkheimian', and as a result so clear to the present-day reader. The contrast between this statement and the legacy of Catholic conservatism, otherwise so obvious and so pervasive in the same work, is so striking that one must look into the reasons for this coexistence. It is all the more necessary to do so since the banal aspects of Cochin's thought have been very harmful to the appreciation of its newness by twentieth-century historians and sociologists.

Unlike the right-wing thinkers of his time, Cochin was not exclusively, nor even primarily, a monarchist, an adversary of the Republic and thereby of the Revolution. He disliked what he called Maurras's 'materialism', his overriding concern with social order. His antecedents were different from those of positivist rationalism. He was a Catholic philosopher, for whom the highest form of knowledge was the knowledge of God, the only intuition able to lead human thought to reality and to unite

30. Augustin Cochin exhibited great bravery during the First World War. Wounded four times – a fact that accounts for the periods of enforced rest that enabled him to write – he always demanded to be immediately returned to the front, where he was killed on 8 July 1916 at the age of thirty-nine.
31. *La Révolution et la libre pensée*, introduction, p. xxvii. The italics are Cochin's.

human beings in the quest for a common goal: that, to his mind, was what had held the medieval world together. In such a world, society existed untroubled by the need to define itself because it was, like the Church, composed of individuals who were separate yet united in God.

For Cochin, a lower form of knowledge and unity, intellectually and chronologically in second place, is scientific thought. It aims at understanding not the richest and most complex reality – God – but the elementary forms of the material world, which it breaks up into conceptual objects, thus making it possible to dominate it by means of the mathematical calculations that reveal its laws. Scientific thought marks the beginning both of a world in which means operate to the detriment of ends and, in the social order, of the rule of law over free individuals, the first step toward the emancipation of 'society' as an end in itself. The last stage of this development, which characterises the end of the eighteenth century and the Revolution, is the domination of society over thought, of words over ideas. It was the era of 'socialised thought', that is, ideology, created by the philosophical societies.

What is most interesting in this construct, founded on a typology of knowledge whose premise is as undemonstrable as the existence of God, is that Cochin established a link between the emancipation of society from transcendent justification and the eventual substitution of society for transcendency as a principle of thought. For this connection allows us to understand why he was both so far from and yet close to Durkheim, so 'reactionary' and yet so modern. The son of Rome's spokesman in the Chamber of Deputies[32] and the prominent professor of the *Bloc des Gauches* were interested in the same problem and looked at the same history, but one saw it as a catastrophe and the other as a new beginning. Durkheim's blasphemy, which retrospectively used society to explain religion, interested Cochin as the end result, the final inversion of a metaphysics without God. Whereas for Durkheim sociology was the science of the laws that govern all behaviour and all societies, in the past as well as in the present, this ambition appeared to Cochin as the ultimate chimera, the appropriation of ontology by society.

Yet, by way of a paradox about which he never clearly explained himself, the Catholic philosopher nonetheless adopted the atheist sociologist's notion of 'social science', based on the assumption that 'by

32. Augustin Cochin's father, Denys Cochin, was first a member of the Paris city council and then, from 1893, deputy for Paris. In this capacity he was one of the French parliamentarians who were closest to the Vatican.

studying social facts sociology encounters deeper causes than well-considered reasons, stated intentions and concerted volitions'.[33] He therefore seems to have accepted, indeed endorsed, the use of sociology for studying the kinds of behaviour that he considered to be totally 'socialised', and whose model is Jacobinism. Cochin thus excludes religious or scientific thought from the field of sociological critique, which is valid only in the limited – and in his opinion secondary – realm of 'socially created' thought.

This selective use of sociology could be criticised on theoretical grounds. To begin with, Cochin uses Durkheim against what he dislikes, and shields from Durkheim what he likes. Moreover, his idealisation of medieval Christian society, which he portrays as based on each individual's relation to God unaffected by social pressure of any kind, is significant only to the extent that it shows the great distance between Cochin's Catholic traditionalism and the positivism of Maurras, who was indifferent to faith as such, obsessed with the Church rather than God, with order rather than truth, with Louis XIV rather than Saint Louis. Still, it is something of a miracle that Cochin, with all his self-righteous nostalgia and shaky philosophy of history, should have discovered, probably thanks to Durkheim, one of the key problems of the eighteenth century and of the Revolution, which no historian has stated in these terms before or after him: Cochin raised the problem of how the French had come to re-invent society under the name of the 'people' or the 'nation', and of how they came to set it up as the new god of a fictitious community.

Present in rudimentary form by 1788, the definition of the people's will by the philosophical societies and the ensuing manipulation of opinion assumed ever greater scope as the Revolution became one with the power of the societies. The terrorism of the consensus about ideas was supplanted by the terrorism of power over people and things – by what Cochin calls the socialisation of persons and then of property. In 1793–4 Jacobinism thus marked the apogee of the societies' rule, for they had developed its tools, the *sections* and the committees covertly directed by the activists; its techniques, which, taken together, constituted the Terror; its regimentation, which sought to bring all social activity in line with ideology; its ambition, which was to rule as the 'people', and thereby to obliterate any divergence between civil society and power:

Living in serfdom under the king in 1789, in freedom under the law in 1791, the people became master in 1793. Now that it governed itself, it did away with the

33. *La Révolution et la libre pensée*, p. 69.

public liberties that had only served to protect it against those who had ruled. If the right to vote was suspended it was because the people ruled; the right to legal defence because it did the judging; freedom of the press because it did the writing; freedom of speech because it did the speaking: the doctrine is perfectly clear; the proclamations and laws of the Terror are but an extended commentary on it.[34]

'Democracy' (taken to mean 'direct democracy') made its way to power in three successive stages. The first was the secret world of the lodges and philosophical societies, which provided the shelter in which it invented its methods; the second was the pressure of the clubs on the great power vacuum called 'the Revolution'; the third was the official rule of the *sociétés populaires* by means of terrorist control over persons and property. As this historical process unfolded the great diversity in the names, the faces, the backgrounds and even the intimate thoughts of the various leaders was of little consequence; if they changed very often, if they lasted scarcely longer than the anonymous leaders of the clubs and *sections*, it was because they too were but the temporary images of revolutionary democracy, its creations and not its chiefs. For once Cochin agrees with Michelet, whom he quotes:

I have seen that these brilliant, powerful speakers, who gave voice to the thinking of the masses, are wrongly considered to be the only actors. They responded to impulse much more than they imparted it. The leading actor was the people. In order to rediscover it and to restore it to its rôle, I have had to cut down to size the ambitious marionettes whose strings it pulled, and who were believed to show the secret workings of history.[35]

Yet Cochin's people was not Michelet's. Both authors realised that the only hero of the Revolution was the Revolution itself. But where Michelet celebrated an immense, ungovernable, unplanned yet blessed force, Cochin analysed a mechanism. His detachment, to be sure, came from his political tradition; but in his case, which was exceptional, distance gave him the intellectual advantage the concept has over emotion.

For his work, while unfinished, is still perfectly self-contained. It is true that the treatment of 1793 lacks the equivalent of what Cochin had done for 1788, the detailed analysis of archival documents, which, for the later period, he was only able to edit for publication. But the conceptual design is so evident, the subject is so clearly delineated, that together they constitute and should be regarded as a work in its own right, that is, a well-stated question: what was the nature of the revolutionary phenomenon?

Cochin was interested in the same problem as Michelet and most other

34. *Ibid.* p. 241.
35. Jules Michelet, *Histoire de la Révolution française*, vol. 1, 1847 preface, quoted by Cochin in *Les Sociétés de Pensée et la Démocratie*, p. 49.

historians of the Revolution. Unlike Tocqueville, he did not attempt to assess the consequences of the Revolution for French history, or to analyse its origins and effects. Like Michelet, he was interested in the break in continuity, that is, what happened between 1788 and 1794. But his great advantage over Michelet and all the other 'event-oriented' (*événementiel*) historians of the Revolution[36] is that he states his objectives and tells us what he is doing. He does not, for example, mix an *analysis* of origins with a *narrative* of consequences, as if the former were contained in the latter. He states explicitly that he is not dealing with the problem of the causes of the Revolution – which might 'explain' 1789 but not 1792 or 1793 – but with the revolutionary dynamic itself. In short, he treats an eminently 'event-bound' (*événementiel*) topic in terms of a strictly conceptual history: where Mathiez or Aulard are fascinated, Cochin wants to understand in the light of Durkheim. No wonder then that he was not well received or even properly understood in the 'guild'. The historians of the Revolution are bound to be upset when anyone dares to bury the saga of human wills that has been entrusted to their safekeeping, along with the heroes they have chosen to love or hate. As for historians in general, they are not – at least in France – in the habit of practising a political history that is not narrative or of conceptualising short-term developments.

Cochin showed both great insight and narrow-mindedness. Throughout his life as a scholar, his research centred on a single idea, which seems to have come to him when he was quite young, shortly after his graduation from the École des Chartes. His extensive archival research – which testifies to a desire, rather rare at the time, to learn about the provincial and local realities of the Revolution – was carried out in keeping with his central intuition. He was at once very close to Tocqueville and very far from him, for he shared with the liberal aristocrat not only the somewhat horrified amazement at Jacobinism that constituted the existential point of departure of both men's work, but also the taste for what I call conceptual history, which eschews the narration of the actors' intentions. This shared feature alone is enough to place them in a category by themselves in the nineteenth- and twentieth-century historiography of the Revolution. But Tocqueville sought the secrets of continuity, Cochin those of the break. That is why the two minds did not follow the same path. Their hypotheses are not incompatible; they are attempts at explaining

36. I should, perhaps, apologise for putting them all together in this manner. I am not concerned here with the literary and psychological genius of Michelet and only want to emphasise the traits he shared with the traditional narrative history of the Revolution.

totally different problems, and both have the merit of being stated explicitly.

When it came to understanding the immediate causes of the Revolution, Tocqueville did feel compelled to attribute major importance to the rôle of revolutionary ideas and to the intellectuals who had produced or popularised them. He explains that rôle by the development of a *democratic state of mind*, a natural product of an increasingly egalitarian society[37] and all the more powerful for being thwarted by the residual existence of aristocratic institutions. In reading, for instance, in volume 2 of *L'Ancien Régime*, the unfinished but thoroughly outlined chapters devoted to the *parlements'* revolt against the king, to the king's capitulation, and to what Tocqueville calls 'the war among the classes', in which the nobility is already disappearing, one cannot help being struck by the importance he attaches to the public spirit, the ideas and the passions of the time. Commenting on a group of texts emanating from various associations, *corps* and communities, for example, he writes:

The very idea of a tempered and balanced government, that is, of the kind of government in which the classes that form society and the interests that divide it counterbalance each other; of a government in which men are important to the general good not only as units but in function of their property, their patronage and their interest ... those ideas were no longer present in the minds of the more moderate men (and to some extent, I believe, not even among the privileged). They were replaced by the idea of a crowd made up of like elements and represented by deputies who were the representatives of *numbers* rather than of interests or persons.

To the last sentence he added a reminder for himself:

Penetrate this idea more deeply and show that the Revolution was even more present here than in concrete facts; and that in the presence of such ideas the facts were almost bound to turn out just about as they did.[38]

A half-century before Cochin, Tocqueville thus also tried to understand what he called elsewhere the 'power of expansion' of revolutionary ideas. Unlike Cochin, however, he never proposed a distinction between ideas and ideology, nor did he concern himself with the collective production of the new revolutionary faith. He was aware of the existence, as early as 1789, of what might be called an irresistible Jacobin trend, but he attributed it to the influence of the *Social Contract*,[39] which is both an error

37. Tocqueville explains this connection most profoundly at the beginning of the second volume of *Democracy in America* ('Influence of Democracy on the Intellectual Movement in the United States').
38. Tocqueville, *L'Ancien Régime et la Révolution*, vol. 2, p. 117, n. 1.
39. *Ibid.* vol. 2, p. 121, n. 3 on the '*radicalism of the moderates*'. Cf. In particular his statement that 'Rousseau's ideas were a flood that for a time submerged an entire aspect of the human mind and of human intellectual endeavour.'

and a misapprehension: most of the men of 1789 had not read Rousseau, and Sieyès, for example, was no more a Rousseauist than Mirabeau or Roederer. Thus a force different from that of books and ideas must have been at work; Tocqueville wondered what it was but was never able to define it.[40] Having interpreted it in a general manner by analogy with religion in his posthumous notes on Jacobinism, he expressed a somewhat horrified astonishment at this analogy: 'A party that openly attacked the very notion of religion and of God and yet derived from its debilitating doctrine the ardour needed for proselytising and even for martyrdom, which hitherto only religion seemed able to impart! ... At least as inconceivable as it is frightening, such a sight is capable of unsettling the most stable intelligence.'[41]

However, he immediately adds a crucially important note, which summarises all the ambiguity of his thinking about the Revolution: 'Must never lose sight of the enlightened character of the French Revolution, its *main* albeit transitory character' [Tocqueville's italics]. For him, the rôle of enlightened thought in the Revolution was thus both an essential factor, since it embodied the event as the actors experienced it, yet also a temporary one, since it masked the true significance of the event, which was the consecration of the centralised State and of democratic individualism. Tocqueville's central conceptualisation, unlike Cochin's, seeks to explain an evolution accomplished over several centuries.

Cochin did not concern himself with the causes that made the Revolution possible; his subject was the birth, at the beginning of the Revolution, of a new cultural legitimacy, equality, along with the development of a new ground-rule for the political game, 'pure democracy' – what we would call direct democracy. Cochin was not really interested in the pre-revolutionary period and studied it very little. Concerning the old monarchy, the old political society and the old legitimacy, he had fashioned an idealised and uniformly superficial vision. He never analysed, for instance, the ways in which the monarchy progressively destroyed corporative society, or the rôle played by the monarchy in the progress of civil equality or of egalitarian ideology. In failing to do so, he conveyed the inaccurate impression that the debate of 1788–9 was located midway between the old corporatist political society and the manipu-

40. *Ibid.* vol. 2, p. 226, marginal note on a comment about Mallet du Pan's memoirs: 'Insurrection against the old world, the old society, where the same aims give rise to the same passions and the same ideas everywhere. Shows how all the passions of liberty rise up together against the common yoke of Catholicism. What is the reason for this? What is really new in this event? What gave it this power of expansion? Must thoroughly research and analyse these questions.'
41. *Ibid.* vol. 2, p. 239.

lation of pure democracy by the philosophical societies; in fact, even at that date, the old legitimacy was regarded as dead and the new one, democracy, had not yet abandoned the principle of representation. It is true that the electoral procedure devised by Necker in January 1789, by preserving certain aspects of the old system of delegation and by failing to organise a genuine political competition, encouraged the manipulation of opinion. Cochin's demonstration of that point is flawless. Nonetheless, it does not necessarily prove that the Revolution was already completely taken over by the lodges and the clubs in the name of direct democracy.

A more fundamental question also reveals Cochin's lack of historical perspective and his decision to focus his analysis on the short term, on the revolutionary dynamic rather than on the history of its formation. This question is: what is the origin of the ideology of direct democracy? In reading our author one is never quite sure whether he sees it as a simple product of the philosophical societies or as something that existed before them, in the century's enlightened thought for example; and if so, in what ways the two histories were related. In fact, this ideology cannot have resulted from the mere mechanical interplay of intellectual associations based on their members' abstract equality. The Compagnie du Saint-Sacrement, in the seventeenth century, was a philosophical society, just as secret as the lodges of the following century, yet it did not live by the same set of ideas. The ideological crystallisation that occurred in the eighteenth century in the philosophical societies and in related circles presupposes two factors which Cochin never, or almost never, analyses:[42] first, the development of certain seminal ideas in political philosophy as a whole and in major individual works; second, the receptiveness of a society that had lost its traditional principles. When the two trends converged, the philosophical societies were able to substitute an egalitarian ideology and the principle of direct democracy for religion, the king and traditional hierarchies. But it took a long time for ideas to change into ideology, and Cochin broaches this history only at its end, at the point where he considers it to be accomplished, that is, around 1750.

In this scheme of things, the seminal idea is that of popular sovereignty, itself derived from the notion of a founding social compact and defined most systematically in Rousseau.[43] Rousseau's political philosophy, which

42. He did write an interesting article about the *Social Contract*, which he had read carefully (Cf. *Les Sociétes de Pensée et la Démocratie*, pp. 27–33). On the other hand, his 1912 lecture on the *philosophes* strikes me as banal and superficial. (This lecture, delivered as one of the '*conférences Chateaubriand*', can be found in *Les Sociétés de Pensée et la Démocratie*, pp. 3–23.)

43. The best history of the development of this concept, from Pufendorf to Rousseau, is still R. Dérathé's *J.-J. Rousseau et la science politique de son temps* (Paris: P.U.F., 1950; new edn, Vrin, 1970).

(unlike the theoreticians of natural law) treats sovereignty as an inalienable right, does not admit of the notion of representation, since for a free people the delegation of sovereignty to representatives is as impossible as its delegation to a monarch. We know that Rousseau had in mind the concrete examples of the oligarchical English Parliament and the noble-dominated Diet of Poland. But in any case his political thought was far too complex and the *Social Contract* far too abstract a book to be truly understood by the majority of his contemporaries. Moreover, the book does not seem to have had a great deal of resonance at the time; its intellectual impact was produced much later by the Revolution. Hence direct democracy, which was indeed, at least as a general trend, the practice of the philosophical societies – all of which more or less convincingly draped their resolutions in notions of the people's interest and later the people's will – resulted far more from a kind of mechanical usurpation of power than from the elaboration of an idea. In Louis XVI's France, civil society had become infinitely stronger than the State, but it lacked the trustees who could take over the State and transform it on its behalf. Among the kingdom's traditional corporate entities, the nobility and the *parlements* cherished that dream of trusteeship, but the former was never able to turn itself into a ruling class on the English model, and the latter never seriously attempted to acquire the political means and the intellectual tools required for their sporadic ambitions. To this crumbling political society, the philosophical societies gave a new fictive appearance of unity by means of the people's will.

Yet although that substitutive legitimacy was indeed accompanied in practice by direct democracy while the Ancien Régime lasted and because of the very nature of the situation, it did not necessarily imply direct democracy in principle. Cochin's analyses presuppose that 'pure democracy' was from the very beginning and throughout the Revolution the only form of political legitimacy. That is to forget that the Revolution, both in its first phase and after Thermidor 1794, also developed the doctrine of a representative régime. Its most systematic theoretician was Sieyès, who extended to every public official the notion of power delegated by the people.[44] It therefore remains to be explained how and why the first of these concepts came to override the second to the point of constituting – as Cochin fully realised – the very core of revolutionary consciousness, the *sans-culotte* credo of 1793. Indeed one can analyse the rush of events between 1788 and 1794 from this perspective and view it as the takeover of the nation by the militants and the ideologues of direct

44. Cf. Sieyès. The best commentary was written by P. Bastid: *Sieyès et sa pensée* (Paris, 1939, new edn, Hachette, 1970). See, in particular, part 2, chapter 6, pp. 369–90.

democracy, a scenario in which the riot functions as the element that 'rectifies' an increasingly fragile representative régime. But if Cochin's analysis of the revolutionary dynamic is correct, if it was really kept moving by the clubs and the popular societies in the name of a fictitious 'people', then it follows that the successive leaders of the Revolution were always both the products and the adversaries of that dynamic. For not only did the logic of those societies proceed by ideological escalation and scission, but also the leaders, far from being the anonymous puppets suggested by Cochin's mechanical analysis, in fact embodied the principle of representative democracy. In this respect the crisis of 31 May – 2 June 1793 marks a pivotal date in the triumph of 'pure democracy'. But even after the expulsion of the Girondin deputies by brute force, the Montagnard dictatorship had not completely merged with that of the societies, since the Montagnard party was concerned with maintaining its parliamentary majority in the Convention. After the execution of the Hébertistes between April and July 1794, Robespierre ceased to be the man of the societies, and the Festival of the Supreme Being was not a celebration by and of the societies, but an attempt to monopolise the ideology for the benefit of the Incorruptible. It is true that the latter did not outlive for long the popular movement he helped 'put on ice', to use Saint-Just's expression; here Cochin's analysis is persuasive indeed. But it does oversimplify the political fabric of the French Revolution when it overlooks all of the resistances, negotiations and forced concessions that accompanied the thrust of the popular societies at every stage. The term 'machine' suggests a kind of mechanically perfect organisation that is largely a figment of the imagination.

In fact the analysis of the French Revolution should distinguish between two conceptions of popular sovereignty, which Cochin failed to keep separate. It is true that, from 1789 on, all the French revolutionaries – from Sieyès and Mirabeau to Robespierre and Marat – viewed popular sovereignty as the source of the new political legitimacy. The nation, consisting of the sovereign people, was assumed to act like a person. Independently of the *fact* that the destruction of the old society provided the State with a far wider field of activity and weakened the resistance to its authority, this conception entailed, indeed demanded *by law*, a strong central power, assumed to be indistinguishable from the people. It is significant that this conception is unknown in English tradition of public law, which is closer to Locke than to Rousseau.[45] But how was the people's will to express itself? Those who felt with Sieyès that it could be

45. Cf. Bertrand de Jouvenel, *Les Débuts de l'État moderne* (Paris: Fayard, 1976), ch. 10, p. 157.

represented were ready to define this representation and to implement the requisite procedures. Their system was inaugurated in French history by the Constituent Assembly, which, by means of a juridical fiction, extended even to the hereditary king the benediction of the new sovereignty. Within the framework of this conception the many-faceted and de-centralised sphere of power was distinct from civil society and therefore had no transcendent authority over society, least of all over the rights of individuals.

Those, on the other hand, who believed with Rousseau that popular sovereignty is inalienable and cannot be *represented* because it is the people's liberty – the imprescriptible natural right that predates the social compact – were bound to condemn not only the monarchy but also any representative system. The law, which is made by the assembled people and expresses the general will, has by definition absolute authority over the people, because it expresses its free will exactly. Here as always, Rousseau is systematic and intransigent; he expresses with metaphysical profundity the logical quandaries of democracy when he postulates that society and power must fit together perfectly. This somewhat desperate demonstration was a kind of window-dressing for the ideology of 'pure' democracy, which in fact devised a spurious system of perfect identifi-cation, thanks to a succession of imaginary equations in which the people became identified with the opinion of the clubs, the clubs with the opinion of their leaders, and these leaders with the Republic.

Cochin was quite correct in viewing this mechanism, which was both practical and ideological, as the very core of the French Revolution. His time-frame for the event, 1788–94, is perfectly consistent with his ap-proach. After 9 Thermidor, and even beginning with the execution of the Hébertistes in April 1794, the mechanism he analyses ceased to be the driving force of events, for at that point society got even with the *sociétés populaires*. This conclusion, incidentally, reveals a bizarre coincidence between Cochin's analysis and that of the young Marx who, in *The Holy Family*,[46] also developed the idea that the Revolution progressively in-vented a fictitious society, culminating in, and achieved at the price of, the Terror. Marx explained that the fall of Robespierre marked the come-back or the re-emergence of real society (which he called 'civil society'). This idea is echoed in the following lines written by Cochin: 'Real society was not the Counter-revolution but, rather, those areas in which the Revolution would lose and in which authority and hierarchy would prevail even after every man and every law had become revolutionary, as

46. Marx, *La Sainte Famille* [The Holy Family], ch. 6, pp. 144–50.

happened in France in Thermidor Year II, the moment the Jacobins' yoke on society had been lifted.'[47]

In another sense it was also normal for Cochin to adopt the time-frame of the Revolution that is most familiar to left-wing historiography, for the problem he sought to elucidate – Jacobinism, the clubs and the *sociétés populaires* – is also the subject that commands the political sympathies of the Left. For both Cochin and Jacobin historiography, the Revolution was a *unit* between 1788 and 1794, and the characteristics it displayed during the Terror were already in place before the meeting of the Estates General. This definition is both true and false, depending on the aspect of the Revolution that is being studied or stressed; but Cochin, unlike Jacobin historiography, has the merit of presenting a clear justification of the definition and of deriving it from the nature of his conceptualisation. If the Revolution was indeed defined by the phenomenon he analyses, it did begin before 1789 and end with Robespierre. Without wishing to revive the nineteenth-century liberal cult of 1789 (*quatre-vingt-neuvisme*), I am not sure that this time-frame does justice to the efforts made in 1790 to establish a representative democracy, and that it does not overemphasise a retrospective historical 'necessity'; yet the time-frame is very consistent, for those were indeed the years when 'pure democracy' was developed and then reigned.

Cochin, therefore, did not see the essence of the Revolution as social strife or a transfer of property. For him it was the beginning of a new *type of socialisation*, founded on ideological communion and manipulated by political machines. Its abstract model went back to the philosophical societies that flourished at the end of the Ancien Régime, in particular to freemasonry, the most elaborate among them. Any counter-argument to Cochin's hypothesis that cites the oligarchical or conservative character of the French Masonic lodges is wide of the mark, for he felt that freemasonry was the *mould* of the new arrangement of society and that it was destined to engender many others, which would draw other audiences and propagate other kinds of consent, although they would all abide by the same logic of pure democracy. During the Revolution, that logic would become the power wielded by ideology and by the anonymous men of the *sections*. As we have seen, this intellectual reconstruction inevitably led its author to a simplification of revolutionary history, the price to be paid for its very forcefulness. Yet it becomes clear that he put his finger on a central feature, not only of the French Revolution but of what it shared with later revolutions, if one realises that he described in advance many

47. *Actes du gouvernement révolutionnaire*, introduction, p. vii.

traits of Lenin's Bolshevism. It is true, of course, that Lenin, unlike Robespierre, was able to work out in advance his own theory of the rôle of ideology and the political machine. But then his theory was patterned, at least in part, on the Jacobin example.

Yet Cochin's work inevitably suggests two problems with which he never dealt. The first is that of the relationship between social practice and ideology. Cochin seems to postulate that there was none, and that the philosophical societies each held together on the basis of shared ideas alone, independently of specific situations and real interests. But if, unlike Marx for example, he considered that this shared ideology had nothing to do with the interests of the individuals and the classes to which they belonged, and that the members of the revolutionary clubs were somehow socially interchangeable, how would he explain the over-representation of certain groups (such as the *avocats* and jurists in 1788–9) in that activity? One can easily understand, in terms of Cochin's own conceptualisation, the early exclusion not of the nobles but of the nobility; for after all the nobility stood for the very opposite of the symbolic revolutionary system and embodied a principle far more than an interest. But as regards the Third Estate, which was in its entirety on the 'good' side, the outstanding rôle played by certain social and occupational groups can be explained only with technical reasons; and it may well be that their long-standing familiarity with democratic universalism in the abstract accounts for the preponderant rôle played by *avocats*, legal practitioners (*hommes de loi*) and intellectuals in general between 1787 and 1794. If the Revolution was a language, it brought to the forefront those who could speak it.

Why was this language invented by the French? That is another fundamental question, and I do not see that Cochin's work provides an answer to it, even implicitly. The 'Enlightenment' was flourishing everywhere in Europe, yet only in France did it foster Jacobinism. Lodges and philosophical societies existed in England and in the German States, yet they did not bring about a revolution there. This formidable issue was faced squarely and systematically by only one historian of the French Revolution, Alexis de Tocqueville, who, having studied the last centuries of the monarchy, came to the conclusion that the French were the most 'democratic' people of Europe and therefore the most inclined to rejoice in this massive and sudden adoption of the *philosophes*' ideas. Tocqueville thus explains 1789 but not 1793. Cochin, on the other hand, accounted for 1793 but not for 1789. He took note of what I shall call the 'enlightened socialisation' of the old kingdom very late in the eighteenth century, when it was already imbued with what interested him, Jacobin ideology. But he thereby locked himself into an interpretation of the revolutionary dynamic that recognises only the mechanical force of society and fails to survey the cultural factors that had long been at work in these imaginary brotherhoods, which were marked by their generosity before they turned to bloodshed. Cochin was never able to forgive Rousseau for Robespierre: that is the most serious flaw in his work. But at least the fact that he could read Rousseau only through Robespierre prevents him from approaching Robespierre through Rousseau and seeing him as an admirer of the *Social Contract* grappling with the constraints of public safety. His Robespierre is not so much the heir of the Enlightenment as the product of the new system called Jacobinism, the beginning of modern politics. That was how Cochin came to grips with the central mystery of the French Revolution: the origin of democracy.